This book attempts to unify the economic analysis of the production process in order to understand the effects of technical change. It is both an analytical representation of the production process, taking into account the temporal, organizational, and qualitative dimensions of production, and a fact-finding model for studying the economic effects of technical change. The inclusion of temporal and organizational aspects allows the author to examine the analytical implications of recent research on the nature of firms and the characteristics of technical change, whilst the model is used to analyse technical changes that involve variations of scale or degrees of flexibility.

This book deals with themes much discussed in recent research in industrial economics and management studies, and is an important contribution to bringing these two areas of research closer together, providing a general framework for the study of production processes.

Production process and technical change

Production process and technical change

Mario Morroni

University of Bergamo

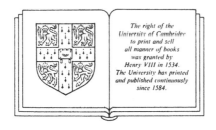

The right of the
University of Cambridge
to print and sell
all manner of books
was granted by
Henry VIII in 1534.
The University has printed
and published continuously
since 1584.

Cambridge University Press

Cambridge
New York   Port Chester
Melbourne   Sydney

CAMBRIDGE UNIVERSITY PRESS
Cambridge, New York, Melbourne, Madrid, Cape Town, Singapore, São Paulo, Delhi

Cambridge University Press
The Edinburgh Building, Cambridge CB2 8RU, UK

Published in the United States of America by Cambridge University Press, New York

www.cambridge.org
Information on this title: www.cambridge.org/9780521119733

First published 1992
This digitally printed version 2009

A catalogue record for this publication is available from the British Library

Library of Congress Cataloguing in Publication data

Morroni, Mario.
Production process and technical change/Mario Morroni.
    p. cm.
Includes bibliographical references and index.
ISBN 0 521 41001 0 (hard cover)
1. Production functions (Economic theory) 2. Technological innovations –
Economic aspects – Mathematical models. I. Title.
HB241.M67   1992   91-3040   CIP
338.5 – dc20

ISBN 978-0-521-41001-4 hardback
ISBN 978-0-521-11973-3 paperback

Contents

**Part 3 Economies of scale, economies of scope and
production flexibility**

Acknowledgements

The main part of this work was written during 1988, when I was a visiting scholar at the Faculty of Economics of Cambridge University. I am grateful to this institution for providing an excellent research environment, and to Geoffrey Harcourt for making my visit possible and for reading and commenting, in his witty and friendly manner, on earlier drafts of this work. I wish to thank Piero Tani (University of Florence) for patiently reading the first (rough) draft of each chapter, providing many helpful comments, and giving his authoritative encouragement. Special thanks are also due to Nicolò De Vecchi (University of Pavia) for his constant intellectual support and most useful suggestions.

I gratefully acknowledge helpful comments on earlier versions from Salvatore Baldone (Milan Polytechnic), Michele Grillo (University of Modena), Samdeep Kapur (University of Cambridge), Michael Landesmann (University of Cambridge), Sandro Marani (University of Venice), Marco Mariotti (University of Cambridge), Ugo Pagano (University of Siena), Cliff Pratten (University of Cambridge), Francesco Silva (University of Turin), Anna Torriero (University of Bergamo), Stefano Zamagni (University of Bologna) and two anonymous Cambridge University Press referees. I am also indebted to Giuseppe Cattaneo (University of Bergamo, Computer Centre) and Giovanni Dugnani (TPA – 'Technologie e Prodotti per l'Automazione', Milan) for their assistance in collecting data for the case studies. With regard to the latter, I wish to express my gratitude to the businessmen and managers interviewed for their interest in the methodology adopted and for providing data from their firms. Moreover, I wish to thank the participants in seminars held at the Departments of Economics of Bergamo University (May 1989), Trieste University (May 1990), Florence University (October 1990), and at the National Research Council (CNR) Group on 'Economic Theory' (October 1990) for valuable comments. Finally, I would also like to thank Joan Hall for her help with the translation of the very preliminary draft of this work, and Anne Stone, Peter Lake and Sheila McEnery for useful suggestions in revising the full final version of this book.

None of the above are, of course, responsible for the statements and interpretations contained in this book. This book is an extensively modified edition of a December 1988 Discussion Paper of the University of Bergamo Department of Economics. The research received financial support from the National Research Council (CNR, n. 85.01221).

Introduction: scope and outline

1   Production process and economic analysis of technical change

The purpose of this book is to present a consistent scheme capable of unifying the economic analysis of the production process in order to understand the effects of technical change. The investigation can be seen from two different points of view: either as a *scheme* of relations between the economic variables of production, open to changes in 'environment' factors (influenced by expectations, industrial relations, institutional aspects), or as a *methodology* useful for studying the economic effects of changes in techniques, and hence for empirical research.

The economic problem of production is far more complex than choosing the combination of inputs: inputs combinations are for the most part technically determined, by their indivisibility characteristics and by their complementarity relations. Consequently economic choice in production mainly concerns combining processes or single phases. This choice involves a host of organizational, temporal and qualitative aspects: harmonizing the productive capacities of the different production phases so as to minimize waste in the use of machinery; trying to exploit possible economies of scale at different operational levels; deciding the volume of production batches and the degree of production flexibility; evaluating transaction costs and on that basis choosing whether to produce components in house or have them produced outside; working out policies for collaboration with other firms; deciding on forms of organization, product differentiation, innovative policies and investments in equipment and human resources. These are just a few of the most important problems related to the economic decisions which lead to the harmonizing and balancing of different processes. Clearly, solving them appropriately determines the competitiveness of firms and of whole industrial sectors.

In determining the size of the firm, a static and purely quantitative representation of the production process does not give due importance to the relationship between the time profile and the organization of production. The production process takes place in historical time; hence the concepts derived from static analysis, based on the hypothesis of reversibility of cost curves, cannot be used. These concepts refer to a logical time (partial or total adaptation) rather than to irreversible historical time. Recently, a few studies, based on John Hicks's work in the 1970s and the analyses of Adolph Lowe and Nicholas Georgescu-Roegen, brought out the importance of an accurate analysis of the production process which takes account of the *temporal* aspects of production (Hicks 1973b, 1976; Lowe 1955, 1976; Georgescu-Roegen 1966, 1971, 1976).[1] This book belongs to this broad line of research. In particular, it develops an analytical representation of the production process useful for evaluating the economic effects obtained or obtainable through changes in techniques. As we shall see, the scheme, presented in the following pages, permits organizational and technical aspects to be considered at the same time. This proves very useful in studying the evolution of production methods, and in interpreting the reasons behind the adoption of certain 'organizational systems'.

Every given combination of inputs (for example, a certain quantity of workers and tools), represented traditionally by a point on an isoquant, may correspond to numerous different ways of organizing production. Clearly, each particular technique represents a specific way of solving the economic and technical problems posed by the organization of a production unit. The organization and division of labour – in a word, the technique adopted – are the result of a complex of elements; among these we can mention the specific characteristics of entrepreneurship and the available labour forces, technological opportunities, social security systems, industrial relations, financial and market structures, and social conditions (in short, the institutional environment).

It is impossible to deal adequately with the phenomenon of technical change unless the functioning modes of the production process as a whole are taken into account. In the *absence* of an analytical representation that takes account of the different economic dimensions of the production process, the detailed analysis of the nature of technical change becomes in fact a mere taxonomy. It is important to underline the close reciprocal relationship between the analysis of the *production process* and the analysis of the *nature of technical change*. If only quantitative aspects of production are taken into account, technical change figures simply as a

---

[1] Among more recent contributions which discuss and develop these different approaches see, for instance: Zamagni (1984b, 1989), Tani (1988), Baldone (1984, 1989), Landesmann (1986), Leijonhufvud (1986), Faber (1986), Amendola and Gaffard (1988), Faber and Proops (1990). As far as the 'time-shape' of production is concerned, see also Frisch (1962) and Winston (1982).

factor that reduces inputs in relation to outputs. On the other hand, if we consider not only quantitative aspects but also the elements of time, organization and size, we can analyse the effects of technical change on the production process, taking account of technical change characteristics such as irreversibility, cumulativity, learning by doing, specificity, uncertainty, etc. That is what I propose to do in this study.

The need to include temporal and organizational as well as quantitative aspects obviously depends on the aims of the analysis.

In some cases it may be useful, for analytical or expository reasons, to concentrate on studying quantities alone. But it is one thing to isolate the quantitative aspects temporarily for analytical purposes – within a model which takes account of the interrelationships between quantities and temporal and organizational aspects – and quite another thing to exclude *a priori* any link between quantities and the time profile and organization of production processes, as occurs in traditional microeconomic analyses.

In many circumstances the simple analysis of quantities is not sufficient. For example, if the aim is to provide a methodology with which to evaluate the effects of technical change, a purely quantitative study can deal with one part only (though a very important one) of the economic effects of the phenomenon. In this case the analysis must extend beyond the quantitative elements to embrace the temporal, organizational and qualitative aspects of the production processes.

The inclusion of these temporal and organizational aspects may enable us to bring into a consistent context certain important analytical elements provided by recent studies on *transaction costs*, on the *nature* of *firms* and *markets*, and on the characteristics of *technical change*. On the other hand, the vast interest aroused in recent years by literature on transaction costs, on the nature of firms and markets, and on determinants and effects of technical change, has helped to fill in part the traditional gap between industrial economics and management disciplines. This book is addressed to readers interested in these fields. Its intention is to contribute to bringing these two areas of research closer, by providing a general taxonomy and methodology for production processes.

What I call the *matrix of production elements* is a useful analytical tool for representing the various dimensions of the production process and understanding the economic effects of changes in techniques. This matrix not only highlights the links between intermediate stages within a given production process, but also makes it possible to consider both the *quantitative aspects*, dealt with in traditional microeconomic analysis (based on the production function or on activities analysis) and the *temporal* and *organizational aspects* which find no place in traditional analysis. The matrix of production elements allows, among other things, changes in production techniques to be classified according to three main forms: 'time-saving', 'inventory-saving', and 'input-saving technical change'. The matrix of production elements is transformed for empirical research, and its applicability is then verified in some case studies. This is the first time an attempt has been made to adopt such a representation of production process in applied analyses, because, as far as I know, no empirical work has hitherto been based on a fund–flow model.

The main purpose of this part of the book is to discuss the theoretical assumptions and implications of the proposed scheme, and to assess its possible empirical applications, leaving to further studies the actual implementation of the model to time series analyses or simulation techniques. In fact, as will emerge in the following pages, the scheme could be applied to historical series or to cross-section data (comparing different processes). If the sample is statistically representative, the economic effects of technical change in the various sectors of economic activity can be studied. Furthermore, the scheme could be used to ascertain the economic effects of possible changes by applying simulation techniques to the current data of a single production process at a given moment in time, adopting specific hypotheses on agents' behaviour and market structure.

In conclusion, this book has a two-fold nature. On the one hand, it is an analytical representation of the production process, on the other, it is a fact finding model for studying the economic effects of technical change. These two aspects are closely linked because clearly the capacity of empirical observations to answer the questions posed by transformations of the production process depends on the adequacy of the framework within which these empirical observations are expressed. It may serve as a useful decision-making tool for changes in techniques within a firm's production unit. These business decisions may involve, for instance, the evaluation of the relationship between (external) transaction costs and internal costs in organizing production in different intermediate stages (in other words, 'buy or make' choice), or generally the problem of investment choice. Moreover, this representation also proves fruitful in analysing problems related to changes in techniques such as variations in dimension of scale or in degree of production flexibility. Computer-based technology tends to link economies of scope with economies of scale by cutting flexibility costs in large plants. This allows the trade-off between economies of scale and production flexibility to be overcome. These last two aspects will be considered at some length in the final part of the book.

2   Plan of the book

The book consists of three parts: Part 1, basic hypotheses and concepts; Part 2, the model and its application; Part 3, economies of scale, economies of scope, and production flexibility. Part 1 is devoted to:

(a) analysing the relationship between the different economic dimensions of production process and the nature of technical change;
(b) introducing some preliminary definitions, such as microeconomic unit, flow and fund, indivisibility and complementarity of production elements and processes, historical and logical time, *ex-post* and *ex-ante* analysis;
(c) discussing the link between efficiency and organization.

The importance of this last point was quite clear to classical economists, who examined the relationship between the time profile of the production process and the organization of labour in determining the size of the production unit. Later, at least until quite recent times, the study of this relationship was largely neglected. As is well known, a reductive approach prevails in which size is simply linked to the configuration of the static (and independent) curves of unit costs of single intermediate stages. This link, between *efficiency* and *organization*, is an essential point in understanding the economic effects of change in techniques. However, readers who are less interested in the theoretical implications of this relationship, and the related debate, and more interested in *applied aspects* and *management studies*, may wish to start from Part 2, perhaps examining the discussion about the assumptions and hypotheses, presented in Part 1, at a later moment.

In Part 2 a fund–flow model is developed which permits temporal and organizational elements to be included in an analysis of the production process. The main analytical tool presented in this part is the *matrix of production elements*, mentioned above. In chapter 9 of Part 2, the applicability of this methodology is verified in some case studies. The cases examined serve mainly as numerical examples of how this methodology can provide a concise description of the production process's principal elements, in terms of its main economic dimensions (quantitative, temporal, organizational, and qualitative) which are influenced by technical change.

Part 3 deals with some of the basic problems in the theory of production for which the proposed scheme may serve as a fruitful analytical tool. Two particular cases of technical change will be examined: varying the dimension of scale and the degree of production flexibility.

The Introduction to Part 3 (chapter 10) discusses the usefulness of the proposed scheme in measuring efficiency changes, as the scale varies, and in ascertaining the economic effects of introducing new information technology or/and new organization systems, which increase flexibility. The concepts of complementarity and indivisibility, introduced in Part 1 are essential to a precise and consistent definition, understanding, and description of *economies of scale*; while it is impossible to deal with *production flexibility* without taking into account the time profile of production processes.

Chapter 11 considers the definition of returns of scale and economies of scale, different methods of collecting data on costs, the problem of the choice of the unit of analysis (such as plant, production unit or firm), the relationship between economies of scale and technical change, the relationship between indivisibility (of processes and production elements) and economies of scale, and, more generally, the underlying causes of economies of scale.

In chapter 12 of Part 3 the following points are discussed: the different meanings of the term flexibility in economic literature, the relationship between flexibility and economies of scope, the link between uncertainty and flexibility, differences between the various industrial organization models (such as traditional artisan production, industrial mass production, small-scale flexible industrial production, large-scale flexible industrial production), the role of organizational and technical aspects in determining production flexibility, the relationship between the elementary process time profile and production flexibility (reducing set-up times is a key factor in determining production flexibility), and the economic effects of computer-based technology.

Part 1

Basic concepts and hypotheses

1 Introduction

The effects of introducing new techniques – especially those involving the application of microelectronics to production processes in market economies – are of increasing interest. During the last twenty years the development of different lines of research has considerably broadened our knowledge of the determinants and effects of technical change, considered as a variation in the method of production and/or in the quality of goods produced. In particular, recent research in innovation has been along the following lines: (a) the nature, sources and procedures of innovative activity;[1] (b) the relationship between technical change and economic growth;[2] (c) the relationship between technical change and market structure;[3] (d) the relationship between innovation, industrial structure, economic development, and international trade;[4] (e) the evolutionary theories of the firm and the theory of transaction costs;[5] (f) the diffusion of new techniques.[6]

There is an increasing need for a representation of the production process, which may be consistent with some of the recent advances, mentioned above, and in particular with studies on the nature of technical change, firms and markets. In the preceding pages the close links between analysing the production process and the nature of technical change have

---

[1] See notes to chapter 2, section 2.2, which analyse the nature of technical change.

[2] See Pasinetti (1981).

[3] Among others: Dasgupta and Stiglitz (1980), Kamien and Schwartz (1982), Stoneman (1983, Part 1), Baldwin and Scott (1987); for more recent literature on game-theoretical analysis of innovative activity and market structure, see the excellent survey by Beath, Katsoulacos, Ulph (1989).

[4] For instance: Freeman (1974), Nelson and Winter (1982), Dosi (1984 and 1988), Dosi and Soete (1988).

[5] On the evolutionary theory of firm see Nelson and Winter (1982), Dosi (1984), Metcalfe (1989); on transaction costs see Williamson (1985), Teece (1980, 1988), Demsetz (1988b), Alchian and Woodward (1988). Finally, see Hodgson (1988) and Langlois (ed.) (1986) for the relationship between these themes and the neo-institutional approach.

[6] For example: Nabseth and Ray (1974), Brown (1981), Metcalfe (1981, and 1988), Sahal (1981, Chapter 5), Rosenberg (1982), Soete and Turner (1984), Stoneman and Ireland (1983), Stoneman (1983 Part 2, 1986, and 1987a Part 2), Santarelli (1987), Antonelli (1989 and 1990), Hagedoorn (1989, Chapter 4), Antonelli, Petit and Tahar (1989).

been stressed. In fact, without a model capable of considering all the main economic production dimensions, a detailed analysis of the nature of technical change appears to be a simple taxonomy. This lack of an appropriate representation of production processes may lead to a dichotomy between the analysis of the nature of technical change and the characteristics of these processes.

The representation of the production process, presented in the following pages, takes account of three *self-evident* and fundamental characteristics of production. First, in order to produce a commodity a technique must be created. Secondly, creating a technique and the consequent production of a commodity takes time. Thirdly, production is characterized by pronounced asymmetries in its component elements. These asymmetries arise from the unequal distribution of the 'individuals' power' and the productive capacity of instruments, and imply that individual agents' ability to influence the market is different.[7]

It is clear that the first two characteristics are closely linked to the temporal, organizational, and qualitative dimensions of the production process. These dimensions characterize the production process together with the quantitative dimension (given by the relationship between inputs and outputs).

As far as asymmetries in production processes are concerned, it can be argued that they are attributable in the last analysis to the factors of indivisibility, economies of scale, specialization, externalities and others such as 'information' and knowledge distribution, specificity of resources, diversity of interests and aims, capacity and ability in labour and negotiations, endowment of resources, and the definition of property rights.

Chapter 2 is devoted to analysing the different economic dimensions of the production process and the nature of technical change. The inclusion of the different production dimensions, i.e. the relationships between quantities of inputs and outputs, between time and organization, and between different qualities of production elements, allows the above-mentioned dichotomy between the analysis of the nature of technical change and the study of the characteristics of production units to be over-come. The importance of this point is evident, since it is closely linked to

---

[7] On this matter Frank Hahn writes 'those who regard power as central to economic understanding must look beyond classical General Equilibrium Theory. I rather count myself among those, and my earlier strictures were directed at the unfortunate fact that no serious work in new directions is available' (1981, p. 132). On the agents' power, considered in a broad sense, Jacob Viner notes that 'the important freedom ... is freedom of choice, but absence of power in the sense of economic resources, or of acquired knowledge and skills ... makes subjective exercise of that freedom of choice little more than indulgence in wishful daydreaming' (1961, p. 47).

the main aim of the book which is to provide a representation of production process which encompasses the economic effects of technical change.

The following chapter gives the main definitions of microeconomic unit, operational level and production element. A single microeconomic unit corresponds to each operational level. The distinction between *fund* and *flow* elements is considered here. Moreover, I introduce the concepts of *economic indivisibility* and *technical indivisibility*, and discuss the implications of *complementary* relationship between production elements in production unit organization and size. Lastly, the time dimension, in the creation of techniques and in the production process itself, is analysed. Production is seen as a sequential process which means taking historical irreversible time into account, instead of logical time.

Chapter 4 shows that economic efficiency cannot be considered *independent* of the production process organization. We shall consider the mutual interdependence of organization, size, division of labour, resources specificity and learning processes. It is clear that the level of demand and the specific characteristics of inputs/outputs (indivisibility and specialization) play an essential part in determining the kind of organization and size of the production units; and that the last two factors (organization and size of the production unit) are closely connected to the production process time profile.

In Part 2 a model of the production process is developed, whereby all main dimensions of the production process can be embraced. As we shall see, this model will allow the links between organization and efficiency to be considered, in addition to those between division of labour and the time profile of equipment utilization.

2 Technical change and the three economic dimensions of production

2.1 The counterpart of Occam's razor

Occam's fourteenth-century dictum against the use of superfluous entities in science is a very important methodological tool.[1] However, if we consider the present state of the art of analyses of the production process and the economic effects of technical change,[2] we must recognize that we often face the opposite threat.

The greatest danger when we consider the production process and technical change is not really so much that of contravening Occam's law, omitting 'shaving' off superfluous entities, as the opposite, that is, ignoring relevant elements for a proper understanding of the phenomenon and thus its effects on the structure of enterprises and markets.[3] The time profile aspects of the production process and the qualitative changes of production and of their individual elements have economic implications far too important to be left to technical specialists, engineers, and experts in industrial relations. Economic theory assumes techniques as given, i.e. deriving from purely engineering solutions to problems. From this point of view, the economist confines himself to the 'simple' task of choosing among many possible combinations of inputs that appear most convenient in relation to relative prices. Economic factors that contribute to the 'formation' of technique thus tend to be neglected, even when they have important implications for *time profile*, *organization*, and *size of production process*.

The exclusion of these aspects from the analysis and the growing

---

[1] 'Entia non sunt moltiplicanda praeter necessitatem', William Occam 1280–1349.

[2] I prefer the expression 'technical change' to the commonly used 'technical progress', because the latter expression implies 'value judgements' (with respect to some definition of the 'aims and ends of human society') which go beyond the range of this study and indeed of economic analysis itself (cf. Pasinetti, 1981, pp. 66–8). For example, one cannot say, on the basis of purely economic considerations, that a new source of energy or a new product represents not only a technical change but 'progress' for humanity.

[3] On the suppression of necessary 'entities' in many scientific processes see K. Menger (1979, pp. 105–33).

segmentation of the studies on innovation, with various theoretical approaches, demonstrate the undoubted difficulty of reconciling, within the same theoretical model, the various dimensions of the production process, relevant to economic analysis. This segmentation of analyses of technical change limits severely the interpretative capacity of the theoretical models used, and at the same time influences even the results of empirical analysis.

The simple quantitative relationship described by means of the set of production or through a Sraffa model (or by a matrix of the Leontief or von Neumann type) provides no information about the functioning of the production process, its timing or its organization.[4] Clearly, these aspects affect economic decisions. As Zamagni observes, given equal coefficients of labour, or in other words, equal hours of work per unit of output, each particular organization of labour can lead to a different degree of utilization of existing plant, and produce a variation in all the other coefficients, without any modification in the state of techniques.

representing techniques through the usual matrices does not allow us to distinguish between variations in the coefficients owing to the introduction of a new technique and variations arising from a reorganization of processes based on the old technique. And everyone knows that the latter depend more on circumstances involving economic variables than on those involving technical variables. (Sraffa was evidently so conscious of the *conceptual impossibility of such a separation that he used intersectoral flow tables only in problems with fixed quantities of goods produced*).[5] (Zamagni 1982, pp. 19–20, my italics)

As shown by classic economists, an increase in demand can allow a reorganization of production which brings about a notable increase in productivity and decrease in unit costs, without necessarily changing the type of tools and equipment. Adam Smith in his celebrated example of the pin factory observed that an increase of demand, and thus of the volume of production of single production units, permits the *transition* from *craft production*, where one worker performs a variety of heterogeneous operations moving from one machine to another, to *line production*, typical of the factory system. Line production may allow an increase in the degree of the division of labour and hence an increase in productivity (Smith, 1776, pp. 14–15, n. 3 by editors). Another consequence of line production, which becomes more important with the growth of fixed capital, lies in the fact that it reduces idle times of production equipment

[4] In this connection, Tani (1988) and Baldone (1989) have recently made some interesting attempts to investigate the relations between sectoral interdependence and the time profiles of production processes. In particular, Baldone (1989) shows the possible use of an input–output model in measuring the effects of structural change, considering not only variations in technical coefficients, but also changes in production times. See also Oda (1990).   [5] Cf. Sraffa (1960). On this point see also Scazzieri (1983).

through the 'saturation of time profile' of production process. This last aspect, together with the need to match (at each given instant of the process) the different productive capacities of the different phases, plays a very important role in determining the size of the production unit. Figure 2.1 summarizes the chain of these relationships; this table indicates only the main flows although there are also causal relationships in the opposite direction to those shown.

In conclusion, it is clear that the level of demand and the specific characteristics of in/outputs (indivisibility and specialization) play an essential part in determining the kind of organization and size of the production units; and that the last two factors (organization and size of the production unit) are closely connected to the time profile of the productive process.

If one does not take into account the various economic aspects of production, it is not possible to obtain an accurate picture of the production process. And, as a result, it is not possible to appreciate the transformation brought about by technical change. There are at least *three dimensions* that must not be neglected by the economic analysis of productive activity and technical change:

(i) the relationship between *physical quantities* of input and output (physical productivity), and, at given prices, between input costs and output proceeds (profitability);

(ii) the relationship between *times* and *modes of execution* (organization of inputs and size of productive units);

(iii) *changes creating new inputs* and/or *new outputs* according to the technological opportunities and the demand conditions (qualitative transformations).

These organizational and temporal elements of production, together with quantitative aspects, were extensively dealt with in the analyses of classic economists. For example, Adam Smith considered these three dimensions of production examining the relationship between efficiency and internal organization (1776, chapters 1, 2, 3), while Karl Marx referred to these different dimensions in discussing the various aspects of the social relationship between producers within the capitalistic mode of production (1867, vol. 1, pp. 165, 426ff., 455ff. and chps. 5, 14, 15, 25; vol. 3, ch. 5).[6]

---

[6] Rosenberg (1976a) contains an interesting critical examination on 'Marx as a student of technology'. A discussion on the antithesis between production, as social relationships among producers, and production, as a natural process, is in Rowthorn (1974). For a comparison between Marx's and Schumpeter's theories of innovation see Elster (1983, chapters 5 and 7) and the recent work by Hagedoorn (1989, chapter 2). Finally, on the division of labour and the factory system in classical economists, see Leijonhufvud (1986).

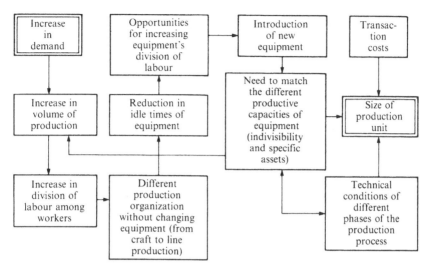

Figure 2.1 Relationships among increases in demand, time profile of the production process and size of the production unit

A theory of the production process which intends to analyse the economic effects of technical change should have a consistent methodological framework, able to include the quantitative, qualitative, and temporal dimensions. Figure 2.2 shows some of the main elements, related with these three dimensions, which can be influenced by technical change.

It is evident that technical change could have aims other than a simple reduction of the quantities of input per product unit. To quote two examples, a change in techniques can be related to the attempt to acquire a stronger position in certain market segments, or to increase the flexibility of production where market conditions are turbulent. In these cases, technical change can involve a change in the quality of input and of output, without any variation in the quantity (size of the production unit and the time profile of production process), or it can have an effect on the time profile and thus on the organization and on the size of the production unit without influencing the quantity and quality of input and output. Nevertheless, it is obvious that a change in a single element can often cause changes in almost all the other elements of the production process. For instance, where a new machine has been installed we can have, among others, the following changes: (i) in the quantities and qualities of raw materials, intermediate goods, inventories, and outputs; (ii) in the kind of work used; (iii) in production time; (iv) in the distribution of shifts; (v) in the number of machines; (vi) in the size of the production unit.

Moreover, some changes in technique can arise from in-house activity

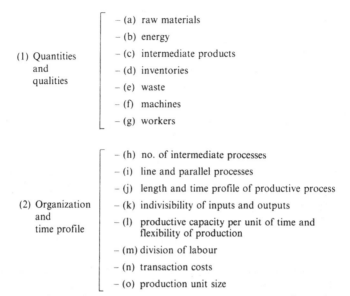

(1) Quantities
and
qualities

- (a) raw materials
- (b) energy
- (c) intermediate products
- (d) inventories
- (e) waste
- (f) machines
- (g) workers

(2) Organization
and
time profile

- (h) no. of intermediate processes
- (i) line and parallel processes
- (j) length and time profile of productive process
- (k) indivisibility of inputs and outputs
- (l) productive capacity per unit of time and
      flexibility of production
- (m) division of labour
- (n) transaction costs
- (o) production unit size

Figure 2.2 Main elements of the production process affected by
technical change

in research and development, other changes come from materials,
equipment or professional services supplied by outside firms. As far as
innovation is concerned, when the choice of buying out intermediate
products or services prevails over the choice of making them in-house, the
production unit will be characterized by a high degree of innovation even
with a modest in-house innovative activity and with low R&D costs (on
this point see Part 2 chapter 9, section 9.1).

For all these technical changes that imply a variation in the production
process, there is a close two-way relationship between the level of analysis
of the production process and that of the nature of technical change. As
mentioned, in the absence of an analytical representation that takes
account of the different economic dimensions of the production process,
the detailed analysis of the nature of technical change becomes in fact a
mere taxonomy. The lack of a suitable representation of the production
process may lead to a sharp dichotomy, present in some studies, between
the analysis of the nature of technical change and the characteristics of
production processes. For example, this dichotomy, between the analysis
of the nature of innovative processes and the study of the behaviour of the
characteristics of production units, can be seen in some parts of Nelson
and Winter's work (1982). In fact, in reviewing this book, Loasby (1983)
justly observes:

In their general theory, every organization is the product of its own history – which is partly, but only partly, shared with other firms. Yet in the models, all firms are alike. They differ in size, but a small firm is simply a large firm in miniature: they all have the same set of decision rules (except when divided into innovators and imitators)...There is no room for the creative intelligence emphasized in the preface.

On the other hand, in most books which discuss literature on innovation, the current forms of analysing the relationship between production process and innovative activity deal only with the approach based on the production function (see e.g. Heertje 1973, ch. 8; Rosegger 1980, ch. 3; Stoneman 1983, ch. 11; Clark 1985, ch. 4).[7] However, it is not really possible to take into account the economic effects of technical change upon the production process, if we do not consider, on the one hand, the temporal and organizational dimensions of production, and on the other hand, the complexity of the nature of technical change. Thus, in the next section we shall be looking firstly at some of the aspects related to the nature of technical change which will serve our analysis.

2.2   The nature of technical change

It is outside the scope of this study to develop the analysis of the nature of technical change. There is a vast and interesting literature on that subject to which I refer the reader.[8] In this section I shall examine only those particular aspects of technical change which are useful for the present study.

Technical change means a variation in the method of production and/or in the quality of goods produced. The distinction between change in processes and change in products is very important – although often the two phenomena are linked in the sense that a change in the product leads to a change in the process and vice versa. It should be noted that the concept of innovation is much broader than that of technical change. In

---

[7] In some reviews, as in Coombs et al. (1987, chapter 2) and Kay (1979, chapter 3), the analysis is broadened to including theories of the firm, based on managerial, motivational, behavioural, evolutionary, transactional and even systems theories. All these theories offer interesting explanations of the behaviour of firms, but they do not illuminate the functioning of the production process. Even in the recent large collections of essays on technical change, references to the production process are very limited (see Dosi et al., eds., 1988; Arcangeli et al., eds., 1991). On the application of production function on applied analysis of technical change see below chapter 9 (section 9.1) and chapter 11 (section 11.3).

[8] On the nature, sources and procedures of innovative activity see, for instance, Freeman (1974), David (1975), Rosenberg (1976b and 1982), Nelson and Winter (1982), Pavitt (1984), Dosi (1984 and 1988), Stoneman (1983 and 1987a), Piatier (1984), Metcalfe (1989).

fact, innovation, though it usually involves a change in production techniques, may be related to changes in market conditions, which have no influence on production processes.[9]

By method of production (or technique) I mean the technical conditions of production, within a specific organizational system (e.g., Taylorism, neo-Fordism, organization for objectives, project organization, etc.) and a specific industrial organization model (such as mass production, large-scale flexible production, small-scale flexible production, traditional artisan production, etc.), belonging to a given socio-juridical form, called the mode of production (feudal, capitalist, or collectivist production). Although these four levels are related to each other, a given mode of production is clearly compatible with the very different organizational systems and industrial organization models which correspond to successive historical phases, or which may coexist within a given phase (on this point see Part 3 chapter 12, section 12.5).

The study of the nature of technical change is very complicated, as it concerns various different phenomena requiring an analysis that crosses the boundaries of traditional disciplines. Even if, as here, we restrict the field of analysis to economic aspects, one cannot but agree with Morton Kamien and Nancy Schwartz (1982, p. ix) that the analysis of the economic aspects of technical change 'involves almost all the difficulties excluded from the standard analysis of competitive equilibrium', e.g. non-convexities, scale economies, indivisibility, externalities, public goods, uncertainty and non-price competition. Moreover, technical change is still a very complex subject because it involves: (a) a high number of variables; (b) changes in variables along with time; and (c) two-way relationships among variables.

Technical change includes, on the one hand, a series of small improvements in machines and the organization of labour, arising from slow processes of learning by doing and learning by using, and on the other, the application to production of the results of systematic planned research carried out by firms and university research institutes, laboratories, private and public bodies, etc. This process, as Luigi Pasinetti writes:

---

[9] Schumpeter, as is well known, distinguished five different types of innovation: (1) the introduction of a new good; (2) the introduction of a new method of production; (3) the opening of a new market (that is a market into which the particular branch of manufacture of the country in question has not entered previously, whether or not this market has existed before; (4) the conquest of a new source of supply of raw materials or half-manufactured goods; (5) the carrying out of the new organization of any industry (like the creation of a monopoly position) (Schumpeter, 1911, p. 66). On the concept of innovation in Schumpeter see Rosenberg (1975 and 1978), Stoneman (1987a, chapter 2), De Vecchi (1988, pp. 27–30).

consists of long and repeated attempts not only to reorganise the old methods of production, to utilise more efficiently the new materials, and to improve the quality of products, but also to invent and apply new methods of production, produce new products, find new resources, and discover new sources of energy. (1981, pp. 66ff.)

Following a taxonomy which is by now widely accepted, we can thus distinguish between *incremental changes* and *radical changes*.

Incremental changes (or minor innovations) are the innumerable small improvements and modifications that occur more or less continuously in any industry. As Nathan Rosenberg pointed out, these minor technical changes, which represent an important portion of total technical change, are mainly connected with the processes of learning by doing and learning by using. In many cases, increases in efficiency arising from learning processes continue even after a radical change in production technique. Rosenberg cites numerous empirical studies on technical change in the different sectors of manufacturing industry, demonstrating that 'the cumulative effects of minor technological changes', upon increase in efficiency and cost reduction, 'were greater than the effects of major technical changes' (1978, pp. 6–8).

Radical changes (or Schumpeterian innovations) are discontinuous events. To quote Schumpeter's famous example, there is no way in which railways could have emerged from incremental improvements in the production of mail coaches. It is worth noting that Schumpeter stated explicitly that his analysis was intended to apply only to major innovations. 'We shall impose a restriction on our concept of innovation and henceforth understand by an innovation *a change in some product function which is of the first ... order of magnitude*' (1939, p. 94, Schumpeter's italics).[10]

Radical changes usually involve the application and spread within the productive processes of a new technology. Technology is a set body of knowledge about techniques; in that sense it constitutes the application of scientific knowledge to production. Technology often refers, not only to knowledge bases, but also to artifacts: the corresponding products and processes (Freeman, 1974, p. 4; Metcalfe, 1989, p. 55).[11] The knowledge implicit in a technology is both practical and theoretical, as it includes 'know-how, methods, procedures, experience of successes and failures

---

[10] 'Innovations [he argues elsewhere] are changes in production function which can not be decomposed into infinitesimal steps' (Schumpeter, 1935 cf. Rosenberg, 1976, p. 300, n. 7). In this respect Rosenberg's view, about the important role played by incremental changes, is in sharp contrast to that of Schumpeter, with its emphasis on the discontinuous nature of technical progress (Rosenberg, 1975).

[11] On the relationship between science and technology, see Rosenberg (1978, p. 13, 1981, pp. 143–4), Dasgupta and David (1987, pp. 323ff).

and also, of course, physical devices and equipment' (Dosi, 1984, pp. 13–14).

Technical change involves production of information, an activity which is often performed under uncertainties and, due to moral hazard, many of the related risks cannot be efficiently insured. Moreover, it has been argued that information has the attributes of a public good, because if one person uses a piece of information it does not physically prevent someone else from using it simultaneously – 'though, of course, the benefit to each will typically depend on whether the other is using it'. Finally, the market for knowledge is imperfect because 'potential purchasers of information could not ascertain its value exactly, since to disclose it would be to convey the information without cost' (Dasgupta and David, 1987, p. 520; cf. Arrow, 1962a).

Patent protection is essential to guarantee high returns on innovative activity and hence the appropriability of its outcomes, even if it involves a social cost due to restricting the diffusion of these outcomes to other firms which lose the opportunity of taking advantage of them. However, not all findings that research generates are patentable. In spite of the negative incentive of possible non-appropriability and spillovers, there are many important reasons that induce private firms still to invest in R&D. In fact, 'R&D not only generates new information but also enhances the firm's ability to assimilate and exploit existing information'. In other words, R&D and specifically basic research are essential to increase 'the firm's absorptive capacity to acquire outside knowledge' (Cohen and Levinthal, 1989, p. 569, see also Rosenberg, 1990, pp. 169f). Moreover, private firms spend on basic research in order to exploit first-mover advantages on new techniques, in situations where it is often very difficult to determine *ex-ante* the border between basic research and applied research (Rosenberg, 1990).

Each different technology implies what has been called a technological paradigm (Dosi, 1982) or a technological regime (Nelson and Winter, 1977), that is to say, 'a common approach to certain technological and productive problems'. Nelson and Winter (1982, pp. 258–9) cite as an example of a technological regime the advent of the DC-3 in the 1930s. The DC-3 was characterized by an all-metal skin, low wings, streamlined body and powerful engines. For more than two decades innovation in aircraft design essentially involved better exploitation of this formula. A 'technological paradigm' (or 'technological regime') embodies an '*outlook*, a definition of the relevant problems, a pattern of enquiry. A "technological paradigm" defines contextually the needs that are meant to be fulfilled, the scientific principles utilized for the task, the material technology to be used' (Dosi, 1988, p. 1127). In other words, it is 'a "model"...of solution of *selected* technological problems, based on *selected* principles derived from natural sciences and on selected material technologies' (Dosi, 1982, pp. 14–15). Thus, 'incremental changes' take place within a given 'technological paradigm', while 'radical changes' imply new 'paradigms'. Any 'technological paradigm' defines a frontier of development of knowledge and abilities. A new 'technological paradigm' may lead to changes, even radical ones, and to a new chain of small improvements within a particular path of development. Such a path of development, called by Nelson and Winter (1977) a natural trajectory and by Dosi (1982) a technological trajectory, is 'the activity of technological trade-offs defined by a technological paradigm' (Dosi, 1988, p. 1128).[12] As we shall see, these processes of selection of innovations along a trajectory defined by a paradigm are tacit, specific and cumulative within the different production units, because of the importance of the phenomena of learning by doing and learning by using.

It should be noted that in some circumstances a new technology may lead to the advent of a new technological system. A technological system is defined by a technology with certain characteristics that pervade all sectors (for example electrical energy or microelectronics). The establishment of a new technological system involves not only the appearance of a new range of products but also a general change in the mode of production and consumption and a social acceptance that brings about changes in education, legislation and custom.[13]

It has been justly observed that 'the conceptualization of technology and technical change based on "paradigms" "guideposts" or whatever name is chosen, also helps in resolving the long debate in the innovation literature about the relative importance of "market pull" versus "technology push"' (Dosi, p. 1141), that is to say, to what extent the technical change is induced by demand (demand push, demand led) or stimulated by the development of technological opportunities. In the light of the foregoing analysis this opposition seems to have little meaning, because demand and technical change both play important roles, although at different moments in the course of development of each paradigm. 'Market conditions exert a powerful influence on the conduct of technological search, but they do so primarily by stimulating, hindering

[12] This definition of technology has some analogies with the concept of the metaproduction function proposed by Hayami and Ruttan (1971). The metaproduction function describes a locus of production possibility points that can be *discovered* within the existing state of scientific knowledge. 'Points on this surface are attainable, but at cost of time and resources. They are not presently available in blueprint form' (Rosenberg, 1978, p. 17).

[13] The notion of 'technological system' has been introduced by Freeman (1974, p. 8); on the interaction between innovation and social structure see also Freeman and Soete (1985, pp. 42ff).

and focusing the search for new technological paradigms' (*ibid.*). In the initial phases of the development of a paradigm, technological opportunities tend to prevail because each paradigm, when established, remains quite 'sticky' in its basic technical imperatives. Demand, in turn, becomes important when major innovations lead to a series of secondary inventions and innovations. So it is clear that the firm is driven by the competitive process and appropriability conditions to improve methods of production and products, so as to bring together the technological opportunities presented by the stimuli and possibilities arising from evolving market conditions, both for raw materials and for finished products. In short, one significant part of the role of the innovative entrepreneur is to bring technological opportunities into line with the potentialities of the market. From this point of view technical change is the product of competitive activity (considered in a broad sense).[14] Dosi (1988) effectively sums up this line of interpretation; he writes: 'each body of knowledge ... contains both the opportunities of technical progress and the boundaries within which "inducement effects" can be exerted by the market, while appropriability conditions motivate the economic agents to explore these technological opportunities as a rent-yielding device' (pp. 1142).

Before going on to present the formal model for analysis of the production process, which enables us to take account of the various dimensions of production and hence to consider fully the economic effects of technical change, it is necessary to discuss a few definitions and assumptions regarding the characteristics of production elements and the production process itself. This will be done in chapter 3.

---

[14] On this theme see the interesting review of the literature on new tendencies in market analysis in Dardi (1990, in particular pp. 62–3 and 81).

3 Production and time: preliminary definitions

This chapter is devoted to the definition and discussion of some concepts and hypotheses used in the course of the analysis. In the first place, the elements of production are divided into funds and flows. This distinction permits us to introduce time into our analysis and to separate those production elements which participate in just one production process from those that participate in several processes. In the second place, we shall discuss the concept of indivisibility of production processes and elements. In particular, we shall examine the role of what I call *economic indivisibility* and *technical indivisibility*, which together determine the organization and size of the production unit. The third aspect, closely connected with indivisibility, is that of *complemental* relationship among production elements; in fact, in most production processes the elements combine according to specific (and numerically limited) proportions. *Complementarity* involves not only fixed coefficients, but, as we shall see, it dominates also many other aspects of production processes. Lastly, we shall analyse the notion of *irreversible historical time* and its implications for the analysis of the production process and technical change.

3.1 The microeconomic unit of analysis

By microeconomic unit I mean an elementary technical unit, or a plant, or a production unit, or a firm or a group of firms. An elementary technical unit is a set of production elements which represent the minimum technical unit that can be activated separately for producing a unit of output within a plant. A plant consists of one or more elementary technical units which perform a process or a sub-process (for instance, weaving, spinning etc.). A production unit, or a business unit, consists of one or more plants situated in one or more departments, within a single 'establishment' or in neighbouring 'establishments'.[1] Hence, a multi-

[1] As observed by Cliff Pratten, in production censuses the term establishment refers to a firm's operation at a single site. In practice different terms are used for these operations such as: plant or works in the steel industry, works in the cement industry and factory in the footwear industry (Pratten, 1988, p. 55).

plant, or integrated production unit operates with many plants located on the same site. The production unit is responsible for organizing the production of a single commodity (or a range of commodities) and the relative production methods.[2] A firm is an organization consisting of at least one production unit. A group of firms is a combination of firms with temporary or permanent collaboration relations (belonging to a constellation, network or financial holding). Each 'microeconomic unit' corresponds to a diverse *operational level*. As we shall see in discussing economies of scale and production flexibility, it is essential to always identify the 'operational level' and consequently the 'microeconomic unit' to which the analysis refers.

Production elements can be divided into flows and funds. The *flow* elements are present either *only* as input (e.g. raw materials and energy), or *only* as output (e.g. the finished product and waste), while *fund* elements perform a service inside the process, entering and leaving the process (for example, a piece of agricultural land, a lathe, a loom, a worker). If durable instruments of production are treated as fund economics there is no need to consider these elements as joint products of the process, or to prolong the duration of the process until they are used up completely (Tani 1988, p. 7).[3] Of course, 'the same commodity may be a flow in one process and a fund in another'[4] (Georgescu-Roegen 1969, pp. 64–5, 1965, p. 85).

To the usual fund elements (land, all kinds of machines and tools, workers) must be added the *stores of commodities* and the *elements in progress* during the successive phases through which the input flow passes to become ultimately the product flow.[5] It is supposed that the 'regeneration' of workers' productive capacity takes place outside the production unit. On the other hand, *maintenance operations* on machines and equipment must be considered as separate production processes (Georgescu-Roegen, 1965, p. 84).

A flow element (input or output) always corresponds to a certain quantity of some material, substance or energy, which enters the production process or emerges from it. On the other hand, a fund element may participate in the production of the product only through the service which it performs, and then it is measured by time. On this point it may be useful to stress the difference between the concepts of *stock*, on one

---

[2] On the production unit as the relevant unit of organization, see Metcalfe and Gibbons (1986, p. 496); see also Chandler (1977).

[3] On definition of fixed capital as a species of joint production, see Sraffa (1960, p. 63), and the recent article by Salvadori (1986), who examines the debate on this matter, cf. Salvadori (1988).

[4] As Georgescu-Roegen himself recognizes, the concepts of flow and fund derive from the classical economists (1986, p. 256). A similar distinction is also used by Lowe (1976).

[5] I prefer to use the definition of element in progress instead of the Georgescu-Roegen's definition *process fund* (cf. Georgescu-Roegen, 1965, pp. 92ff.; 1971, pp. 249–40).

hand, and of *flow* and *fund*, on the other. It is true that stock consists in the accumulation of a flow and it decumulates through a flow, but, according to the above definition of flow, the opposite is not always true: 'a flow does not necessarily represent either a decrease or an increase in a stock of the same substance' (Georgescu-Roegen, 1971, p. 223). Hence, a flow may result from a qualitative transformation due to a production process. As far as the difference between stocks and funds is concerned, it should be noted that stock may be accumulated or decumulated in a single instant, while a fund participates to several production processes and its 'decumulation' requires a duration. Georgescu-Roegen gives a good example of this difference between stocks and funds: with 'a box [that] contains twenty candies, we can make twenty youngsters happy now or tomorrow, or some today and others tomorrow, and so on'. But with one hotel room, that probably lasts 1,000 days more, 'we cannot make one thousand roomless tourists happy *now*. We can only make one happy today, a second tomorrow, and so on, until the room collapses' (Georgescu-Roegen 1971, p. 226).[6] By definition, a fund cannot be 'decumulated' in a short (or infinitesimal) interval or even within the duration of a single elementary process.

As we shall see in the following chapters, the definitions of flow and fund make it possible to take account of the levels of use of production elements. It is clear, for instance, that the utilization of each fund is characterized by a specific time profile, with some possible idle times, and that the utilization time profiles of various funds strongly influence the organization and size of production units. Industrial production, whatever its organizational form, and technical changes both reflect the economic necessity to reduce to a minimum any periods of fund idleness.

3.2   Indivisibility

Most of the fund elements (e.g. ovens, pipes, containers, most tools and equipment) are indivisible, while the flow elements are mostly divisible (with the important exception of the components to be assembled). By examining the degrees and timing of utilization of inputs one can evaluate the element effects of the indivisibility of processes on the productive structure, production costs, and the size of the production unit.[7]

---

[6] A general discussion of the relationship between the concepts of stock and flow is in Clower (1959) and Patinkin (1965, chapter 11). Clower and Patinkin give a definition of the stock and flow related only to the time dimension, while Georgescu-Roegen considers the functional definition of flow in relation to his analysis of the production process.

[7] As is well known, production theories, based on models of general economic equilibrium, assume absence of indivisibility, because convexity and indivisibility are incompatible concepts. In fact, if some kind of indivisibility is present, the assumption of convexity on the production possibility set is precluded. When the production possibility set is not

A process is indivisible if indivisible goods appear among its elements (as inputs or as outputs). For a process to be divisible, however, it is not enough for its constituent elements to be divisible. In fact, even where the inputs and outputs are completely divisible, a process may be characterized by a particular size above or below which it cannot take place.

For the purpose of this analysis it is useful to distinguish between what I call *economic indivisibility* and *technical indivisibility*. The former is present when it is impossible to exchange less than a given unit of a particular commodity (a length of cloth, a bushel of corn). The second refers to the impossibility of dividing a particular commodity, once it is exchanged, into amounts usable for production or consumption (in this case the length of cloth and the bushel of corn are technically divisible, while a refrigerator or a loom is not).

We are dealing with strict technical divisibility if a given economic unit x of a given commodity is usable in fractions corresponding to x/n, with $n > 0$, and if the operation of division is reversible – that is to say, if by reaggregating the single fractions we obtain again the original economic unit (i.e. if $x/n \cdot n = x$). Whereas, if the operation of division is irreversible, we are speaking simply of technical divisibility. A very simple example may clarify the difference between strict technical divisibility and technical divisibility. A box of washing powder and a 4-carat diamond are both technically divisible, but only the washing powder is strictly technically divisible, because once the diamond is cut the original commodity cannot be recovered in its original form.

Divisibility, as I have defined it, clearly cannot be confused with the possibility of exchanging a given commodity available in continuously increasing size.[8] For example, it is possible to produce and exchange a series of ovens of continuously increasing diameter, but a given oven of a given diameter is obviously an economically and technically indivisible commodity.

Within this scheme, the presence of technically indivisible flow elements, such as components to be assembled, is not a serious problem because in general such components are used in large quantities. In fact the

convex there may not be equilibrium solutions that maximize profit at given prices, see, for example, chapters 3 and 7 in Arrow and Hahn (1971), and chapter 2 in Tani (1986), cf. Koopmans (1957, p. 25). Integer programming, which requires integer solutions, is a way to deal with indivisibility of inputs, within optimization problems. For the definition of integer convexity see Frank (1969, pp. 34ff, cf. Baumol, 1961, pp. 566–7).

[8] Chamberlin (1949) underlines this possibility (which can be considered as 'divisibility in the long-run analytic context'), when he writes that 'There are a number of ways in which units of different economic entities may be "divided"...[A] steam boiler may be "divided" in manufacturing by making it smaller (or larger) and again the gradations are infinite' (p. 180).

'economic significance' of indivisibility 'is relatively less when the number of units is large' (Arrow and Hahn, 1971, p. 62). On the other hand, the economic indivisibility of some flow elements may make it necessary to maintain large stocks of goods, with major consequences for production costs. For example, certain raw materials are bought in large quantities, and hence stock management becomes a financial operation before it is an industrial one. Economic indivisibility is not the only reason why firms hold large stocks of flow elements, other reasons often given are the instability of demand for final products or the need to produce in large batches. However, the most serious consequences for the organization of the production process, and thus for the size of the production unit, arise from the indivisibility of fund elements (equipment and workers).

Indivisibility can be seen not only in relation to exchangeable quantities, but also in relation to time. In fact, in a situation of technical divisibility, if funds could be bought and sold in the necessary proportions with no economic loss (except for normal wear and tear) there would be perfect economic divisibility and no fixed costs. Thus, economic indivisibility prevents payment for production elements in exact correspondence with the quantity used and the time strictly necessary for their use. This causes fixed costs which in turn lead to an increase in the unit cost when the quantity produced decreases. In short, economic indivisibility depends not only on the specific market conditions that make it necessary to buy some goods in quantities or batches established by custom and regulations, but also on the presence of sunk costs. Sunk costs consist mainly of the contractual costs of selling capital goods. They mainly arise from losses in capital goods prices owing to imperfect and asymmetrical information between buyer and seller (see chapter 12). As we shall see, one way to reduce indivisibility and sunk cost irreversibility is to hire machines instead of buying them, or to buy less durable equipment, or to settle sub-contracting relationships.

Note that economic indivisibility and technical indivisibility have very different effects on the level of utilization of funds. Economic indivisibility entails that in certain periods some of the funds involved in the production process may be unused; in other words, they will have periods of idleness (for instance, a lorry that cannot travel on some days of the week, or a machine that does not operate during the night break). On the other hand, the technical indivisibility of funds means that in operation they may run below their full productive capacity (for instance, a lorry that travels half-empty or below its optimal speed).

The factory system, sub-contracting production, hiring equipment represent three attempts to overcome the problem of indivisibility of production funds, so as to make full use of their productive capacity. The need to render compatible the different productive capacities of indivisible funds is a factor in determining the scale of the production process. In fact, to avoid using individual machines at sub-optimal levels the overall scale of a production unit must be equal to the lowest common multiple of the productive capacities of the individual machines. In this regard, the fund–flow model, presented in Part 2, proves particularly useful for studying the 'combination' of individual funds' productive capacities.

Indivisibility of some production elements may explain the large size of a production unit and is an essential concept in understanding the phenomenon of increasing returns of scale. In chapter 11, the importance of distinguishing between indivisibility of process and indivisibility of production elements will become evident. As we shall see, even if indivisibility of process does not imply increasing returns of scale, increasing returns of scale always imply indivisibility of process. Moreover, indivisibility of some production elements – which always implies increasing returns – is not the sole cause of increasing returns of scale. In fact, increasing returns of scale may arise from several forces, such as technical, statistical and organizational factors, which are in some cases independent of the indivisibility of production elements.

3.3   Complementarity

The presence of both indivisible funds and limitational flows (i.e. inputs that are transformed in strict proportions during the production process) implies a low possibility of substituting the production elements. In the last section we saw that apart from agricultural land most funds are indivisible. If a production element is indivisible, it combines with the other elements through a relationship of complementarity rather than of substitutability; that is to say, a fixed-coefficient type of production prevails. On the other hand, flexible coefficients need total divisibility; only in this case is it meaningful to speak of a given piece of equipment's adaptability to variations in the quantities of other inputs. Robertson's famous example of the shovels is illuminating in this connection. As Stigler writes on this point:

The law of diminishing returns requires full adaptability of the form ... of the 'fixed' productive services to the varying quantity of the other productive service ... when the ditch-digging crew is increased from ten to eleven, the ten previous shovels must be metamorphosed into eleven smaller or less durable shovels equal in value to the former ten ... if the true marginal product of eleven laborers is to be discovered.[9] (1939, p. 307)

---

[9] Cf. Robertson (1930, p. 47) and J. Robinson (1953–4, p. 115). Later in the text Stigler points out that 'Illustrations of perfect adaptability are ... difficult to find ... The historical

In general, the various production elements combine in certain determined proportions, and each machine requires a fixed number of workers. In other words, machines and labour tend to be complementary. The absence of substitutability in the short run (after the choice of the plant) may depend upon the indivisibility of funds, and the consequent insufficient adaptability of the 'plant'. However, in certain circumstances, due to the specific technical characteristics of the production process, the substitutability is not guaranteed even with perfect divisibility of funds. In all these cases we cannot calculate the marginal productivity.

Complementarity may concern, not only plants and machines, but also the organization of labour services which often involves indivisibility of process, because of the peculiar characteristics of team-production. There is the well-known example of two men who are jointly able to lift heavy cargo onto lorries. In a team-production, not only is the total output 'not the sum of separable outputs of each of its members' (Alchian and Demsetz 1972, p. 779),[10] but there are skills specific to a given organization, therefore team members' skills are, at least in part, non-individually appropriable, and this means that there is 'a degree of non-transferable synergy'. Firm resources, and in particular the human ones, are team specific, because of the 'collective nature of co-operators' skills' and work organization.[11] Therefore, it is impossible to determine each team member's marginal productivity.

Complementarity is expressed by the presence of *limitational flows*. It is hard to conceive of a form of textile production in which yarn could be replaced by machine-hours or man-hours (though some working arrangements or maintenance operations may reduce yarn waste). If in order to measure the marginal productivity of labour we keep the quantity of yarn constant (as well as the machine hours, of course) and increase the quantity of labour, we shall obtain no increase in output, 'with the consequence that the marginal productivity of labour would appear to be

connection between agricultural land and the law of diminishing returns may explain in part the failure of economists to recognise the difficulties in short-run applications of the law' (p. 314, n. 18). However, according to agricultural experts the technical complementarity relationships among inputs tend to prevail even in agriculture (see, for instance, Polidori and Romagnoli (1987, p. 345) and Romagnoli (1989, p. 205).

[10] Edwards and Starr have recently emphasized the importance of indivisibility in the use of labour, arguing that in the current standard texts on microeconomics 'indivisibility (or other nonconvexity) of labor is seldom made explicit' (1987, p. 193–4).

[11] Here team-production is considered in a stronger sense than Alchian and Demsetz's definition (1972). In consequence, the marginal productivity of each member of the team-production is not 'costly to measure', but is simply not measurable at all. My notion of team-production is, in many respects, close to that of Marshall (1890, p. 626) and Aoki (1984, pp. 28–9). For further discussion on the distinction between assets specific to a particular job and assets specific to a given organization see chapter 4, section 4.1.

zero' (Tani, 1986, p. 64). The distinction between funds and flows makes it clear that there is no possibility of substitution, for example, between the sewing machine, which represents a fund, and the fabric used for making shirts, which is a flow element (transformed in the production process thanks to the services of the funds) (Georgescu-Roegen, 1979, p. 129; cf. Schneider, 1934, p. 68).

Considering limitational inputs and complementary relationships between inputs, the economic problem, in production of a certain commodity, is no longer a simple problem of optimal inputs combination, but involves choosing a combination of processes, or single phases, largely characterized by indivisibility of inputs. The practice of separating the analysis of variations in proportions (partial or short-term adaptation) from variations in quantities (full or long-term adaptation) seems to be misleading, as there are good reasons for thinking that the proportions and quantities vary together. Relationships of complementarity (and fixed-coefficient production) involve a variation in proportions especially in the case of an increase in the absolute quantities of the inputs – that is to say, when moving onto a larger scale of production. On the whole question, therefore, the usual reasoning has to be reversed so that fixed coefficients should be considered the general case, while variable coefficients should be considered a particular case, or more precisely, a *curiosum*. The assertion that variable coefficients are the general case, which include fixed coefficients as a special case, is theoretically untenable, because, as pointed out by Giovanni Dosi, 'reversibility and variable coefficients, on the one hand, and irreversibility and fixed coefficients, on the other, yield radically different properties of the object of inquiry' (Dosi, 1984, p. 303; cf. Pasinetti, 1981, pp. 203–4).

Complementarity among the different production elements also concerns interdependencies among the productive capacities of the various phases or stages of production. Imbalances among the productive capacities of the various phases of production are a very important factor in determining the size of the productive unit. The necessity of combining the productive capacities of single machines and single stages of the production process according to specific relations of complementarity means that an increase in scale takes place in discrete jumps (chapter 6, section 6.3).

Similarly, a technical advance that speeds up one stage or phase of the production process induces a concentration of innovative forces aimed at speeding up the other stages or phases as well. In this regard Nathan Rosenberg cites the technical evolution that characterises the history of the textile sector: 'Kay's fly shuttle led to the need for speeding up spinning operations; the eventual innovation in spinning in turn created the shortage of weaving capacity which finally culminated in Cartwright's introduction of the power loom' (1969, p. 112).[12]

Complementarity is a prominent feature not only of single phases or single machines within a production process, but also of the components of a given (intermediate or final) commodity and of consumer demand. This creates interdependencies among the single technical changes. For example, the 'improved designs of automobile engines have led – through the achievement of higher speeds – to the invention of improved braking systems.' Similarly, to someone constructing a hi-fi system it is obvious that the benefits of a high-quality amplifier are lost if it is attached to a low-quality loudspeaker (Rosenberg, 1969, pp. 111–12). So the improvement of a single component of an intermediate or consumer good may create a disequilibrium with the other components or with other goods linked to it by relations of complementarity. Hence it may lead to an investment of resources to restore the equilibrium, bringing about a particular sequence and timing of innovative activity.

3.4   Historical time versus logical time

The process of creation of a technique, and the production process linked with it, requires time. The technical conditions of the production process are in fact the fruit of the history of the production unit, depending on the preceding sequence of choices and on the specific model of accumulation of knowledge and experience. Therefore, in order to study the phenomenon of technical change we must examine this particular path of development which leads to the adoption of a technique, through a certain chain of choices and limitations.

It should be quite obvious that *static analysis*, which eliminates historical time from the field of investigation, is not a useful instrument for working out the economic effects of technical change. It would not be worth mentioning this problem, were it not for the fact that static analytical tools are often erroneously applied to questions beyond their range of applicability (i.e. 'application outrunning applicability'). My criticism here is not directed at static analytical tools as such, but at their improper use in the analysis of technical change.

In fact, it is legitimate to compare two or more different 'states' represented, for example, by different production sets, or two different plant cost curves, or again two different wage–profit curves.[13] In static

---

[12] This phenomenon was first highlighted by scholars who studied the industrial revolution, see, for instance, Marx (1867, vol. 1, p. 505).

[13] For example, in Sraffa's model the different wage–profit curves are interpretable as a comparison of possible self-reproducing states. As is well known, this representation has been useful in the debate of the sixties on the vacuity of the concepts of the marginal

analysis, any given state of equilibrium is taken to be determined by current parameters only, so that equilibrium 'can be treated as self-contained'.[14] Historical time is replaced by logical time in which, as in space, it is possible to move in either direction.[15] But technical change takes place in irreversible historical time, in which the different 'states' represented by successive techniques are not independent but linked by a causal relationship. Moreover, these techniques are adopted in production processes whose length (and so the *time dimension*) is one of the variables directly influenced by technical change. Therefore, the evaluation of the effects of technical change on the production process cannot be accomplished through a simple exercise of comparative static analysis, comparing equilibria before and after adoption of a new technique. The basic point is that economic analysis of technical change should involve taking account of the process of creation of techniques which is usually assumed to be exogenously determined.[16]

Alfred Marshall long ago emphasized the *irreversibility* of production conditions (and the associated cost curves) in the presence of technical change and learning by doing. On this question, Marshall observes that 'The statical equilibrium is only an introduction to economic studies; and it is barely even an introduction to the study of the progress and development of industries which show a tendency to increasing return' (Marshall 1890, p. 382; cf. Sraffa 1925, J. Robinson 1971, p. 54).[17] Wilfred

product of capital and the demand curve for capital. In this connection see J. Robinson (1980a, b), and Harcourt's essay on the contribution of Joan Robinson and Piero Sraffa to economic theory (Harcourt, 1986a). For an overall evaluation of the debate mentioned above see two books which have become classics: Harcourt (1972), and Bliss (1975).

[14] For the definition of static analysis see Hicks (1965, p. 32, and 1973b, p. 178). Hicks (1973b, 1976) has developed an approach derived from the Austrian theory of Böhm-Bawerk and Hayek. With regard to the treatment of the production process by the Austrian school, see, in particular, C. Menger (1871, pp. 68, 157), Böhm-Bawerk (1889, chapter 11), Hayek (1941, pp. 70–84, 113–25). For a critical analysis of Hicks' neo-Austrian representation of production process, see Baldone (1984) and Zamagni (1984b). On the distinction between historical time and logical time see Termini (1984).

[15] '[In] space we can move either way, or any way; but time just goes on, never goes back' (Hicks, 1976, p. 135). On the relationship between irreversibility of time, expectations, decisions to invest, conditions of uncertainty, see Carabelli's book on Keynes (Carabelli, 1988, pp. 188–9, 216, 239). On this point see also Faber (1986, Part 3), Faber and Proops (1990, chapter 4).

[16] It need hardly be mentioned here that this contradiction, characteristic of modern economic theory, is not present in classical political economy, where the analysis of technical change is incorporated in a dynamic analytical context. On the distinction between economic theory and political economy see Lunghini (1975). On the process of creation of new techniques see Lowe (1955, pp. 582–4, 1976, pp. 35–47), see also Amendola and Gaffard (1988).

[17] It should be noted that Marshall does not proceed to the analytical demonstration of short and long-run equilibrium. That demonstration was carried out for the first time by Edgeworth and Pigou on the basis of the law of variable proportions, considering the firm

Salter, almost a century later, points out 'the absence of a suitable theoretical framework' in analysing changes in productivity...

when we are interested in movements through time, a system of analysis is required...[which] considers the way in which the present grows out of the past...[Static] long-period theory has only limited application to such problems involving time...certain adjustments to changing conditions take long periods of time to work themselves out, particularly when capital equipment is involved.[18] (1960, pp. 4–6, passim)

As Joan Robinson reminds us, differences in techniques are introduced successively through time as research and development goes on responding to historical changes, not merely to shifts from one technique to another at an instant of time; in fact, 'techniques are blueprinted only when they are about to be used', and 'any change in the ratio of capital to labour involves a reorganization of methods of production' (J. Robinson 1980a, pp. 87–9; 1980b, p. 10).[19] In this connection Geoffrey Harcourt points out that:

for each point on the Salter iso-quant there will be a different production process, and associated with each process there will be a fund of technical knowledge specific to that technique. Knowledge and experience do not just appear independently of the firm's actions....Each process has its own past and this past will dominate the future possibilities available to the firm. (Harcourt 1976, pp. 111–12)

Therefore, as argued by Rosenberg (1975), within the representation based on production isoquants we end up by transferring most technical changes under the label of inputs substitution. On the other hand, Luigi Pasinetti brought out very clearly, in an article published in 1959, the

---

simply as a production function (Edgeworth, 1913, pp. 209–15; Pigou, 1920, Appendix 3). This new approach abandons the detailed study of the relationship between organization and efficiency, which was characteristic not only of the classical economists but also of Marshall's analysis itself. See, for instance, Moss (1984), Morroni (1985), Loasby (1988).

[18] Salter tries to overcome these difficulties by using a vintage model, which enables him to take account of the presence, within one and the same industry, of production techniques belonging to different epochs. Salter's methodology has been the object of numerous criticisms. First, the vintage approach does not distinguish between new techniques that change processes and those that change products. Secondly, this approach tells us nothing about the sources of technological change. Why, for instance, is equipment belonging to vintage v better than that of vintage $v-1$? (see Stoneman, 1983, p. 7).

[19] The 1980b paper has not yet been published; the quotation is taken from a passage cited in Harcourt (1986a, p. 104). Joan Robinson criticises the frequent error of introducing historical events into a timeless picture: 'if we are to introduce decisions into a model [for instance moving from a point on an isoquant to another point], we must introduce time. Decisions are taken in the light of beliefs about their future consequences' (1980a, pp. 87–9). Joan Robinson's conception of time in economic reasoning follows the best tradition of two great Cambridge economists: Marshall, with regard to the limits of static analysis, and Keynes, with regard to the theory of expectations.

concrete impossibility of distinguishing between a *change* of the production function and a *movement* along the same production function. This is due to the fact that, when 'we come to actual observations ... what we can observe are not entire production functions, but only actual combinations of factors' (1959, pp. 271–2).[20]

John Hicks too, in *Capital and Time* and in his most recent works, seems to agree that the notion of the blue book, contained in the concept of the production function, is useless for the analysis of technical change. He observes that 'the notion of a "technology" as a collection of techniques, laid up in a library (or museum) to be taken down from their shelves as required ... in itself is a caricature of the inventive process' (1973b, p. 120).

The path of development, selection and adoption of techniques is based on a 'flow' of small continuous changes. These day-to-day adjustments are – it should be emphasized – *cumulative*, *irreversible* and *specific* to each single production unit. In fact, as highlighted by the evolutionary approach to technical change, firms learn from experience and 'possess mechanisms for maintaining memory over time in the face of changes in personnel' (Metcalfe, 1989, p. 57). This is a source of irreversibility in the development path of single firms. The degree of irreversibility of economic choices about production processes influences the level of strategic flexibility (see chapter 12).

Moreover, the in-house techniques improvement process is based on the unwritten and tacit knowledge of the machine in use and the problems to be solved in that given production unit. This knowledge is strongly selective in the sense that it involves mainly not so much a body of general information about techniques, as concrete or practical knowledge about the use of specific machines and equipment.[21] This knowledge is expressed in the ability to perform operations efficiently, in relation to the optimal use of resources, and effectively, in relation to achieving objectives.

This 'ability to do' is based on each operator's fundamental knowledge; it develops through the formation of professional skills, which are generated both by the production process and by the process of innovation.[22] The acquired professional skills sometimes act as a brake on further changes. In fact, the accumulation of specific knowledge may lead

---

[20] On this point, see also Kaldor (1957, p. 265), Harcourt (1962, p. 133), Marzi and Varri (1977, p. 15).

[21] A similar concept may be found in Hayek's definition of 'practical knowledge' (Hayek, 1945). In this article the author analyses, on the one hand, the importance of 'day to day adjustments' in changing agents' beliefs and in determining economic decisions, on the other, the relationship between division of labour and the 'dispersed', 'incomplete' and 'contradictory knowledge ... which all the separate individuals possess' (*passim*, esp. pp. 519, 522–3, 527–8).

[22] For further elaboration on skills see point C of the organizational scheme in section 8.2 (chapter 8).

to a crystallization of experience and roles which in some cases make those skills inadequate for new technologies. This may create a strong resistance to change in methods of production.

As has been observed, these elements of tacit and specific knowledge 'are not and cannot be written down in a "blueprint" form and, therefore, cannot be entirely diffused either in the form of public or proprietary information' (Dosi 1988, p. 1131).[23] Everyone who uses a computer knows that there is a vast difference between being informed about the characteristics and capacities of the different kinds of software on the market and being able to use one of them effectively. The latter ability comes only through a tedious process of learning by doing. It is not enough simply to know the sequence of operations to be performed; one must acquire the ability to carry out chains of routines not directly deducible from the list of the sequence of operations (Egidi, 1986 and 1989).

In medium and large-sized production units, organized according to the 'factory system', specificity involves something different from the simple sum of equipment or even the sum of individual people's knowledge (in this connection, see Nelson and Winter 1982, p. 63). In fact, this specificity concerns mainly the way in which production elements are organized and employees' knowledge (of techniques) are utilized within the definition of particular routines, linked in turn to the model of division of labour adopted. On the other hand, in craft workshops or very small production units this specificity can often be identified with the specificity of knowledge and skills of single individuals, and with aspects of the origin and history of the founder or proprietor–entrepreneur (level of qualification and skill, knowledge of technologies and markets, relations with suppliers and customers). In a few words, the specificity of a single production unit relies upon different organizational and technological forms, upon differences in ability to translate information (which is not distributed equally and without cost) into knowledge and, more in general, upon a variety of responses to the evolution of environmental conditions which has determined its development path.[24]

Given this specificity of knowledge regarding the techniques for each single production unit, the number of possible choices at any given moment is quite limited, and in cases of technical change it is not always

---

[23] 'Of course, this does not imply that such skills and forms of tacit knowledge are entirely immobile: people can be hired away from one firm to another or can start their own firms…learning procedures of one firm may be imitated by other firms' (Dosi, 1988, p. 1131). On tacit and specific knowledge about production techniques see Nelson and Winter (1982, pp. 59–60).

[24] On the variety of behaviour among different firms in an evolutionary perspective see, for instance, Metcalfe (1989), Metcalfe and Gibbons (1986).

known *a priori*. On this point Mario Amendola and Jean-Luc Gaffard are very clear, innovation is

the process through which a new technology is developed step by step from an initial impulse as a particular answer to given problems in a specific environment... This process has an essential sequential character, in the sense that at each given moment different paths are open and different decisions can be taken leading to different alternative developments; but not all the conceivable developments are feasible, because of constraints and endowments that have gradually accumulated along the particular path that has led to the present state. (1988, p. 4)

A change in techniques used may arise simply from experience and the realization of formerly unutilized potentialities of equipment already in use; just as the improvement of an existing plant or the construction of a new plant may incorporate techniques that were formerly unknown. In dynamic terms, the long run can be seen as nothing but a 'slowly changing component of a chain of short-period situations', in which different techniques coexist within the same production unit (see, e.g. Kalecki 1971, p. 165; Lowe 1976, pp. 10–11). In our scheme we shall take account not only of the time dimension relative to the creation and adoption of a technique, but also of the time dimension within which the production process using that technique is carried out. This time dimension contributes to determining the organization of the process, and at the same time is usually strongly influenced by technical change; while technical change may consist, in turn, in a reduction of production times for single phases of the production process.

3.5   *Ex-ante* and *ex-post* analysis

Finally, with regard to the time dimension, it should be noted that in the study of the production process a fundamental distinction must be made between *ex-ante* analysis and *ex-post* analysis. By *ex-ante* analysis we mean the examination of possible ways of organizing production to correspond with a desired productive capacity, using given inputs and a given technology. *Ex-post* analysis, on the other hand, is the study of the production process of an actually operating unit.[25]

Thus *ex-ante* analysis corresponds to a 'plan' of the production process, on the basis of given hypotheses on agents' behaviour and market structure, assuming as given the availability of inputs. *Ex-ante* analysis

---

[25] This distinction has many analogies with that presented in Hicks (1973b): 'The process may be regarded in two ways: *ex-ante* and *ex-post*. When it is regarded *ex-ante*, it is simply a plan... Regarded *ex-post*, it is the set that underlies the actual achievement, such as is recorded in "historical" accounts' (p. 14). On this distinction see also Tani (1986, pp. 237–9).

provides the answers to a series of important questions. How can the firm reduce idle time for the equipment used? How can it reconcile the different productive capacities of single indivisible elements? What is the optimum size of the production unit given the existing technology and relative prices – or, in other words, which intermediate products should be produced internally and which should be brought in from outside? What division of labour (distribution of qualifications and jobs) will give the highest productive efficiency and at the same time maximize the advantages of learning by doing? It is useful to divide the *ex-ante* analysis of the production process into two different sequences or stages (see chapter 6). The first step is represented by the 'plan' of what we call the '*simple* production process' – that is to say the production process which is not yet organized according to criteria of cost minimization. The second step is the 'plan' of the '*organized* production process' (whether linear, parallel or in some other form) based on criteria of efficiency and efficacy.

By contrast, *ex-post* analysis aims to elucidate the productive characteristics of a given process actually in operation. One may study the effects of technical change in order to evaluate variations that have occurred in the past (comparison of the same production process at different points in time), or in order to evaluate the effects of the application of a new technique where the choice is constrained by technological opportunities, market conditions, and the skills and abilities available within the firm or on the market. In the first case, *ex-post* analysis is applied to production processes at different times, on the basis of historical data on the production unit. In the second case, after beginning with the *ex-post* analysis of a given process in a production unit, one moves on to an *ex-ante* analysis simulating the effects of certain changes.

4 Division of labour, specialization and economic efficiency

In this chapter I will examine the relationship between organization and economic efficiency, and the influence exerted on this relationship by the characteristics of production elements (such as specialization, specificity, indivisibility and complementarity). In particular, I pose the following questions: what is the relationship between division of labour and specialization? How can the various organizational models influence the degree of division of labour? How are indivisibility, complementarity of resources and the size of the production unit related? The scheme presented in the following chapters is meant to provide useful analytical tools for dealing with these problems.

4.1 Learning processes, specificity of resources and different organizational systems

In economic literature division of labour and specialization are often considered to be synonymous (see e.g. Arrow 1979, p. 154; Landesmann 1986, p. 290; Pagano 1988, pp. 6–7).[1] However, these two phenomena should be kept quite distinct, as they do not always coincide.

The division of labour is obviously encouraged by the opportunity of exchanging (or bartering) goods and services. Exchange, however, is not the only form in which the division of labour takes place; as is well known, in addition to the *social* division of labour between different activities of productive processes, regulated by the market, there is the *manufacturing* (or technical) division of labour among various jobs, which is regulated by the organization of the firm.

An increase in the division of labour (social or technical) may favour the *specialization* of labour, defined as the acquisition of specific abilities (job-specific skills) which provide a comparative advantage in the performance of a given task. In the light of this definition, it is clear that usually the longer it takes to learn a job the greater is the specialization.

---

[1] Arrow argues: 'I think of specialization or division of labour (which I take to be the same thing) as primarily specialization in knowing how to do things' (1979, p. 154).

However, if division of labour is increased to the point of greatly simplifying the job to be done, it tends to nullify the element of specialization, or job specificity skills. The comparative advantage is lost, the need for training time is reduced, and in the end the simple task can be assigned even to a person who has not developed any specific skill.

Thus, the economic advantage of a very pronounced technical division of labour derives less from the increase in skill and ability, put forward by Adam Smith,[2] than from reduced training costs within and outside the productive unit. This aspect – the possibility of lowering costs by reducing the levels of qualification required for the workers – has been stressed above all by Ure (1835) who, unlike Smith, does not take into consideration the social effects arising from the de-skilling of workers' tasks.[3]

On the other hand, an increase in production and in the division of labour means that each job can be assigned to the appropriate qualification level, thus avoiding the need for any worker to perform tasks requiring lower qualification levels than that for which he is paid. In other words, if all the work were executed by one workman, this person would have to possess sufficient skill to perform the most difficult task. Charles Babbage argued that by dividing the work to be executed into different operations, each requiring different degrees of skill, the entrepreneur can pay for the precise skill required for each operation (1832, pp. 172–3). An appropriate division of labour, then, permits a more efficient allocation of the various abilities and qualifications.

Another important element in the relationship between division of labour and specialization is the level of specificity of resources. As mentioned, specialization can assume two different aspects: it may involve abilities specific to a particular job or specific to a given organization. In the first case, changing to another productive unit does not involve the loss of the comparative advantage acquired through the learning process

---

[2] According to Adam Smith, the division of labour permits: (i) an improvement in dexterity of the workmen in carrying out a single operation; (ii) a saving in the 'time commonly lost in passing from one sort of work to another'; (iii) the introduction of new machines that facilitate and shorten the work (Smith, 1776, pp. 17–21, 212). Moreover, Adam Smith observed that the division of labour arises from the human propensity for exchange (and barter), not in the diversity of individual intelligences and talents: these are the effect rather than the cause of the division of labour (pp. 28–30).

[3] The two divergent consequences of the division of labour (increase and decrease of training times) are brought out by Pagano (1988), cf. Dosi (1988, p. 1113). On the negative social effects of a pronounced technical division of labour Adam Smith observes: 'The man whose life is spent in performing a few simple operations ... has no occasion to extend his understanding. He ... generally becomes as stupid and ignorant as it is possible for a human creature to become' (1776, p. 734).

(which represents an economy external to firms), while in the second case the acquired abilities are not transferable and cannot be re-used.[4]

Alfred Marshall brought out clearly this second aspect of specificity. He refers to the example of a 'head clerk in a business', who has

> an acquaintance with men and things, the use of which he could in some cases sell at a high price to rival firms. But in other cases it is of a kind to be of no value save to the business in which he already is; and then his departure would perhaps injure it several times the value of his salary, while probably he could not get half that salary elsewhere. (1890, p. 520)

In the capitalist mode of production, characterized by high mobility, investment in learning processes and training costs specific to a particular organization are not advantageous to workers or to firms, because if the employment is terminated both suffer a loss.[5] Consequently, in the absence of special contractual safeguards, there will be a tendency to restrict as much as possible the learning process specific to a particular organization. In most firms, skills specific to the organization are restricted to a few people whose jobs are regulated by 'contracts that have superior properties for safeguarding employment' (Williamson, 1986, p. 53). The formation of skills specific to a given organization gives both employer and employee some 'contractual power' because of the loss which each could suffer if the employment were terminated. In this case the analysis is made more complex by the presence not only of specific resources but also of uncertainty, in the sense of incomplete information, and by the possibility of opportunistic behaviour on the part of the agents. This limits the competitive conditions and leads to special contractual forms. However, the result of these contracts is very uncertain; it depends on the information possessed by the agents, on their ability, and on prevailing contractual customs.

It is noteworthy that along with certain forces, which tend to favour job-specific learning processes by reducing the degree of technical division of labour, there are other forces that work in the opposite direction, actually increasing the technical division of labour. The prevalence of one or the other set of forces depends largely on the specific characteristics of the elements of production; it varies from one sector and from one historical moment to another.

At the time when Adam Smith was writing there was a progressive reduction in the complexity of the operations performed by each worker as the technical division of labour increased. This permitted the

---

[4] According to Aoki (1984) the presence of firm-specific resources leads to an 'organizational rent' and a bargaining process, which regulates its distribution among 'firm-specific resource-holders' (pp. 31–3).

[5] On the relationship between specificity of resources and division of labour see Pagano (1988, pp. 8).

introduction of machines to carry out the simplified operations, which in turn favoured a further division of labour. But this relationship between division of labour and accumulation, which played an important role in the early decades of the industrial revolution, has been partly reversed by technical change. Since the middle of the last century, in many cases machines have carried out more and more complex tasks, and this has led to a reaggregation of the different operations performed by numerous workers.

We might look at the evolution of pin manufacture, reexamined recently by Pratten (1980). Between 1860 and 1920 many separate operations, from which the benefits of the division of labour were obtained, were replaced by new machines which allowed the complete mechanization of the main processes of pin making. The directly productive labour was homogenized, while at the same time there arose new administrative and technical-organizational roles that were not present in the organization observed by A. Smith and later by Babbage.

On the one hand, we can see the unification of skills and training for certain workers involved in production, so that an intersectoral occupation is developing for a 'process operator', who is mostly assigned duties of control and maintenance. On the other hand, we see an accentuated specialization in the other, 'indirect' functions or services (for example, marketing, design, software etc.), which are connected with innovations in products and/or processes.

Thus technical change seems to feed the demand for more and more specialized services, with a high degree of indivisibility and discontinuity in use, as they are not required continuously over time in some production units. Hence production units tend to buy out these services in the so-called services-for-industry sector which develops to meet the demand (Momigliano and Siniscalco, 1982; Gershuny, 1983). Using these 'specialized' services outside the production unit also brings the advantage of flexibility and reduction of the risk involved in innovative activity.

In some cases, numerous elements may arise that favour a system with relatively little technical division of labour. Such factors include:

(a) the specific characteristics of the labour supply in relation to levels of qualification and to expectations regarding the type of work involved; resistance to repetitive tasks;
(b) the impossibility of dividing up or reducing certain tasks;
(c) intrinsic characteristics of the product or of the technology adopted;
(d) the need to increase the product's reliability;
(e) the particular characteristics of the market.

All these elements can lead to an organization of labour that takes full advantage of learning processes, to a modification of contractual norms, and in some cases even to a redefinition of property rights. Moreover, this interpretation can also shed light on systems involving participation and co-management that regulate employment and organization in some large Japanese firms.

The necessity for the production unit to adapt rapidly to the qualitative and quantitative changes has led to the creation of organizational systems based on principles of maximization of flexibility (for production flexibility, see chapter 12). The need for rapid responses and for adaptation to continuous changes required by a turbulent environment, has favoured thus the rise of organizational structures based on: (i) horizontal and vertical recomposition of labour; (ii) increasing integrative functions; (iii) redefinition of roles according to objectives; (iv) control concentrated on the results of the production process.

One effect of this has been to reduce the level of division of labour. At the same time, Tayloristic or 'bureaucratic' organizational models may be difficult to apply because these models have little capacity to adapt and respond to the continual changes which some product markets increasingly require. Instead, new models arise which can ensure more consensus and personal responsibility on the part of employees and the capacity to make the firm's strategic objectives their own, with an increase in quality of production and a decrease in monitoring activity during the process.

There are very complex problems, however, in the diffusion of this type of organizational approach on a wide scale. On the one hand, the flexibility and versatility of electronic technologies facilitate the spread of organizations 'according to objectives and results'. On the other hand, the choice of decentralizing objectives, responsibilities and modes of control appears difficult, and in any case discretionary and specific to each national or firm context. This choice may modify even the power structure within the organization to such an extent that it may slow down the application of some new technologies.

In conclusion, although the division of labour may be favoured by the definition of property rights which characterizes capitalist production, it cannot be asserted, as is done by some scholars (e.g. Braverman 1974; Bowles 1985)[6] that the general tendency of the capitalist system of production is towards increasing segmentation of tasks: in fact, as we have seen, there are various forces that favour an opposite tendency. The assumption that in capitalist production there is an innate general

---

[6] One cannot but share Pagano's observation that 'the "control" argument can either reinforce (as Braverman maintains) or weaken and even, sometimes, invert the de-skilling strategy' implicit in the Babbage–Ure division of labour. 'In some situations employers can increase discipline and productivity of some groups of workers by involving them in their jobs and factory life – strategy that may imply reskilling...jobs' (Pagano, 1985, p. 18, n. 1).

tendency towards de-skilling is based, in my opinion, on the error of treating as a characteristic of capitalist production a tendency which is actually present only in some specific organizational models limited to specific historical situations. For these models a good organization is one in which functions, tasks, organizational structures, jobs, procedures and processes are specified as fully as possible, and rationally interconnected through a pre-ordained plan, in order to ensure maximum overall efficiency and maximum predictability and governability of the single parts. If there is only 'one best way' of producing a given commodity, as in the production–function model there is only one efficient combination of inputs for a given vector of prices. From this point of view, there are some obvious analogies between Tayloristic organizational models and the analysis of the production process based on the production function.

The evolution of organizational systems, however, has demonstrated that the 'one-best-way' models generally correspond to a specific productive context characterized by environmental elements that can provide a high degree of predictability and stability (Hellriegel and Slocum, 1974, p. 71). These in turn favour the consolidation of predictable 'static' organizational models, which work rather like a clock, and whose primary objective is efficiency (understood only as maximization of the quantity produced at given cost). In considering the evolution of organizational systems, we have to take account of the changes in historical and environmental conditions – in other words we must consider the peculiarities of the variables that make up the environment of each production unit, and the adaptive responses provided by the production unit itself, in a complex of reciprocal interactions. The organization of the activity of a production unit should thus be seen in terms of an analytical approach based on organic models.[7] According to these models, a production unit is considered as a complex organization whose single parts (structures and roles) are open systems that carry out specialized functions. These individual parts of the organization, which are linked by a 'network' of information exchanges and economic and social relationships, interact according to game rules which they can often influence. In such a context, decisions are made in a situation of imperfect knowledge and uncertainty (see Egidi, 1986, 1989). Furthermore, every decision on changes in techniques implies a subjective element. In other words, it always presupposes an option, an innovative choice. For instance, it is possible that in single production units the mechanistic model will continue to prevail even in environmental situations that might suggest a

---

[7] A similar argument is developed by the 'contingency theory'. From the vast body of literature on contingency approaches see, for example, Hellriegel and Slocum (1974). On adaptive responses in a changing environment see Burns and Stalker (1961).

different organization, based on an organic model. All this determines a variety of behaviour among production units, based on different degrees of adaptation to the evolution of environmental conditions.

4.2   Economic efficiency and production organization

In the last section we concluded that the 'mode of capitalist production' is compatible with different organizational models corresponding to different historical and environmental situations. We shall look more closely at one aspect of the problems mentioned above: the possibility of increasing economic efficiency by changing the organization of the production process.

Recently Oliver Williamson (1986, p. 207) stressed some advantages of Smith's pin-making example, in contrast to the tenet that this famous example 'does not afford the ideal illustration of the division of labour', and that it is a pity 'that Adam Smith did not go a few miles from Kirkcaldy to the Carron Works to see them turning and boring their cannonades instead of to his silly pin factory – which was only a factory in the old sense of the word' (Ashton 1925, p. 281; Clapham 1913, p. 401).[8] In my opinion, however, this view cannot be accepted for two reasons. The first is that Adam Smith's example was probably not based on 'field studies', but was apparently taken (without credit) from the accurate illustration given under the entry 'Epingle' in Diderot and D'Alembert's *Encyclopédie* (1751) (see Arrow 1979, p. 153).[9] The second and more substantial reason is that the example of the pin factory suited Adam Smith's analytical objectives. As we know, he aimed to bring out the strong connection between the market extent, the division of labour and capitalist accumulation on the one hand, and the increased productive power of labour on the other. Then, a very simple technology, divisible into different stages, was particularly appropriate for demonstrating the effects of an increased scale of production on the division of labour, and hence on the economic efficiency of production. Adam Smith's example brings out the fact that the change from craft production to factory production is not initially characterized by the use of a different technology – in fact initially the technology remained the same – but by an increased demand which favours a more efficient distribution and organization of workers within the process. This expansion of the market – which may be due to numerous factors including easier transport and increased urban concentration – leads to the development of the division of labour, which in turn causes increased productivity and reduced costs. In short, Adam

---

[8] Both these passages are in Williamson (1985).
[9] For a further discussion on this point see P. Bianchi (1984, p. 35).

Smith's illustration demonstrates that economic efficiency cannot be considered independent of internal organization, which likewise cannot be considered independent of the extent of the market. It is worth stressing that in Adam Smith this reasoning is incorporated into a dynamic analytical context in which the conditions of economic development are analysed.

An example may be useful to show the links between economic efficiency and production organization. Suppose that initially two workers share the eighteen different operations belonging to eight different intermediate stages, in such a way that each worker carries out nine operations in four intermediate stages. For the sake of simplicity, let us assume that these eighteen operations are divided in such a way that they take the same time. Then an increase in production, opens two different possibilities:

> either it may keep the same type of organization, producing in parallel with each worker continuing to perform four intermediate stages; or
>
> it may reshape the organization of production, instituting a linear sequence in which each worker performs the minimum number of operations.

When the quantity produced increases to the point of making it possible to hire eighteen workers, we shall obviously have the maximum technical division of labour achievable with that particular process and those particular technical conditions. Even though the tools in this example remain the same, the eighteen workers may have a much lower level of skill and specialization (in terms of training times) than the two original artisans, as each of them is asked to perform much simpler operations. Thus, an increase in the scale of production permits a *reorganization* that does not involve a simple multiplication by *n* of the *quantities* of inputs, but also brings about a *qualitative* change at least in the labour inputs. In this case the increased division of labour not only increases the productivity of labour, but also reduces the level of specialization (i.e. the acquisition of specific capacities) and with it the unit cost of the labour.

There is a contradiction, however, between the proposition that a firm can increase its profitability by expanding the scale of production and the theory of perfect competition. This contradiction, which Alfred Marshall noticed,[10] was highlighted later by Piero Sraffa. In the case of increasing

---

[10] Marshall holds, however, that single firms meet obstacles to their development which prevent the tendency to increasing returns. These obstacles arise from the concurrence of various elements: (a) the prevalence of external over internal economies; (b) the life cycle of single firms; (c) imperfections in the market. These considerations lead Marshall into

returns to scale for a single firm, the development of a firm implies that it is able to dominate the entire market, driving all others out of a given business. This obviously entails a movement towards monopoly conditions (Sraffa 1925, pp. 41–2; 1926; 1930).[11] As Kenneth Arrow observes in this connection, 'this dilemma has been thoroughly discussed; it has not been thoroughly resolved' (Arrow 1979).[12]

Finally, as far as the relationship between economic efficiency and organization is concerned, it should be noted that Adam Smith examines the effects of increased segmentation on the productive power of labour, but he does not discuss another consequence of factory production. At the time he was writing, this aspect had not yet become prominent because of the relatively small involvement of fixed capital, but in the following years it was to take on more and more importance. I refer to the opportunity of using factory production to reduce periods during which production tools are *idle*. This aspect was brought out later by Babbage (1832, p. 169) and Rae.[13] In our example, if the two artisans perform eight intermediate stages (four each) and one intermediate stage at a time, the tools of six intermediate stages remain idle at any given time. It is clear that, in the previous example, only the employment of eighteen workers, as many as there are different jobs, will permit *constant* utilization of production tools. Obviously, the greater the cost of the equipment used, the more desirable it is to reduce idle times. As we shall see better in chapter 5 (which is devoted to an analytical description of the production process), factory production, and in particular, line production, allow drastic reduction in the idle time of production tools. Once the formal model on

the sphere of dynamic analysis (external economies due to technical progress and the life cycle of firms) and into hypotheses of market conditions that are not perfectly competitive (the particular demand curve for the single firm). Marshall emphasises the dangers of putting the static theory of partial equilibrium 'in definitive form', because 'the further it is pushed into its most remote and complicated logical consequences', the further it gets from real life (1890, pp. 238–9, 305–6, 315n., 379–82).

[11] A second analytical result of Sraffa's 1925 and 1926 articles is the demonstration that falling (or rising) long-run supply curves, for an industry as a whole, are incompatible with the hypothesis of *ceteris paribus* necessary in the *partial equilibrium* analysis of perfectly competitive markets. This second point is often forgotten in current textbooks, in spite of its relevance and the lucidity and breadth of the author's exposition.

[12] In terms of the axiomatic theory of production increasing returns involve the non-upper convexity of the production set and hence the possibility of *non-existence* of the equilibrium.

[13] Rae asserts: 'If any man had all the tools which many different occupations require, at least three-fourths of them would constantly be idle and useless. It were clearly then better,...[that each man restrict] himself to some particular employment' (1834, p. 165), cf. J. S. Mill (1844, p. 129). Recently Georgescu-Roegen has returned to the analysis of the effect of eliminating idle time of fund elements, underlining the importance of this element in understanding the factory system. Cf. Leijonhufvud's interesting article (1986, pp. 206ff.).

fund element time profiles is introduced, it will be apparent that multiplying the number of funds in order to reduce the problem of idle time and the under-utilization of productive capacity makes it possible, but not necessary, to introduce greater division of labour. We shall see in chapter 6, section 6.2 that line production may be compatible with very different levels of division of labour and it is in fact possible to imagine line production with little division of labour.

Part 2

The model and its application

5   Introduction

Part 2 contains an analytical representation of the production process which is useful for ascertaining the economic effects of changes in techniques and, at the same time, handle the particular characteristics of production elements and processes, such as indivisibility, complementarity and irreversibility.

In chapter 6 the features of the elementary production process are examined, using an *ex-ante* analytical representation, mainly based on Georgescu-Roegen's production model. In recent years this model has aroused increasing interest, because time can be included in the analysis of production (Georgescu-Roegen 1966; 1971; 1976).[1] In particular, the Roegenian fund–flow model explains the logic of the factory system. The chief difference between the factory system and the craft production system is in reducing idle times and achieving the maximum time economy. As will emerge in the following pages, the introduction of the factory system is not a technological innovation, but an economic and organizational one, since it is independent of technology (in fact, primitive techniques can be used in a factory system). Finally, chapter 6 covers the relationship between the size of the production unit and the need to coordinate the different productive capacities of various indivisible funds, in order to reduce idle times. We shall see that the presence of indivisible funds involves an increase in the overall production level of a particular commodity, but not necessarily an increase in the scale of the single production unit. This will lead to some considerations as to the alternative between internal or external growth model of the firm.

The general characteristics of what I call the *matrix of production elements* are explained in chapter 7. This matrix enables us to consider, on

---

[1] The general properties of the Georgescu-Roegen model are discussed by Tani (1976, 1986, and 1988), Mariti (1980), Scazzieri (1983) and Zamagni (1984a). As far as we know however, the fund–flow model has not been used as a methodological basis for applied researches in industrial economics, though the contributions of Landesmann (1986), Lejonhufvud (1986), Wodopia (1986), Cantalupi (1986), Piacentini (1987, 1989), Polidori and Romagnoli (1987), Romagnoli (1989), and Benvenuti (1988) contain useful suggestions for feasible applications.

the one hand, the interconnections between the different intermediate stages (inside or outside the production unit) and, on the other hand, the quantitative, temporal, organizational and dimensional aspects of production. The matrix therefore provides an analytical and synthetic representation coping with the main aspects of the production process which are significant for economic analysis. The matrix of production elements also allows three main forms of technical change to be identified: 'time-saving', 'inventory-saving' and 'inputs-saving'.

In chapter 8 the matrix of production elements is divided, for applied analysis, into two different tables, giving an *ex-post* description of the production process: the *quantitative and temporal matrix* and the *organizational scheme*. The quantitative and temporal matrix takes into account the 'process time', the quantities of flow elements and the hours of services rendered by funds elements; while the organizational scheme summarises some information implicitly included in the above matrix, provides further information on the temporal profile of production process, the organization and size of the production unit, and the characteristics of production elements. Thus from the quantitative and temporal matrix, and the organizational scheme one can obtain a more detailed picture of the production processes considered, and of the organization and size of the production unit, than is possible using traditional methods of analysis based on static assumptions and referring to quantities alone.

In chapter 9 the applicability of this methodology is verified in some case studies. As mentioned, the cases examined serve mainly as numerical examples of the capacity of the quantitative matrix and the organizational scheme to provide an analytical representation of production process. Further studies may be addressed to the actual implementation of the model to time series, and cross section analysis, or to simulation techniques. To consider organizational and technical aspects at the same time proves very useful in studying the evolution of production methods. The possibility of summing up the different production process aspects in a relatively small amount of 'data' permits useful comparisons to be made between different processes at a given point in time (cross section analysis), or the same process at different points in time (on the basis of historical series of data).

Comparing different processes before or after the technical changes, may be useful if it is true that often even the single firms have some difficulties in precisely evaluating the overall effects of their innovative activity.[2] If the sample is large enough to be statistically representative, the

---

[2] For instance, Nelson and Winter (1982) notice that some case studies conclude that the calculations made by many firms regarding the effects of innovations tend to be

economic effects of technical change in the various sectors of economic activity can be evaluated. Furthermore, by applying simulation techniques to the current data of a single production process at a given time, the scheme could be used to ascertain the economic effects of possible changes. Then, this model may prove to be fruitful in simulating decision making processes. The recent development in information technology has provided interesting opportunities for these simulation techniques which could represent tools for answering business decision problems.

haphazard, and that even *ex-post* many firms had little idea, quantitatively, how profitable the innovation turned out to be (cf. Nabseth and Ray, 1974).

6   Production as a sequential process

In chapters 6 and 7, we will deal with the *ex-ante* analysis of the production process i.e., a 'plan' of a feasible production process (chapter 3, section 3.5). First we shall consider a '*simple* elementary production process', i.e. an elementary process before it has been organized according to criteria of full utilization of the productive capacity of the funds. Then we shall go on to the analytical description of an '*organized* elementary process', which maximizes the productive capacity by using line and parallel production, and through the utilization of a number of funds that renders the various productive capacities compatible.

6.1   The elementary process

Before turning to the notion of elementary process, let us look again at the definition of fund and flow (chapter 3, section 3.1). The *flow* elements are present either as input only (e.g. raw materials and energy) or as output only (e.g. the finished product and waste), while *fund* elements perform a service inside the production process, entering and leaving several processes (for example a loom, a worker).

The elementary production process is the process whereby an 'economically indivisible unit' of output is obtained by means of an 'elementary technical unit' (or a 'chain' of 'elementary technical units' operating in sequence). As mentioned, an 'economically indivisible unit' is the minimum exchangeable unit which is not subsequently reducible for exchange purposes in a specific market (for instance, a piece of cloth of so many yards, a packet of detergent of so many kg., a certain model of a car or computer). An 'elementary technical unit' is said to be the minimum technical unit which can be activated separately.

The elementary process is defined by an analytical boundary (or a border) that determines the object of our analysis, i.e. the output, to which the elementary process is referred, and the inputs used in that process (Georgescu-Roegen, 1969, pp. 62–3). Thus, the boundary of an elementary process defines the level of vertical integration. For instance, the transformation of worsted and washed wool into a piece of cloth, or into

54

a jacket, are both elementary processes at two different levels of vertical integration. The location of the process analytical boundary, in relation to the 'chain' of different intermediate stages, depends upon the purpose of the analysis, and in applied researches, also upon the characteristics of the production unit under consideration.

Let T_{SEP} be the duration of a 'simple elementary process' (SEP) from the starting time (O), when the process begins with the input of raw materials, to the moment when the process is completed (T), with the production of a unit of the commodity under consideration obtained through the transformation of those raw materials. For the sake of simplicity, in this section we shall assume the absence of any kind of inventory, while we shall remove this hypothesis from the following section. It is clear that if flow elements are left for a certain time in the warehouse, or between different operations or intermediate stages, the duration of the elementary process under consideration becomes longer.

During the periods when a given fund actively enters the production process, the degree of use of its productive capacity may vary, i.e. in operation it may run below its full productive capacity. So it is necessary to take into account for each fund, not only the 'utilization time', but also the degree of use. Clearly, productivity and costs are influenced, not only by the 'duration' of the production process, but also by the rate of the total productive capacity of each fund actually used. As we shall see in the following analysis, the ways in which a production unit may eliminate periods of idleness and minimize the under-utilization of the productive capacity of the different fund elements affect not only its costs, but also its size and organizational structure.

Let us assume that the number of elements involved in the process is finite, and that each element is a homogeneous entity, cardinally measurable.[1] For each individual element of the production process, whether input or output, a *function of time* can be determined within the closed interval $T_{SEP} \in [0, T]$. I, H, K are respectively the total number of output flows, input flows and funds. We define $G_i(t)$ ($i = 1, 2, ..., I,$) the functions indicating, at time t, the cumulative quantity of the ith outflow, $F_h(t)$ ($h = 1, 2, ..., H$) the functions indicating, at time t, the cumulative quantity of the hth inflow, and $S_k(t)$ ($k = 1, 2, ..., K$) the functions indicating, at time t, the cumulative quantity of the services of the kth fund. By convention we can give a positive sign to the functions of outflows $G_i(t)$, that come out of the process, and a negative sign to the functions of inflows $F_h(t)$ and the functions of funds $S_k(t)$. According to the definition,

---

[1] The following analysis in this section is mainly based on Tani's formalization of Georgescu-Roegen's model (Tani 1988, 1976, 1986; and Georgescu-Roegen, 1966, 1971, 1976). However, I have preferred to use different symbols to indicate variables, in particular output flows are distinct from input flows.

$G_i(0) = F_h(0) = S_k(0) = 0.$ As $G_i(t)$, $F_h(t)$ and $S_k(t)$ are cumulative functions:

$$G_i(t_{m+1}) \geqslant G_i(t_m)$$
$$F_h(t_{m+1}) \leqslant F_h(t_m) \qquad m = (0, 1, 2, ..., M-1),$$
$$S_k(t_{m+1}) \leqslant S_k(t_m). \qquad \text{where } t_0 = 0, \text{ and } t_M = T$$

The production process can thus be represented by a vector of functions of time:

$$[G_1(t), G_2(t), ..., G_I(t), F_1(t), F_2(t), ..., F_H(t), S_1(t), S_2(t), ..., S_K(t)] \qquad (6.1)$$

Figure 6.1 presents an illustration of a possible shape of these functions. This is an example of the analytical representation of an elementary process for the production of a given commodity, in terms of the following co-ordinates:

Flow co-ordinates
  Outputs
      (1) product $G_1(t)$,
      (2) waste $G_2(t)$.
  Inputs
      (3) from nature $F_1(t)$,
      (4) raw material $F_2(t)$,
      (5) energy $F_3(t)$.
Fund co-ordinates
      (6) worker $S_1(t)$,
      (7) loom $S_2(t)$,
      (8) area of plant $S_3(t)$.

In the list of flow coordinates two outputs are shown (the product and waste), but we can assume any number of output flows. In the case of joint production we shall have many elementary processes, with as many different durations and characteristics as there are output flows. In addition, natural resources such as water, air and solar energy, which do not involve monetary costs for the firm, are included among the input flows.

$G_i(t)$ are always monotonic non-decreasing output functions, while $F_h(t)$ and $S_k(t)$ are always monotonic non-increasing input functions. $G_i(t)$ and $F_h(t)$ may be discontinuous functions because I assume that, in certain cases, flows may exit from the process, or enter the process, in a finite quantity in an infinitesimal interval of time (such as respectively the output function $G_1(t)$ and the input function $F_2(t)$ in Figure 6.1). Flow elements are measured in the specific physical unit: the amount of flow is given by the number of physical units in relation to the production process

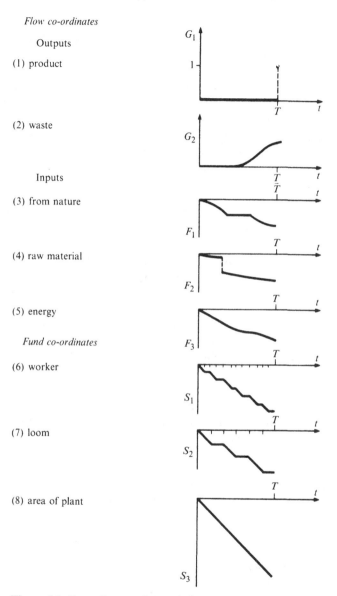

Figure 6.1 Co-ordinates of cumulative quantities of the production elements in a simple elementary process

time (the former is the vertical axis, the latter is the horizontal axis). As observed (chapter 3, section 3.1), they may be decumulated and cumulated in stocks in an infinitesimal interval of time. Consequently, a flow may exit or enter the process in a single instant.

On the contrary, $S_k(t)$ cannot be discontinuous functions. $S_k(t)$ are always continuous functions because services provided by funds cannot be accumulated and decumulated in an infinitesimal interval. In fact, their use involves a lapse of time. In other words, they are used over time. Services provided by funds are measured in minutes or hours. Then the amount of services is given by service-time in relation to the time of the process (as a continuous variable). Therefore, in Figure 6.1, which depicts the possible shape of functions $S_k(t)$, the vertical axis gives the number of hours or minutes of services provided by the fund under consideration (multiplied by the coefficient expressing the degree of use) and the horizontal axis gives the duration of the simple process.

Variations in the *slope* of the graph of function $S_k(t)$ depend on changes in the *degree of use* of the fund under consideration during the production process. Let us suppose that the degree of use of the kth fund varies, at each moment, from 0 (when it is not in use) to -1 (when the fund's productive capacity is fully utilized). Therefore, the slope of $S_k(t)$ will range from 0 degrees (a straight line parallel to the axis of the abscissae), and $-\pi/4$ (maximum degree of use corresponding to $-45°$, first derivative equal to -1). For the sake of simplicity, suppose that in each segment, where the function $S_k(t)$ is less than zero and derivable, the intensity of use is constant, as in Figure 6.1. Let us also assume that the degree of use of workers' fund is constant and equal to -1, while in the case of fund elements such as plant or equipment the degree of use may vary between 0 and -1.

Calculating the derivative with respect to time of $S_k(t)$ (where it exists), we obtain a function $U_k(t) = (dS_K(t)/dt)$, which represents the slope of the function and then the degree of use of the kth fund at each moment of the elementary process. Thus:

$$S'_k(t) = U_k(t). \tag{6.2}$$

Figure 6.2 shows the possible shape of the step-function $U_k(t)$ referred to a worker, a loom and the plant area. The value of $U_k(t)$ may vary between 0 and -1. In fact, as mentioned, when the slope of $S_k(t)$ is $0°$ (with a line parallel to the horizontal axis), the first derivative, and the value of $U_k(t)$, will be 0; when the slope of $S_k(t)$ is between 0 and $-\pi/4$ ($-45°$) the first derivative, and the value of $U_k(t)$, will be between 0 and -1; finally, when the slope of $S_k(t)$ achieves its maximum $-\pi/4$ ($-45°$), the first derivative, and the value of $U_k(t)$, will be -1.

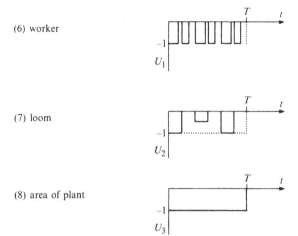

(6) worker

(7) loom

(8) area of plant

Figure 6.2 Fund co-ordinates according to degree of use in a simple elementary process

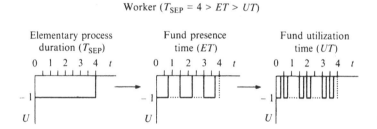

Worker ($T_{SEP} = 4 > ET > UT$)

Elementary process duration (T_{SEP})

Fund presence time (ET)

Fund utilization time (UT)

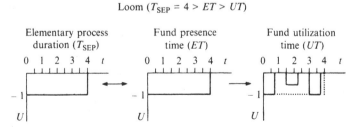

Loom ($T_{SEP} = 4 > ET > UT$)

Elementary process duration (T_{SEP})

Fund presence time (ET)

Fund utilization time (UT)

Figure 6.3 Differences in presence time and utilization time between two funds during a simple elementary process
Note: Equal $\leftrightarrow$ More $\rightarrow$

Functions $U_k(t)$ may allow the various time profiles of funds to be compared. Figure 6.3 illustrates a very simple example in which the time profiles of two funds are different. This is a result of the unequal distribution of funds *presence times* and *utilization times* in relation to the production process *duration*, which is the overall time necessary for transforming the raw materials required in the unit of commodity under consideration. As shown in section 3.2 on indivisibility, differences in time profiles of funds depend upon the fact that some funds (e.g., the loom, in Figure 6.3) must be present, i.e. available in the plant, during the whole duration of the elementary process, even if they remain inactive during the pauses when the process is suspended (unless they are used in other processes). By contrast, other funds (like the worker, in the same example) must be present only when the process is in operation. Moreover, the times of (actual) utilization of the funds (both the loom and the worker) may be shorter than the presence time of the elementary process, because of various organizational and technical interruptions. This causes further periods of fund idleness.[2]

In the next section we shall see that the functions $U_k(t)$, which allow the various time profiles of funds to be compared, are very useful for the analytical representation of methods whereby firms try to solve the problem of underutilization of indivisible fund elements.

6.2   Parallel and line production

In the following pages we shall examine the way in which it is possible to organize a production process in order to make compatible the different productive capacities of the various indivisible funds and to reduce as far as possible idle times. We shall see that the duration of an '*organized* elementary process' is notably below that of a 'simple elementary process' for the reduction of idle times.

Where a single elementary process employs a single indivisible fund at $\frac{1}{3}$ of its productive capacity (with no idle time), it is possible to perform three parallel elementary processes, in order to make full use of its productive capacity (see Figure 6.4). It is clear that if the elementary process simultaneously uses three different types of indivisible funds, and uses different proportions of the productive capacity of the three funds (let us say $\frac{1}{3}, \frac{1}{4}, \frac{1}{6}$, without idle time), the number of elementary processes to be activated in parallel is the lowest common multiple of the number of elementary processes carried out simultaneously by the single funds (see Figure 6.5). In this case the whole operation will use four units of fund A, three units of fund B, and two units of fund C, in order to produce in

---

[2] For a closer examination of the different definitions of the production process time profile, see chapter 7, section 7.2.

(a) *indivisible fund utilized at 1/3 of its productive capacity (1 elementary process)*

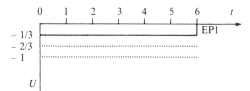

(b) *Indivisible fund fully utilized (3 elementary processes in parallel)*

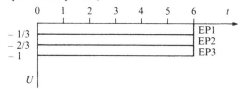

Figure 6.4 Parallel production with three simple elementary processes
Note: Three elementary processes in parallel make full use of the productive capacity of the fund. The maximum degree of use is equal to -1. The duration of the simple elementary processes is equal to 6.

parallel twelve elementary processes. When indivisible funds are used, therefore, reducing the unused productive capacity to a minimum leads to an increase in the number of elementary processes and hence in the volume of production.

If we now consider the possibility that the indivisible funds undergo periods of idleness, parallel production is no longer sufficient to reduce the excess of productive capacity (see Figure 6.6). In this case we must have recourse to line production, activating one process after another in a predetermined sequence. In fact, in the very simple case of an elementary process that uses just one indivisible fund at $\frac{1}{3}$ of its productive capacity and which is active for $\frac{3}{6}$ of the duration of the elementary process, inactive for $\frac{2}{6}$ and, finally, active again for the remaining $\frac{1}{6}$, it will be necessary to employ four different units of the same fund, producing thus in parallel three elementary processes that start at spaced intervals of $\frac{T}{6}$, where T is the duration of the 'simple elementary process' ($T = T_{\mathrm{SEP}}$) (see Figures 6.6 and 6.7).

This regular interval in the activation of the elementary processes, which permits the elimination of idle times, corresponds to the greatest common sub-multiple of the intervals of use and idleness of the element involved (in our example $\frac{1}{6}$), on the assumption that these intervals are commensurable. In this way, it is possible to identify the 'minimum scale size' of the linear process (in terms of quantity produced) that will permit

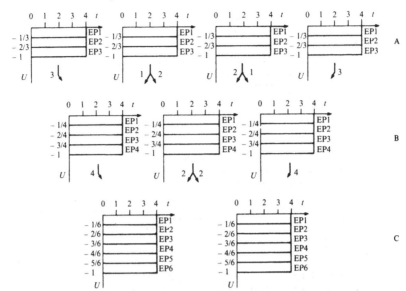

Figure 6.5 Parallel production with twelve organized elementary processes

Note: The parallel production with twelve organized elementary processes involves the use of three different types of indivisible funds with different productive capacities (4 units of fund A with productive capacity of 3 elementary processes and 2 units of fund C with productive capacity of 6 elementary processes). Figures near arrows indicate the number of elementary processes which are performed by the following fund. If we ignore, for the sake of simplicity, the time of moving semi-finished products from one fund to another, the duration of the organized elementary processes considered is equal to 12 units of time.

the total elimination of idle periods (Tani, 1986, p. 219; 1988, p. 10). In our example the number of elementary processes carried out in line production will thus be twelve (at any t) and the capacity of the single funds will be fully utilized at each moment of the elementary process. Every semi-finished product is kept in a warehouse $\frac{2}{6}$ of the duration of the 'organized elementary process', before passing from fund C to fund D. Clearly, in line production, once the process is established, finished products will come off the line regularly *in rapid succession*. In the present case the interval between them will be $\frac{T}{6}$.

Georgescu-Roegen (1969) writes that the factory system, for this extraordinary property to achieve the maximum time economy, 'deserves to be placed side by side with money as the two most fateful economic innovations for mankind'. This innovation is 'economic' and not technological, 'because the economy of time achieved by the factory

(a) *1 simple elem. process*

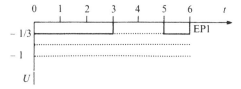

(b) *3 simple elem. processes in parallel*

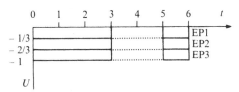

Figure 6.6 Parallel production with three simple elementary processes with idle times
Note: The duration of the simple elementary processes is 6 units of time with 2 units of idle times.

system is independent of technology. Nothing prevents us from using the most primitive technique of cloth weaving in a factory system' (p. 68).

Comparing examples 1 and 2 shown in Figure 6.7, it is clear that line production may be compatible with very different degrees of division of labour (on this point see Tani 1976, pp. 82–3). Figure 6.7 shows two out of many possible cases. Here we have three contemporaneous parallel production processes performed by each fund and activated in line at regular intervals of $\frac{T}{6}$, using four different funds. In example 1, funds A, B and C perform in sequence the first, second and third stages of the three parallel processes, while fund D repeats stage four of the three processes throughout the whole duration of the elementary process. By contrast, in example 2 the division of labour is at a maximum: the four funds perform only one stage out of the total four stages: fund A keeps repeating the first stage, fund B the second, fund C the third and fund D the fourth. This example demonstrates that line production is a precondition for the division of labour, but does not in itself make the technical division of labour necessary.

6.3   Babbage's factory principle and firm's growth

Naturally, the number of elementary processes performed, and with them the volume of production, rises considerably if the elementary process uses different types of fund elements, each characterized by different

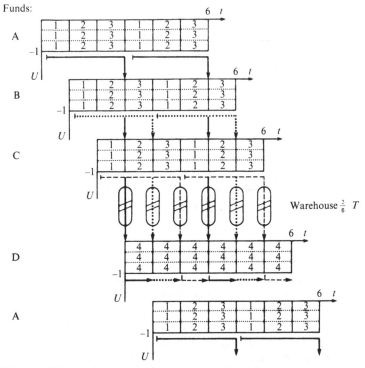

Figure 6.7 Line production with three organized elementary processes activated in parallel at equal regular intervals: two examples of different division of labour among funds
Example a – four funds (A, B, C and D) of which one is specialized (fund D).

distributions of idle time and intensity of use at each moment. In fact, in the presence of specialized and indivisible funds a high volume of production is necessary to render compatible their different productive capacities. Once a scale is established that eliminates idle times for the fund elements on the basis of different intervals of use and idleness for the various fund elements, 'any expansion in the scale of production of such a system would have to occur in discrete jumps of (integer) multiples of the scale achieved. If this rule were not followed, production would be conducted "less efficiently"' (Landesmann 1986, pp. 308–9).[3] Therefore, in accordance with Babbage's Factory Principle, 'efficiency reversals over certain ranges of increases in production levels can only be avoided if the

[3] Concerning the necessity of harmonizing the various productive capacities of indivisible inputs see also Schneider (1934, p. 96).

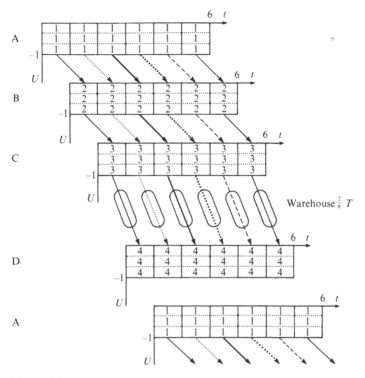

Figure 6.7 See facing page
Example b – four specialised funds (A, B, C and D).

scale increases take place in discrete jumps, that is, according to integer multiples of the scale at which full utilization of work-capacities was achieved' (*ibid.*). With discontinuity of techniques, even within the static analysis, there is no real curve of economies of scale but a series of cost curves corresponding to different plants and different technologies.[4]

However, the need to coordinate the different productive capacities of the various fund elements does not necessarily involve an increase in the size of the firm or the production unit. In fact, if the process is decomposable into different stages that are separable in time and space, according to the definition of decomposability which we shall examine in chapter 7, this need to coordinate the different productive capacities implies an increase in the overall production of a particular good, but not necessarily an increase in the scale of the single productive units. The use

---

[4] On the discontinuity of cost curves, see Sylos Labini (1956, pp. 57ff.) and R. Bianchi (1974, pp. 71–6).

of indivisible funds 'may lead to more production of the final commodity, but at the same time it may permit the sub-division of that production into a number – even a large number – of productive units which are more specialized than those involved in the previous technique...' (Tani, 1976, pp. 83–4).

As observed, these considerations are the basis of Marshall's theory of the industrial district (*ibid.*). In fact, the advantages of large-scale production can generally be obtained if a large number of small producers are grouped in a single area. In the *Economies of Industry*, Alfred and Mary Marshall write:

We shall find that some of the advantages of division of labour can be obtained only in very large factories, but that many of them, more than at first sight appears, can be secured by small factories and workshops, provided there are a very great number of them in the same trade...small factories will be at a great disadvantage relative to large unless many of them are collected together in the same district....The localization of industry promotes the education of skill and taste, and the diffusion of technical knowledge.[5] (Marshall and Paley Marshall 1879, pp. 52–3 passim)

The existence of an industrial district – characterized by infrastructures, skills and professional abilities specific to some particular manufacture – favours the external growth of firms. This model of the growth of firms, 'from the inside out', is the opposite of the traditional view of firm's growth from within, through increasing both direct investment and employment. The external model of firm's growth through co-operative inter-firm linkages is often based on a 'constellation' of firms with a leading firm and a cluster of complementary organizations or a 'network' of independent firms with collaborative relationships. In spite of the small dimension of single firms, these co-operative linkages enable certain economies of scale to be achieved through high overall production volumes.[6] Alongside the undoubted advantages provided by co-operation agreements and the development of an industrial structure, based on small dimensions, possible risks of fragmentation and fragility for industrial

---

[5] On this theme see the interesting essays by Becattini (1979) and Bellandi (1982).
[6] The firm's external growth model is examined in Lorenzoni and Ornati (1988) and Håkansson (1989), who analyse the formation of constellations and networks of firms. On inter-firm forms of collaboration (such as, licensing, franchising, venture capital, consortia, joint R&D, complementarity and auxiliary relationships) see Richardson (1972), Teece (1980, 1988), Mariti and Smiley (1983), Kay, Robe, and Zagnoli (1987), Zagnoli (1988), Lorenzoni and Ornati (1988), Mariti (1989), Semlinger (1990), Walsh (1990). Finally, a growing body of literature is being devoted to industrial districts and the growth of small firms; see, for instance, Brusco (1982, 1986), Storey (ed.) (1983), Fuà and Zacchia (eds.) (1983), Piore and Sabel (1984), Russo (1985), Barca and Magnani (1989), Goodman's Introduction to Goodman et al. (eds.) (1989), Amin (1989b), Rey (1989), Sforzi (1989), Tinacci Mosello (1989), Capecchi (1989), Storper (1989).

firms must not be forgotten (in certain cases, for example, difficulties in raising finance, in innovating production processes, or in providing adequate working conditions).

To sum up, if the production processes can be divided into different intermediate stages, a high volume of production may be obtained by a large number of specialized firms. This would lead to an increase in the size of the whole sector rather than of individual firms. The decomposability of the production process into different intermediate stages, together with other elements (like transaction costs), is an important condition in determining the size of the firm. Chapter 7 will be devoted to an analysis of the decomposability properties of the elementary process and the development of a scheme useful for studying the relationship between the various intermediate stages.

7   The matrix of production elements

7.1 ˙ The decomposability of an elementary process

An elementary process is *decomposable* if it is possible to identify *individual intermediate stages* (or sub-processes) separable in time and space, and which are linked by the fact that the product of one stage is an input to (at least) one other stage. An elementary process may embody any degree of vertical integration. In a vertically integrated production process, the elementary process includes all the operations carried out along the production *filière* (or cluster), through the different intermediate stages leading up to the finished product. An elementary process is defined as 'vertically integrated' when it includes the whole chain of the *filière*, so that the inputs are represented by services of labour and capital goods funds, and the output is the final commodity. In the case of a 'vertically integrated' process, therefore, intermediate goods are not explicitly taken into consideration.[1]

A *filière* consists of the total of technical and transaction operations needed to obtain a finished product from a given raw material. 'A *filière* includes many types of activities which contribute to the production of a commodity, using a process that can be broken down into many phases, from the production of raw material and equipment to the marketing and services connected with this commodity' (Montfort 1985).[2]

The structure of a *filière* is rarely linear – that is, characterized by a chain of successive intermediate stages and operations, beginning with a given raw material and ending with a single final commodity. In many cases this structure includes ramifications of an 'implosive' or 'explosive' kind. We speak of an 'implosive' *filière* (or part of one) when different operations and raw materials converge, or are assembled, to produce a

---

[1] On the concept of the 'vertically integrated production process' see Pasinetti (1981, pp. 33–4, 127–30). For the links between the analysis of *filière* and Pasinetti's model see Arena, Rainelli, and Torre (1984, pp. 319–20).

[2] The analysis of *filière* has been developed mainly for examining the degree of interdependence among sectors using Leontief's input–output tables. See Bellon (1984), Arena, Rainelli, and Torre (1984), Jacquemin and Rainelli (1984), Dufour and Torre (1985), Moran (1985).

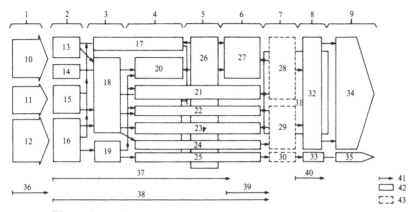

Figure 7.1 *Filière* of the textile industry
Key: 1 Supplying; 2 fibre preparation; 3 spinning; 4 weaving of spun threads; 5 finishing; 6 making up; 7 product/market; 8 sales; 9 consumption cycle; 10 agricultural raw materials; 11 forestry (cellulose); 12 chemical raw materials (petroleum); 13 washing combing (wool, cotton); 14 hackling (linen, jute); 15 artificial fibres; 16 synthetic fibres and threads (polyamides, polyesters, etc.); 17 non-woven fabrics (felt, etc.); 18 spinning; 19 twisting; 20 weaving of finished product; 21 knitting (sweaters, stockings, socks, underwear); 22 household linens; 23 drapery materials; 24 carpets; 25 industrial applications (packing, drainage, etc.); 26 finishing (dyeing, velvets, etc.); 27 making up (cutting, sewing); 28 clothing; 29 textiles for the home; 30 industrial products; 31 marketing; 32 distribution (independent, integrated, etc.); 33 direct distribution; 34 consumption by households (income, fashion, prices, etc.); 35 industrial consumption; 36 (INSEE definition): agriculture, paper pulp (chemical); 37 (INSEE definition): textile; 38 current definition of the textile-apparel plant; 39 (INSEE definition): apparel; 40 (INSEE definition): sales; 41 technical relations between industries; 42 industrial definition of sectors; 43 types of market. *Source*: Bellon (1984).

single final commodity. In this case, the various technical operations which follow one another often use technologies which have nothing to do with each other, so the unifying element of the various phases is the finished product. Contrariwise, an 'explosive' *filière* (or part of one) begins with a single raw material or intermediate product and ends with the production of a multiplicity of commodities. Even very different final processes (such as the production of furniture and the production of banknotes) may constitute transformations of a single raw material (such as wood) and may have the same production *filière* at the beginning of the manufacturing process. A single *filière* will often include alternating linear

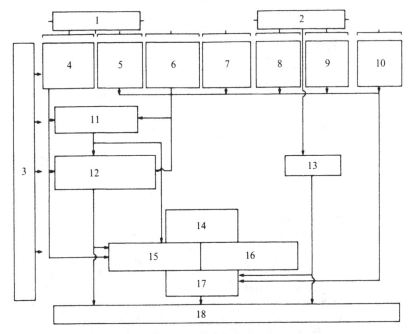

Figure 7.2 *Filière* of the automobile industry
Key: 1 Production and initial processing of steel and non-ferrous
minerals; 2 basic chemical and parachemical industries; 3 production
of machine-tools, robots, etc.; 4 production and processing of special
alloys for cars; 5 production of electrical material for cars;
6 production and initial processing of plastics for car components;
7 insulating and glueing materials for cars; 8 automobile paints;
9 glassworks; 10 fabrics and seat coverings; 11 various plastic and
metal components; 12 electrical, metal and plastic components (engine
and body components), chassis; 13 tyres; 14 vehicle design;
15 manufacture of engines and mechanical components; 16 bodywork
manufacture; 17 assembly line and finishing; 18 distribution and
services. *Source*: Fenneteau (1985).

phases and implosive or explosive phases (see Figures 7.1 and 7.2,
regarding the textile and automobile industries).

A production process may be decomposable into different intermediate
stages, such that the output of one process becomes the input of the
following one in the chain of the *filière*. In economic analysis the
decomposability of processes is considered in relation to the *possibility* of
giving to various 'semi-processed' products (which cross the 'frontier' by
passing from one stage to another) an 'independent existence' (Tani,
1976, pp. 78–9). In concrete terms this means that they can be moved from

one place to another, and thus 'remain unaltered for a certain time outside the production process' (*ibid.*). An elementary process is called 'non-decomposable' when it cannot be separated into two or more elementary processes.

Of course, the different intermediate processes within a decomposable process may be performed by a single production unit or by several production units, which in turn may belong to the same firm or to different firms. The choice between in-house production and market procurement depends upon a series of economic reasons, among which *transaction costs* play an essential part. Transaction costs are generally defined as costs of exchanges and contracts, that is to say, the costs of using markets.[3] The cost of exchange may also include costs of auxiliary transformation processes (for trade), product packaging and transport. Although transformation costs for trade are often neglected in analysing transaction costs, they have considerable importance in many activities where the semi-finished product requires a specific process to give it an independent existence outside the production process where it originated. Many examples could be given of products which require specific transformation where production is not integrated: among these we could mention the case of cellulose pulp to produce paper, or glass paste; both have to be dried and hardened to be transported outside the production unit. In fact, for molten glass to be utilized outside the production unit, additional costs of hardening and packaging must be borne, while its reuse entails liquefying by heating. Obviously these costs do not arise in a vertically integrated production. Finally, among transaction costs, we have to include costs concerning inventories, related to delivery times, and the quality control of semi-finished goods bought outside. In the case studies further on, we shall see that quality control is of considerable importance among transaction costs.

The *technical characteristics* of the production process and the transaction costs cannot be seen as the only elements which determine the size of a firm. It is clear that the choice of producing intermediate commodities in-house or purchasing them outside may be influenced by the difference in production costs of diverse organizational structures. For instance, the presence in a certain area of specialized firms in a single intermediate stage, which enjoy 'specific-product economies', may induce some other firms to buy out the semi-finished product of that intermediate stage or to establish subcontracting relationships. Thus a comparative

---

[3] Williamson (1985) distinguishes between *ex-ante* contracting costs and *ex-post* contracting costs (p. 40). On transaction costs definition see also: Coase (1937), Goldberg (1985), Grossman and Hart (1986), Demsetz (1988b). For a discussion on exchange and transaction costs in a neo-institutional perspective, see Hodgson (1988, chapters 7, 8, 9).

advantage in some intermediate stage is an important element in favouring inter-firm agreements. In this connection, as indicated in chapter 6, a wide range of mixed forms between market and hierarchy, based on complementary relationships among firms, exist in the various sectors.

As far as the integrated production is concerned, we also have to consider the 'organizational costs' which concern the costs of moving the semi-finished product from one intermediate stage to another within the production unit. These costs therefore consist mainly in transport costs (energy and tools for moving goods) and in costs of storing the intermediate products, between one sub-process and the next. The cost of warehouses depends, obviously, on the quantity of semi-finished goods stored and the length of time during which they remain unused in the form of inventories. If we want to take these costs into account, therefore, we must include *time* in our analysis of the production process.

The scheme presented is particularly well-suited to studying the relationship between different related intermediate stages performed by the same production units or by different production units, because it subdivides the production process into various intermediate stages according to the definition of decomposability formulated above, and because it analyses the production process time profile. Considering the links between various intermediate stages and the time dimension of production processes allows different costs in relation to firms' different organizational and dimensional structures to be explained.

7.2   Time profile of the production process: some further specifications

I shall consider in detail the theme of the temporal dimension of the production process. The whole length of the production process can be broken down into different periods of time, or sub-periods, such as raw materials delivery time, machine time, technical and organizational inventories time, process breaks (nights, holidays, seasons). Then there are several production time profile definitions, according to different sub-periods under consideration. For the purposes of the analysis of an organized elementary process we may consider:

(1) *Net process time* (NPT_{OEP}). The 'net process time' or 'gross machine time' is the time required for producing a unit of commodity by means of an elementary technical unit (or a chain of technical units), excluding all interruptions apart from loading, tooling-up (or set-up), and maintenance breaks, relative to single funds. Therefore the 'net process time' excludes: (a) all pauses which may permit the elementary technical unit to be used in other elementary processes, within the overall duration of the

elementary process considered, such as breaks due to the technical need to let semi-finished goods settle or mature and breaks due to storage caused by the different productive capacity of the single phases and by internal movements; and (b) all breaks caused by specific regulations on process conditions or by seasonal variations (such as nights, holidays etc.). Obviously, the 'net process time' is a theoretical length of time, in the sense that it is derived from the simple addition of the partial times.

(2) *Process time* (PTI_{OEP}). 'Process time' is given by the sum of 'net process times' plus breaks due to periods of time in which semi-finished products lie in technical inventories for maturing or settling. It should be noted that technical inventories are an integral part of the whole process because the semi-finished goods exit from technical warehouses, transformed according to the production needs.

(3) *Working time* (WT_{OEP}). In addition to all technical breaks contained in 'process time', 'working time' also takes into account organizational inventories, related to all interruptions in the use of funds for organizational reasons, such as breaks due to differences in the productive capacity of individual process phases, or to internal movement times.

(4) *Duration* (T_{OEP}). In chapter 6 the overall 'duration of the elementary process' was defined as the actual total time starting from the moment when the process begins (with the input of the first raw material) to the moment when the process is completed with the production of a unit of commodity. The 'duration' includes, therefore, all kinds of interruptions. A production process which, in terms of 'net process time' can be concluded in twenty-one hours, can actually be as long as several months as a result of various interruptions such as technical and organizational breaks, and any pauses due to shift regulations, working conditions and seasonal variations (e.g. nights, holidays).

(5) *Response time* (RT_{OEP}). This is the time lapse between the order being received and the delivery of the finished product. The 'response time', in some sectors, constitutes an important competitive element in a production unit. As for delivering semi-finished goods, processing the customers' orders and distributing outputs may also be seen as different intermediate stages.

(6) *Gross duration* (GD_{OEP}). 'Gross duration' includes the time needed for receiving raw materials, and goes, therefore, from the moment when the order is placed by the production unit up to the completion of the elementary process. Delivery time (from the order being placed) of raw materials represents a transaction cost, which varies greatly from sector to sector and from region to region. In many transformation processes, such times represent an important part of the total length of the production process and so can create significant organizational and financial

problems.[4] The delivery of inputs, which determines the difference between the gross duration and the duration, may be considered as a separate intermediate stage, within the whole elementary process.

(7) *Financial time* (FT_{OEP}). This is the period of time between paying for the raw materials and selling the product. I shall assume, for simplicity, that 'financial time' is equal to the 'duration' of the organized elementary production process.[5]

It is evident that these time dimensions of the production process are closely linked because 'net process time' is part of 'process time', 'process time' is part of 'working time' and 'working time' is part of 'duration', which is in turn part of both the 'response time' and the 'gross duration'.

The introduction of new techniques usually makes significant variations in production process' time profiles and may influence these various time dimensions of production process in different ways. For instance, technical changes, which permit the speed of machines to be increased or to reduce interruptions by simplifying loading, maintenance and set-up operations, contribute to reducing 'net process time' (point 1). As we shall see in Part 3 (chapter 12), decreasing set-up times is an essential element in determining technical flexibility in a mix of products.

'Process time' (point 2) is, of course, strongly influenced by technical production characteristics. As mentioned, certain semi-finished goods have to be matured (to settle), sometimes for long periods, between one production phase (or intermediate stage) and another. Therefore, there are significant quantities of semi-processed goods stored in technical warehouses. In this kind of production, great importance is attached to changes which reduce technical storage time.

The second important reason for semi-finished goods having to remain in the warehouses for long periods is batch production or the different productive capacities in the various phases. As we shall see, a better balance between the productive capacities of different phases or organizational changes, like adopting a 'just-in-time' production system, allows a reduction in organizational inventories and in the size of batches, shortening the 'working time' (point 3).

Organizational changes, which affect the structure of working shifts and process interruptions, can bring about a notable reduction in the

---

[4] For example, in the textile sector, running the raw materials warehouse is such an important function that it is managed personally by the owner–entrepreneur or, in managerial firms, by the top levels of the company hierarchy. On the textile sector, see chapter 9 below.

[5] Coutts, Godley, and Nordhaus (1978, chapter 3) have made an interesting analysis on the time lags between production costs and final prices. The authors estimate, in various 'industrial groups' and under different assumptions on pricing policies, the lapse of time between a cost increase and the completion of the corresponding price increase, on the basis of the cost structure, the 'period of production' and the stock/output ratios.

'duration' of production processes (point 4). In fact, differences in the time profiles of equipment utilization, due to the particular structure of shifts (i.e. the number of hours in which equipment is in operation), can explain remarkable differences in unit costs.

Introducing new technologies, or just reorganizing production, may reduce 'response times' (point 5). Think of the application of computer-aided design (CAD) or of computer-aided manufacturing (CAM). In fact, implementing computer-based technology decreases the time needed to collect orders (from customers) and to transfer these orders to production lines according to the specific characteristics required.

Finally, improvements in transportation and communications may cut down the delivery times of raw materials, and so the 'gross duration' (point 6). Moreover, some technical advances might make it possible to produce necessary inputs near the production unit, thus reducing the gross duration.

7.3   The matrix of production elements

If an elementary process is *decomposable*, it can be represented by a matrix of function of time, which I call *matrix of production elements* or matrix **L(t)**. The *matrix of production elements* is not present in Georgescu-Roegen's works,[6] nor, as far as I know, in the literature on the subject; nevertheless, this matrix may be considered as a development of some elements drawn from his analysis of the production process and, in particular, from Tani's related formalization, considered in chapter 6. As we shall see, the matrix of production elements is useful in microeconomic analysis because it brings out the links between intermediate stages and, at the same time, enables us to deal with quantitative, temporal and organizational aspects of production.

For the time being, let us consider the matrix $L(t)$ of production elements regarding the *ex-ante* analysis of an 'organized elementary process'. Each element of matrix $L(t)$ indicates, at time t, the cumulative quantities of production elements going in and/or going out in each intermediate stage of a decomposable organized elementary process.

Matrix $L(t)$ has as many columns as there are intermediate production stages, and as many rows as there are process elements, that is:

$$L(t) = \begin{bmatrix} G_{ij}(t) \\ F_{hj}(t) \\ S_{kj}(t) \end{bmatrix} \tag{7.1}$$

In matrix $L(t)$, $G_{ij}(t)$ indicates, at time t, the cumulative functions of ith

---

[6] Georgescu-Roegen (1979, p. 108, and 1986, p. 263) worked out a matrix representing the inter-industrial flows of an economy as a whole, in order to determine the energy consumption of an economic system.

($i = 1, 2, ..., I$) outflow or *intermediate out/input flow*, leaving (or entering) the production of the jth ($j = 1, 2, ..., J$) intermediate stage; analogously, $F_{hj}(t)$ indicates the cumulative functions of the hth ($h = 1, 2, ..., H$) *inflow*, entering the production process of a given j^{th} intermediate stage; and finally $S_{kj}(t)$ indicates the cumulative functions of the *services* of the kth ($k = 1, 2, ..., K$) *fund element*, used in the production of the jth stage. As already mentioned, I give a positive sign to the functions of output flows $G_{ij}(t)$ and a negative sign to the functions of input flows $F_{hj}(t)$ and of funds services $S_{kj}(t)$. Production elements (inputs and outputs) are defined by their specific characteristics and by their date of availability.

$G_{ij}(t)$ are non-decreasing monotonic output functions of t, while $F_{hj}(t)$ and S_{kj} are non-increasing monotonic input functions of t. Functions $G_{ij}(t)$ and $F_{hj}(t)$ may be discontinuous. On the contrary, $S_{kj}(t)$ are always continuous functions. Functions $S_{kj}(t)$ give us not only the time profile of services of the various funds (note being taken of the idle times), but also the degree of utilization during the time in which these funds are in operation.

Obviously, throughout the whole duration of the 'organized elementary process' it is usually possible to obtain more than one unit of output. In other words, within the duration of an elementary process, that is, the overall time required to produce a single commodity – say thirty days for producing a piece of fabric from raw wool – a production unit may produce thousands of similar commodities. Of course, the total quantity produced may vary according to whether the elementary process is organized in series and/or in parallel, or according to the duration of pauses, or the inventory on hand. Moreover, in the case of 'joint production', an elementary process yields technically inseparable products. Even the production of waste may be considered a form of joint production. As is well known, in joint production the average productivity of the single elements cannot be calculated in relation to the single commodity under consideration, but must refer to the total of all goods produced within the elementary process. 'Joint production' should be distinguished from 'multi-production', that is to say, production connected for economic reasons. When there are shareable fund elements, the advantage of multi-production 'lies precisely in the possibility of using fund elements continuously (or at least reducing their intervals of inactivity) and of saturating their production capacities by using them in different processes' (Tani, 1986, p. 215). Multi-production may involve a differentiated product, or a vast range of products differing greatly among themselves. Multi-production, in providing the opportunity of economizing on certain shareable production elements, leads to *economies of scope* (chapter 12, section 12.2).

$$L(t) = \begin{bmatrix} G_{1,1}(t) & G_{1,2}(t) & - \\ G_{2,1}(t) & - & - \\ - & G_{3,2}(t) & G_{3,3}(t) \\ - & G_{4,2}(t) & - \\ - & - & G_{5,3}(t) \\ - & - & G_{6,3}(t) \\ F_{1,1}(t) & - & - \\ F_{2,1}(t) & F_{2,2}(t) & F_{2,3}(t) \\ S_{1,1}(t) & - & - \\ - & S_{2,2}(t) & - \\ - & - & S_{3,3}(t) \\ S_{4,1}(t) & S_{4,2}(t) & S_{4,3}(t) \\ S_{5,1}(t) & S_{5,2}(t) & S_{5,3}(t) \\ S_{6,1}(t) & S_{6,2}(t) & S_{6,3}(t) \\ S_{7,1}(t) & S_{7,2}(t) & S_{7,3}(t) \end{bmatrix}$$

Figure 7.3 Matrix of production elements

With 'joint production', matrix $L(t)$ has to include all outflows produced within the elementary process, while with 'multi-production' it is generally possible to represent the production process of each single commodity by calculating its specific input requirement. We can then identify as many matrices $L(t)$ as there are different types of outputs produced within the process, although the elementary process of each commodity is not independent from the elementary processes of other commodities belonging to the same range of products.

Let us look for purely illustrative purposes at the example shown in Figure 7.3 of an 'organized elementary process', decomposable into three elementary intermediate processes, that employs two input flows and four funds. Assuming that each intermediate stage produces a waste product, we have six output flow functions [one function of the final output flow $G_{5,3}(t)$, two of the intermediate output flows $G_{1,1}(t)$ and $G_{3,2}(t)$, and three of the waste flows $G_{2,1}(t)$, $G_{4,2}(t)$ and $G_{6,3}(t)$]. It can be seen that the intermediate output flow of one sub-process becomes an input flow in the following one [$G_{1,1}(t)$ becomes $G_{1,2}(t)$, and $G_{3,2}(t)$ becomes $G_{3,3}(t)$]. As far as input flows coming from outside the production unit are concerned, the first is utilized only in the first intermediate process [function $F_{1,1}(t)$], while the second input flow is used in all three intermediate stages [functions $F_{2,j}(t)$]. Each of the first three funds are used in only one sub-process [respectively functions $S_{1,1}(t)$, $S_{2,2}(t)$ and $S_{3,3}(t)$], while the fourth fund is used in all the intermediate process [functions $S_{4,j}(t)$]. Finally we have to consider the functions regarding organizational inventories [functions $S_{5,j}(t)$], the semi-processed output in technical warehouses [functions $S_{6,j}(t)$], and the quantity of output constantly in progress on machines [functions $S_{7,j}(t)$].

Thus far, we have conducted an *ex-ante* analysis of a production process, considering a 'model' or a 'plan' of a possible elementary process organized according to the criteria of maximizing the funds' productive capacity. However, the matrix of the elements of production can be applied also in an *ex-post* analysis, to evaluate the impact of technical changes on historical data concerning processes in actual operation. In fact, it is possible to compare two or more matrices of the production elements related to different moments in time.

An important effect of technical change is to save time. Even if a reduction in the 'process time' usually leads at some time to a decrease in the requirement for some elements, these two phenomena must be kept analytically distinct. In fact, saving time, on one hand, and reducing inputs' requirement, on the other, may be independent, or a 'reversal relationship' may exist whereby, in many significant circumstances, a decrease in the 'process time' can be obtained through increasing the requirement for some inputs or changing the (quality of) inputs used. Moreover, technical change may involve, for a given elementary process, a decrease in some inputs and an increase in other inputs. This kind of technical change is known as 'locally progressive' and 'locally regressive'.

Referring to matrix $L(t)$, I can indicate three main forms of technical change. A variation in techniques is said to be:

(a) '*time-saving*' if it reduces the 'total process time', by decreasing 'total net process time' (i.e. total gross machine time) and/or technical inventory breaks;

(b) '*organizational-inventory-saving*' if it reduces the quantity of semi-finished goods in organizational inventories;

(c) '*inputs-saving*' if it reduces the quantity of input flows or of services of funds which enter the elementary process directly (such as energy, raw material, workers and fixed capital). More precisely, when the required quantity of one or more inputs is reduced while the quantity of all the other inputs does not increase.

Of course, these three forms of technical change may appear separately or may be combined. As mentioned, in certain circumstances, a 'time-saving technical change' may involve an increase in inputs requirements and vice-versa. On the other hand, 'organizational-inventory-saving technical change' is an intermediate form, between *a* and *c*, because it allows both a cut in the length of the production process (the duration), as well in the quantities of inputs (semi-finished goods in organizational-inventories).[7]

As far as the calculation of the 'total process time' (PT) is concerned, it is easily obtainable from the sum of the 'process time' of the individual intermediate stages (PTI_j), that is:

$$PT = \sum_{j=1}^{J} PTI_j \qquad (j = 1, 2, ..., J) \tag{7.2}$$

The 'process time' of each intermediate stage is, in turn, the sum of the single periods during which the transformation process operates, hence it excludes pauses due to organizational inventories or interruptions of the elementary process itself (such as nights, holidays etc.). The presence of alternating periods in which the elementary process operates and does not operate allows instants t_m $(m = 0, 1, 2, ..., M)$ to be specified so that the 'process time' of a single intermediate stage can be determined in the following way:

$$PTI_j = \sum_{p=1}^{P} PTI_p, \qquad (p = 1, 2, ..., P) \tag{7.3}$$

where $PTI_p = t_{m+1} - t_m$ $(m = 0, 2, 4, ..., M-1)$, with $P = (M+1)/2$. If $P = 1$, then $M = 1$ and the process does not break off and the process time is equal to the duration $(PTI_{OEP} = T_{OEP})$; see example (a) in Figure 7.4. By contrast, example (b), in the same figure, shows a process time with two interruptions, hence $P = 3$ and $M = 5$.

Furthermore, technical change involves not only variations in the necessary quantities of inputs and outputs, or time profiles or production organization, but also changes in the *qualitative characteristics* of production elements. In this last case a meaningful comparison between different techniques (before and after the change in production element quality) requires consideration of:

(i) the qualitative characteristics of outputs which are relevant for the markets;
(ii) functions of cost and revenue.

The qualitative characteristics of outputs may be understood in terms of ability to meet consumers' needs and expectations. For some outputs

---

[7] Matrix L does not consider 'response time' or 'gross duration', but these time dimensions can be obtained by computing the duration of backward or forward intermediate stages (such as the raw material transport process or distributing of the final product) and adding them to the duration of the elementary process under consideration.

(a) Process time equal to the duration of an organized
    elementary process (no interruptions) $PTI = T$

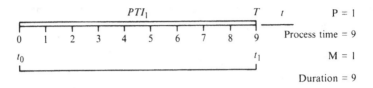

(b) Process time less than the duration of the organized
    elementary process (2 interruptions) $PTI < T$

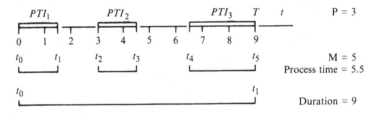

Figure 7.4 Duration and process time of an intermediate stage

the simple physical characteristics may be a sufficient indicator of their
quality. Measuring the qualitative characteristics of most industrial
artifacts, however, is very complex. Recent studies have proposed a
'composite measure' of the economic and technical performances of
products. This approach allows technical change *per se*, in any given
industry, to be measured on the basis of the evolution of intrinsic product
characteristics (Sahal 1983, pp. 153–4; Saviotti and Metcalfe 1984, p. 147;
cf. K. E. Knight 1985; Esposito 1990).[8] Following this approach, it is
possible to associate to the relevant output of a given matrix $L(t)$ an n-
vector x, whose components indicate the intensity of performances of the
elementary process relevant output. Thus we have the row-vector:

$$x = [x_1 \, x_2 \ldots x_n], \tag{7.4}$$

where x_n denotes the nth performance. For instance, in the computer
industry, examined by Sahal (1984) and Knight (1985), possible indices of

[8] On different techniques of analysing product quality see also Swann (1986, chapter 2).
Finally, on engineering production functions see Wibe (1980).

performance are computational speed (in 1,000s of operations/second), computational cost (in 1,000s of operations/£) and memory capacity (in 1,000 of bytes); in the aircraft industry, analysed by Esposito (1990), possible indices are speed, comfort, safety, cost-effectiveness (given by the inverse of direct costs). For motor cars, Saviotti and Metcalfe (1984) give an example of a list of performances (or service characteristics): speed, number of passengers, luggage space, ventilation, comfort, radio and other instruments, pollution, noise, space occupied, danger to occupants and to other people. Another performance characteristic is given by the reliability of the product. Reliability may be measured by the incidence of consumers' complaints about defective units, by the duration of the average interval between one repair and another and by the average life of the product. It should be stressed that in applied research the composite measure of performance indicates, of course, only the main characteristics representable by quantitative indices; in fact, not all qualitative characteristics which have market significance are easily measurable in quantitative terms and some of them may elude any quantitative evaluation.

Saviotti and Metcalfe (1984) in their analysis of the output quality include a second set whose components represent technical characteristics. Among the output technical characteristics they mention are: for an engine – type, size, number of cylinders, bore, stroke, compression ratio, carburettor, injection and position; for transmission – number of gears, syncromesh, automatic, semi-automatic, clutch, type of drive wheels; for the braking system – disc/drum, power braking, circuits; for suspension – independent, shock absorbers, hydropneumatic, etc. As suggested, taking also technical characteristics into account may prove fruitful in analysing the adoption and diffusion processes of innovations. In fact, output may be described as a combination of two sets of characteristics (service and technical characteristics), that gives the efficiency with which a set of technical characteristics can supply a certain level of services. 'Within this framework there will then be several possible dimensions of technological change': (i) change in absolute values of elements of the two sets mentioned above; (ii) change in the balance of elements of two sets, change in the pattern of mapping between two sets (Saviotti and Metcalfe 1984, p. 142).[9]

---

[9] The authors present a third set whose elements are the production process characteristics (pp. 144, 147). However, their examination of this issue, which is the main theme of the present book, is brief. An interesting feature of Saviotti's and Metcalfe's approach is that it makes it possible to compare production process, and technical and performance characteristics. Moreover, a 'technological regime' can be defined as consisting of a given *list* of technical characteristics, and a 'technological trajectory' as the pattern of improvement of the various elements of the technical characteristics (p. 145). For the

In conclusion, the qualitative characteristics of outputs may be assessed at three different levels: (a) from the list of physical characteristics; (b) by a performance set (or service set); (c) by comparing performance set with technical characteristics set. It is obvious that the way of measuring the qualitative characteristics of the output depends very much upon the type of commodity under consideration and the aims of the analysis. Whatever level of detail and disaggregation we consider necessary to our study of quality, it is worth noting that the analytical representation of the production process, presented above, allows the transformation of the production processes to be linked to the change in quality of production elements within a consistent framework.

As far as the second point is concerned, in order to obtain costs and revenue functions of a production process, we must multiply each function of the matrix $L(t)$ by its price, denoted respectively by P_i, P_h, P_k. We have thus:

$$Z(t) = \begin{bmatrix} G_{ij}(t) \cdot P_i \\ F_{hj}(t) \cdot P_h \\ S_{kj}(t) \cdot P_k \end{bmatrix} \tag{7.5}$$

Let us suppose that (a) the input flows and funds services (machines, equipment and premises) are paid for at the beginning of the elementary process; and (b) labour and the output of the production unit are paid for at the end of the process. Since it is assumed that the input flows are paid for at the beginning of the process, the cost of inventories increases (due to interest) over the period of the elementary process.

The monetary cost of labour can be calculated very simply: the number of hours of presence is multiplied by the hourly cost of the corresponding level of occupation. However, for funds consisting of equipment and machines the cost calculation is more complicated, since the cost of their services depends not only on the time of presence but also on the intensity of use. It may be postulated that each machine is able to carry out a finite quantity of production processes. On the basis of the average intensity of its use one can then determine the period of technical depreciation and thus calculate the cost per hour of use. For the real estate of an establishment the calculation of the hourly cost presents few difficulties, as it is given by the relation between annual depreciation and the total hours worked. Finally, the hourly cost of the products in progress and semi-finished products held in warehouses is measured on the basis of the rate of interest on the value of the locked-up monetary capital. In short, the hourly cost of fixed capital (equipment and premises) depends on the

definitions of 'technological regime' and 'technological trajectory' see chapter 2, section 2.2 on the nature of technical change.

degree of utilization and therefore it is not independent of the production organization.

There are firms which sell some of their intermediate products, and others which use up all their semi-finished products internally. In the first case, the matrix shows the price of the goods produced by the separate intermediate stages, while in the second case, it shows only their cost, which is the sum of the costs of input and fund service elements. The cost of inventory and products in progress refers to the 'historical cost', on the basis of transformation costs, and not to their 'opportunity cost', which may differ according to whether the various goods can be assigned a price (if they are sold) or simply a cost (if they are merely utilized in the next intermediate stage). Hence, the cost of inventories and goods in progress is calculated as the *interest* on the current 'transformation cost' of the goods, which is given by the sum of flow costs, labour and machine services. It excludes, then, all other costs (such as the costs of inventories and premises depreciation, of parallel service processes of administration, organization, planning, marketing, distribution, etc.).

A comparison of the functions of costs enables us to evaluate some of the effects of technical change, in relation to a given elementary process. Considering the three main forms of technical change, presented above, and assuming prices as given, we have three definitions. Then technical change is said to be:

(i) '*technical–inventory–cost-saving*' and/or '*goods-in-progress–cost-saving*', if it is characterised by a reduction in 'total process time'. In fact, 'time-saving technical change' causes a decrement in costs by decreasing technical inventories and/or total interest on monetary capital locked-up for the semi-finished goods in progress;

(ii) '*organizational–inventory–cost-saving*', if it is characterised by a reduction in organizational inventories;

(iii) '*inputs–cost-saving*', if it involves a decrease in inflows and funds services requirement.

Cost and revenue functions in matrix $Z(t)$ should be considered very important variables affected by (and influencing in turn) technical changes. Nevertheless, in the case of a production unit being able to influence the prices of inputs and outputs, it may not always be possible to isolate variations deriving from changes in relative prices from those that come from qualitative changes of the goods under consideration. Moreover, variations in cost and revenue functions represent only a part of the problem under consideration. For example, some technical changes facilitate reorganization, which increases production flexibility without remarkable corresponding effects on cost. In other instances, the main purpose of technical change concerns the strengthening of the market position of the production unit in relation to some particular segments. Such strengthening can be achieved by altering the quality of the product through incorporating new techniques, which do not always necessarily reduce production costs. All these problems will be discussed in chapter 8 which is devoted to the possibilities of applying the matrix of production elements to empirical research in order to study the economic effects of technical change.

8 Transformation of the matrix of production elements for empirical research

In the course of the foregoing analysis we have seen that a production process may be represented either by a matrix or by a vector of functions of time of the different production elements, depending on whether or not the process is decomposable into different intermediate stages. The matrix of production elements (or the vector) contains information on the main variables characterizing the quantitative, temporal and organizational aspects involved in the economic analysis of the production process. Data on production techniques can be obtained directly from the functions that compose the matrix, or can easily be deduced from them by formulating a few *ad hoc* hypotheses (especially with regard to the use of the services of funds). However, for the purposes of empirical analysis it is preferable to *transform* the matrix of functions of time of production elements into two separate tables: the *quantitative-temporal matrix* and the *organizational scheme*. This transformation of the matrix of production elements makes it possible to 'standardize' the data of the different elementary processes under consideration, and thus create a homogeneous data base on which to make the comparisons required for empirical analysis.

The differences between theoretical and empirical representation arise from the fact that the matrix of production elements with respect to time is constructed according to theoretical criteria of consistency, while the quantitative and temporal matrix and the organizational scheme derived from it correspond to the requirements of empirical analysis. Hence the two later tables take account of criteria of efficiency and efficacy in relation to the availability of data and the possibility of a concise representation which is as quantitative as possible and which lends itself to comparison.

Before going on to illustrate the quantitative-temporal matrix and organizational schemes we must consider the important problem of determining the 'analytical frontier', as defined in chapter 7. In other words, we have to select the output to which the elementary process refers, the production elements, and the elementary technical unit of plant necessary for its production (i.e. the minimum unit which can be activated separately). Since the aim of this book is to study production processes in relation to the economic effects of technical change, it suffices to consider a product which is representative of the whole range of outputs. In contrast, in *manufacturing accounting* it would obviously be necessary to calculate as many matrices as there are different types of product. It should be noted that if the mix of outputs varies over time, the representative commodity must also vary.

Of course, the number of intermediate stages and production elements to be considered depends on the aims of the analysis, as well as the characteristics of the elementary process in question and the availability of reliable data. In this connection we should note that, according to the purposes of the analysis one can use different levels of disaggregation, developing single parts of the two tables and considering a larger number of elements related to the type of problems in the area of interest. For example, one can obtain a more accurate description of the quantitative aspects or of the organizational ones, or of those related to the labour market. Moreover a set of output performances may be related to the matrix of production elements, in order to assess the qualitative characteristics of products. In fact, as we have seen, it is possible, at least within certain limits, to represent the qualitative characteristics of a product by means of quantitative indices. Whatever the level of disaggregation of the single parts, it is essential, for the reasons explained in the foregoing chapters, that the analysis of the individual aspects forms part of a scheme which can take account of all the different economic dimensions of the production process at one and the same time.

In the next section I shall analyse the *quantitative–temporal matrix*, and in the following section I shall deal with the *organizational scheme*. The quantitative–temporal matrix indicates the quantities of each output and input flow and the time of services provided by each fund. As we shall see, the organizational scheme summarizes some information implicitly included in the quantitative and temporal matrix. It gives further information on the temporal profile of production process, providing also additional data on the production process organization and on the size of the production unit. The data in each table complement each other: the two tables are different, mutually complementary tools of a single interpretative scheme.

8.1   The quantitative and temporal matrix

The quantitative and temporal matrix shows the dated input and output flows, and fund services, required by an elementary technical unit (or a 'chain' of elementary technical units) to produce one 'economically indivisible unit' of the product emerging from an 'organized elementary process'.

The production elements are defined by their physical characteristics. The quality of the output can be seen as a combination of characteristics which may satisfy consumer needs or expectations. The specific characteristics of labour services may be expressed by skill, educational level, and actual job performed, while the characteristics of machines may be expressed by size, power, speed and vintage.

In the quantitative and temporal matrix (which for simplicity, I shall henceforth call matrix A_{pt} or the production matrix) the columns indicate the different intermediate stages considered, while the rows show the quantities of input and output flows, and of productive services provided by fund elements necessary to produce one unit of the final commodity. This unit of the final commodity appears as the output of the last intermediate stage. Obviously the different intermediate stages comprising a decomposable elementary process are not necessarily elementary in themselves, that is to say, they do not necessarily involve just one unit of intermediate product. Finally, matrix A_{pt} includes also the quantities of semi-finished products lying in technical and organizational inventories.

Let us define matrix A_{pt} as:

$$A_{pt} = \begin{bmatrix} a_{11}\, a_{12} \ldots a_{1J} \\ a_{21}\, a_{22} \ldots a_{2J} \\ \ldots \ldots \ldots \ldots \\ a_{Q1}\, a_{Q2} \ldots a_{QJ} \end{bmatrix} \tag{8.1}$$

where pt – the subscript of A_{pt} – denotes the 'total process time' of the elementary process, while a_{qj} indicates the quantity of the qth ($q = 1, 2, \ldots,$ Q) output or production element of the jth ($j = 1, 2, \ldots, J$) intermediate stage.

The quantities shown in each row are homogeneous and hence summable quantities. The measurement of the quantities of the flow elements used within the production process is very simple, because each of these elements is a substance or material or form of energy easily measurable in its own normal units of measurement. On the other hand, as far as fund elements are concerned the quantities employed in the process are measured by the hours of services rendered. With regard to workers, in chapter 3 we assumed that their capacity to work throughout the production process is maintained by operations outside the process itself. In the case of funds constituted by plant, agricultural land and machinery, we adopted the hypothesis that these operations, which guarantee the maintenance of productive capacity, occur within parallel production processes. These maintenance processes also involve funds (workers and equipment) and flows (components which must be regularly changed and those that break accidentally). For example, in the latter case the new oil coming in is considered as an input flow, and old oil going out as a waste output. The same applies to new parts installed and old ones being replaced.

The measurement of services provided by funds is based on the time of their presence (man hours) or their utilization (machine hours). In the case of plant it is quite easy to take account of the intensity of use of a fund in relation to its productive capacity. Generally, the latter decreases in relation to wear and tear, according to the number of elementary processes carried out. Note that the number of machine hours and man hours should not only be referred to homogeneous elements (such as workers of the same category or machines of the same type and age), but should always be associated with a given type of organization. Fifty man hours performed by one worker are quite different from fifty man hours performed by five workers. Moreover, from a given number of workers and hours worked one can obtain a higher or lower productivity depending on the organization of production (which for example may be linear or in parallel, with a greater or lesser degree of division of labour and cooperation). As argued in chapters 3 and 4, the organization of labour service often involves indivisibility, because of the peculiar characteristics of 'team-production'.

Since the output of an elementary process is by definition equal to an 'economically indivisible unit' of the corresponding commodity, the quantities of input flows and of services of funds in matrix A_{pt} represent indices of physical cost, or the technical coefficients of production, for the elementary process under examination. As in traditional input–output analysis, these coefficients correspond to the quantities of production elements necessary to produce one physical unit of the final commodity. From the inverse of the input flows and services of funds, involved in the elementary process, we obtain an index of 'physical average productivity' for each input flow or service of a fund.

If we look again at the example in Figure 7.3 (p. 77) and apply it to the definition of the quantitative matrix, we obtain Table 8.1. The sum of the coefficients shown in the rows corresponding to intermediate products is zero when the production unit uses up the whole intermediate product of the preceding intermediate stage and does not buy any part of the intermediate product from outside. The last two rows indicate the quantity of semi-finished products in inventories and in progress (on machines) necessary to produce a unit of the final commodity.

By comparing two (or more) matrices A_{pt} of an elementary process operating at different times, one can evaluate the effects of changes in production techniques on the duration of the elementary process and on

Table 8.1 *The quantitative and temporal matrix for a given 'total process time'*

Production elements	Intermediate stages (IS)			
	1	2	3	TOTAL
Output IS1	$+a_{1,1}$	$-a_{1,2}$	–	0
Waste output IS1	$+a_{2,1}$	–	–	$+a_{2,4}$
Output IS2	–	$+a_{3,2}$	$-a_{3,3}$	0
Waste output IS2	–	$+a_{4,2}$	–	$+a_{4,4}$
Output IS3	–	–	$+a_{5,3}$	$+a_{5,4}$
Waste output IS3	–	–	$+a_{6,3}$	$+a_{6,4}$
Input IS1	$-a_{7,1}$	–	–	$-a_{7,4}$
Input IS1, 2, 3	$-a_{8,1}$	$-a_{8,2}$	$-a_{8,3}$	$-a_{8,4}$
Services of fund IS1	$-a_{9,1}$	–	–	$-a_{9,4}$
Services of fund IS2	–	$-a_{10,2}$	–	$-a_{10,4}$
Services of fund IS3	–	–	$-a_{11,3}$	$-a_{11,4}$
Services of fund IS1, 2, 3	$-a_{12,1}$	$-a_{12,2}$	$-a_{12,3}$	$-a_{12,4}$
Organization inventories	$-a_{13,1}$	$-a_{13,2}$	$-a_{13,3}$	$-a_{13,4}$
Technical inventories	$-a_{14,1}$	$-a_{14,2}$	$-a_{14,3}$	$-a_{14,4}$
Elements in progress	$-a_{15,1}$	$-a_{15,2}$	$-a_{15,3}$	$-a_{15,4}$

requirements for input flows and services of funds, in producing a representative commodity.

Variations in input requirements and services of funds often serve as *indirect indices* of variations occurring in the time profile of the production process. In fact, as seen in chapter 7, a change in the production process time profile may have immediate effects on the input requirements. However, this correspondence is not always guaranteed, as in many cases changes in the time profile of the elementary process may be reflected only partially, or not at all, in the quantities of production elements. Therefore, in chapter 7 I distinguished 'time-saving', 'organizational-inventory-saving' and 'inputs-saving technical change'.

Comparing two elementary processes after a technical change, we may obtain two quantitative and temporal matrices, say A_{pt} and, after the change in techniques, $\hat{A}_{pt}$. The 'total process time' of A_{pt} is denoted by PT, while the 'total process time' of $\hat{A}_{pt}$ is denoted by $P\hat{T}$. Hence we have:

(1) $PT > P\hat{T}$, $a_{14,j} \geqslant \hat{a}_{14,j}$, $a_{15,j} = \hat{a}_{15,j}$, $\forall j$, if technical change is time-saving;

(2) $a_{13,j} > \hat{a}_{13,j}$, $\forall j$,
if technical change is organizational-inventory-saving;

(3) $a_{qj} \geqslant \hat{a}_{qj}$, $q \neq 15$, $\forall j$,
if technical change is input-saving.

The comparison of different matrices A_{pt} makes it possible to assess possible differences in productivity owing to wear and tear on machines, or simply to different intensities of use (attributable both to different levels of demand and to certain technical improvements that make the machines run faster).

As argued above, technical change may bring a variation in the inputs required per unit of product and, at same time, a change in the inherent qualities of the commodities. For instance, a variation in the dimension of scale usually implies also a change in technology and/or in the organization of production, with a modification in the quality of production elements. Change in quality may concern inputs, semi-finished products and final output for consumers. The techno-economic performance of inputs (both flows and funds) is analysed by the quantitative–temporal matrix and, as we shall see, by the organizational scheme. The quality of semi-finished goods is measured by the percentage of defective goods within the process, indicated in the organizational scheme. Finally, as suggested in chapter 7, when the definition of physical characteristics of the matrix A_{pt} relevant output is not sufficient, it is possible to associate this output with an n-vector x, whose components indicate the intensity of its performances:

$$x = [x_1 \, x_2 \, ... \, x_n] \tag{8.2}$$

On the other hand, it is possible to compare costs and profitability, which means multiplying the physical quantities by their respective prices, which we take as given. Multiplying each element of matrix A_{pt} by its price we obtain matrix V_{pt}, whose elements represent the revenue and costs of the elementary process under examination. Thus we have:

$$V_{pt} = [v_{qj}] = [a_{qj} \cdot p_q] \tag{8.3}$$

In calculating the prices and costs of inputs and outputs we shall follow the same criteria as those adopted earlier in the case of the matrix of functions with respect to time of the production elements. With regard to the cost of workers' services the calculation is very simple: one need only multiply the number of hours worked by the hourly cost.

The cost of plant, however, is estimated on the basis of annual technical depreciations calculated according to the degree of utilization. Calculating the cost of plant services is particularly intricate due to the fact that each intermediate stage may use machines of different vintage (hence with different levels of depreciation), and machines with different degrees of utilization. Furthermore, the period of technical depreciation has a conventional value, while the interest rate calculated by firms is strongly differentiated because of the particular characteristics of financial markets. For simplicity I shall follow a practice widely adopted in manufacturing accounting, and consider the cost of parallel maintenance processes as a percentage of the cost of equipment. Thus the overall cost of services of funds constituted by equipment is given by the interest on the monetary cost of equipment plus depreciation (in relation to a given productive capacity, and based on the number of hours of actual use and on the intensity of use) plus maintenance fees, as a percentage of the monetary cost of the equipment. For the sake of simplicity I disregard any depreciation of the value of equipment due to the appearance on the market of new and more efficient equipment.

The hourly cost of premises is not difficult to calculate: one need only divide technical depreciation by the number of hours worked. Finally, as we saw in chapter 7, for semi-finished goods in progress and inventories one calculates the cost of the locked-up monetary capital given by the interest rate on their current transformation cost. This cost can be calculated directly from matrix V_{pt}. It is clear that the hourly cost of equipment, premises and inventories depends on the intensity of utilization of funds and on their possible idle times. Therefore, it is linked to the way in which production is organized.

The prices of waste output has a positive sign only if it brings in a revenue (through recycling); but if the waste product involves an additional cost, as often happens, the corresponding price has a negative sign.

Matrix V_{pt} shows the industrial costs. The general costs, covering costs of administration, R&D activity, advertising and marketing, sales and distribution, are included in the gross mark-up on direct costs. However if the parallel processes of administration and organization, marketing, distribution etc. can be considered as intermediate stages, according to the definition given earlier, then whenever the aims of the analysis require it they can be represented alongside the industrial intermediate stages within the quantitative matrix and the organizational scheme. In this case the output of the parallel intermediate stages of administration and organization, marketing, distribution etc. appears as an intermediate product used as an input by the other intermediate stages performed by the same production unit, and possibly by other units belonging to the same firm or other firms. For example, in the case of a 'constellation of firms', operating on the basis of collaborative agreements and 'mutual interdependence with regard to the objective of producing complex final product', it is very common for a production unit to perform some administrative and organizational intermediate stages for other units belonging to independent firms (Lorenzoni, 1983, pp. 218–19).

The study of production costs by intermediate stages also permits a comparison between in-house costs and those registered by outside production units specialized in certain operations or intermediate stages. The costs of specialized subcontractors represent an indirect index of the efficiency of integrated production. In fact it is clear that, if the price set for a given intermediate commodity by an external subcontractor unit, plus transaction costs, is less than in-house costs, it may be profitable to decentralize that intermediate stage.

As we have given a positive sign to output flows and a negative sign to input and fund service flows, the sum of the elements of each column gives us a gross margin which indicates the gross profitability of each intermediate stage. The comparison of several matrices referring to elementary processes taking place at different times may be a useful way of evaluating the changes in gross mark-up and the effects of technical change on costs.

The definitions of 'time saving', 'organizational-inventory-saving' and 'inputs-saving technical change' may be applied to costs, assuming prices as given. Consequently, technical change may be considered as:

(i) technical-inventory-cost-saving and goods-in-progress-cost-saving;
(ii) 'organizational-inventory-cost-saving';
(iii) 'inputs-cost-saving'.

However, variations in inventories and inputs costs may depend not only on a change in inputs requirements, but also in their quality or in their price. Summing up, costs are influenced by inputs prices and quality, and by the elementary process time profile. Time profile in turn depends upon the production unit organization and size. Thus, it is necessary to focus on organizational and dimensional aspects, which are – as we know – closely linked; this I propose to do in the following section.

8.2   The organizational scheme

Though the quantitative and temporal matrix uses the concepts of flow and service of a fund (both referred to time), it is in some ways akin to fixed-coefficient production models. In particular, the treatment of quantitative aspects in matrix A_{pt} has some points in common with the activities analysis approach, especially with regard to the concept of fixed coefficients (cf. e.g., Koopmans ed. 1951; Dorfman 1953; Manne 1961; Manne and Markowitz 1963; Baumol 1961). Production time profile and organization, considered in the 'quantitative–temporal matrix' and in the 'organizational scheme' are for the most part neglected in economic literature[1] because of the analytical difficulties which the theory encounters in dealing with the specific characteristics of technologies (indivisibility, complementarity, externalities, etc.) and the irreversibility of time. These difficulties have been discussed in earlier chapters.

The 'organizational scheme' summarises or develops data provided by the production matrix, according to the purposes of the analysis. It also gives further information on the time profile and the dimension of scale of the elementary process considered. As we have seen in previous chapters, temporal, organizational and dimensional aspects are closely inter-connected: the size of a production unit is in fact influenced, not only by the presence of possible economies of scale and by the amount of transaction costs, but also by the time profile of the different intermediate stages and in some cases by the indivisibility of fund elements. Thus, in comparing elementary processes taking place at different times, we can use the organizational scheme to supplement the information provided by the 'quantity and temporal matrix' so as to take account of any trans-formations undergone by a production process in terms of organization, time profile and production unit size.

As we shall see in chapter 9 (Table C2, p. 131), each column of the organizational scheme corresponds to an intermediate stage, except for the last column which presents the overall data on the elementary process. The rows are divided into six blocks or sections dealing with: (A) output; (B) time; (C) workers; (D) plant; (E) demand characteristics; (F) characteristics of quality and reliability of the product.

Table 8.2 lists the main row elements present within the 'organizational scheme'. The first block concerns the daily (internal and external) production volumes. From this section it is possible to work out the effects of possible supply relations with outside production units by noting whether the input flows of a given intermediate stage have been (wholly or partly) produced internally, and whether the output flow of a given intermediate stage has been (partly or completely) sold outside.

The second block registers the term profile of the decomposable elementary process. For each individual intermediate stage, it indicates: 'net process time', 'process time', 'working time', 'duration', 'response time', (i.e. the time elapsing from receipt of the order to delivery of the goods) and 'gross duration' (which includes the raw materials purchase time).

As mentioned in chapter 7, 'net process time' is the 'gross machine time' including set-up, loading and maintenance operations. 'Net process time' excludes any kind of organizational and technical breaks which may

---

[1] There are a few exceptions, for example, some analogies can be found in certain features of the tables in which Babbage (1832) illustrates the division of labour in pin manufacture.

Table 8.2 *The organizational scheme*

(*A*) *Output*
A1 internal production per day of each single intermediate stage
A2 external production per day of each single intermediate stage
A3 production of each single intermediate stage sold per day

(*B*) *Time*
B1 net process time
B2 process time
B3 working time
B4 duration
B5 response time (from receipt of order to delivery)
B6 gross duration (total time of production process from issue of purchase
    order for raw material to sale of product)

(*C*) *Labour*
C1 (who) number of workers by occupation, shifts, sex, age and education
C2 (how) tasks, jobs, and skills by occupation
C3 (where) employees/machine ratio

(*D*) *Plant*
D1 machines by type (number, time and intensity of use)
D2 adaptability (variations in quantity produced)
D3 flexibility (variations in product mix, minimum batch)

(*E*) *Demand*
E1 quantitative variations
E2 qualitative variations

(*F*) *Quality of products in progress*
F1 average incidence of defective intermediate products during course of
    process (internal failures)

---

allow use of the same fund in other elementary processes. The data on the 'net process time' of individual intermediate stages allow any variation in physical equipment productivity, due to innovations in loading, setting-up and maintenance operations or to changing the machine speeds, to be highlighted. 'Process time' is given by the sum of 'net process times' plus breaks due to periods of time in which semi-finished products lie in technical inventories. 'Working time' also takes into account interruptions in the use of funds for organizational reasons. The overall 'duration' is the actual time between the moment when the input flows begin to enter the process and the moment when the finished product, obtained by transforming these inputs, is ready for sale. It includes any seasonal pauses, night stoppages, Sundays or holiday times. The quantity of goods held in warehouses is closely linked to the difference between the 'duration' of the elementary process and 'net process time'. As we shall see in Part 3 (chapter 12), recent innovations, introduced by computers and flexible automation systems, help to reduce the elementary process 'duration' by permitting a reduction in the batch sizes. The duration of the elementary process is strongly influenced by the organization of production and stocks, by the technical characteristics of processes and materials, and by regulations governing labour relations. 'Response time' may be seen as the sum of the length of backward and forward intermediate stages in processing customers' orders and distributing the final commodity. It may be useful to insert, in the organizational scheme, data on 'response time', even if, for the sake of simplicity, the backward and forward intermediate stages are not included in the quantitative and temporal matrix, because in many markets they are significant in determining the production unit competitiveness, and because they may be strongly influenced by the introduction of new processes of products or simply by reorganization of production. Finally, section B considers the 'gross duration' of the production process. 'Gross duration' includes the time required to obtain raw materials, and hence goes from the moment when the production unit orders raw materials (or semi-finished goods) to the moment when the elementary process is completed. Consequently, it is given by the 'duration' of the backward intermediate stage of delivery of raw material and intermediate goods, added to the 'duration' of the elementary process under consideration. Delivery time for raw materials from suppliers represents a transaction cost, which varies greatly from sector to sector and from region to region. In many transformation processes these times represent an important part of the overall production process 'duration', and hence create substantial organizational and financial problems.

By studying the differences between 'process time' and 'duration' we can take account of the *efficacy*, which is represented by the adequacy of the response in relation to the market. Efficacy may consist not only in the intrinsic characteristics of a product, but also in the duration or response times of its production process. It is clear that, at any given rate of efficiency, which is expressed by the ratio between output and inputs in a moment of time, we might have very different 'durations' of the production process. A reduction of the 'duration' or 'response times' in relation to the 'process time', owing to a change in the organization of production, increases the efficacy of production where the response time is essential for determining the quality of the output or where a shorter 'response time' permits a more timely response to changes in demand. This last element is important in all productions characterized by rapid evolution in the product's design and qualitative aspects, e.g. in all

productions affected by fashion. Moreover, in some areas of manufacturing, but especially in service industries, the 'duration' and the
'response times' of the production process form part of the inherent
qualitative characteristics of the product and represent important elements
of competitiveness. For example, this is true not only of transport services
but also of most personal services (like health), and bureaucratic services
(such as issuing documents and permits, assigning pensions and
contributions, etc.). In all these cases not only is the quantity of input per
unit of output important, but also the difference between 'process time'
and the 'duration' or 'response time'.

In chapter 9 we shall apply our scheme of analysis to the study of a few
production units belonging to the textile sector of the manufacturing
industry, but this methodology may also prove very useful for the study
of production processes in the service sectors, where the difference
between 'duration' and 'process time' becomes important, as in many
cases it determines the efficacy of the service. In conclusion, efficacy is
closely connected with the quality of the product in the broad sense, i.e.
in terms of its response to the preferences expressed by the market, or its
capacity to satisfy the consumers' demands in relation to the quality and
the delivery times of products and services supplied.

Block C (Table 8.2) looks at the services performed by employees. This
section of the table gives information on the number of workers in terms
of: (i) occupational position; (ii) job specification; and (iii) skills. The first
point indicates the numerical distribution of the different occupational
positions among workers in the various intermediate stages, according to
shifts, sex, age and educational level. An eventual comparison of several
matrices referring to different moments will make it possible to identify
the intermediate stages that need more or fewer workers. The analysis of
changes in required occupational positions can be carried out by
ascertaining the types of work focused upon by the 'new demand for
labour'. Thus, one can see, for example, whether a change in production
techniques leads to retraining of old skills, absorption of young workers,
changes in average educational levels, expansion or contraction of the
female component of the labour force. In substance, these data permit the
identification at microeconomic level of certain important effects of
technical change on the conditions of the labour market.

In the second part of section C, I examine the distribution of jobs
according to tasks, occupational positions and the corresponding skills.
The different occupations in fact correspond to tasks that often require the
performance of different jobs, in other words *jobs are subsets of tasks*.[2] The

---

[2] I call a 'job' what Markowitz and Rowe (1963) call an 'elementary task': 'These
  tasks...can be broken into more elementary tasks, as analysed in time and motion

content of tasks is valued on the basis of the amount of time devoted to the different jobs, such as: (1) loading and unloading of machines, transport from machine to machine or from intermediate stage to intermediate stage; (2) the transformation of input flows; (3) organization; (4) maintenance work; and (5) innovative activity.

The skill level corresponding to each occupational position can be defined as the 'work capacity', or combination of abilities and 'practical knowledge' necessary for performing a task or function (including a combination of jobs). These abilities and capacities have to do with both efficiency (optimal use of resources) and efficacy (attainment of objectives).[3] In the organizational scheme I consider five different aspects which together characterize the skills attributed to the different occupational positions: (i) the complexity of the activity performed and the specialization possessed, expressed by the average time required for training inside and outside the production unit; (ii) polyvalence, i.e. the capacity to perform several jobs and functions; (iii) autonomy and control/self-control; (iv) degree of interaction with other workers inside and outside the intermediate stage; (v) flexibility, defined as the capacity to adapt readily and adequately to unforeseen events or changes that may occur or be reflected in the production process.

Comparing several organizational schemes thus enables us to take account of changes in relations between occupational positions, jobs and skills. For example, one can ascertain to what extent the evolution of the distribution of occupational positions reflects a real change in jobs and levels of skills linked with changes in methods of production. Then one can see if the technical change makes the assigned tasks more complex, with a consequent rise in skills and levels of specialization, or if, on the contrary, it leads to an impoverishment of the skills with lower levels of specialization and hence shorter training times.

Finally, the third point of block C (Table 8.2) shows the man/machine relation in each intermediate stage, or the (direct and indirect) allocation of employees to the different machines. The man/machine ratio is an important index of the effect of investments on labour demand.

Block D is devoted to equipment and individual machines. The main data concern the number per type, utilization time (hours per day and days per year), speed, set-up, loading and maintenance breaks, and idle

studies' they write. The authors utilize the concept of elementary task in analysing the possibilities of substitution between two machine tools ('one-for-one substitution') on the basis of their different efficiencies in performing various tasks (pp. 313–14). My definitions of skills, tasks, and jobs have some points in common with the corresponding definitions used by Landesmann in studying the relationship between a 'job-specification programme' and the 'set of available work-capacity' (1986, pp. 288–9).

[3] On 'practical knowledge' see above, chapter 3, section 3.4.

time per day. Furthermore, block D concerns the characteristics of *adaptability* or *non-adaptability* in response to variations in the *quantity produced*, and characteristics of *flexibility* or *rigidity* in response to variations in the *product mix*. This section poses basically the following questions: (i) is it possible to vary the quantity produced without incurring significant cost increases? and to what extent, compared with normal productive capacity? (ii) Is it possible to vary the type of product without serious increase in costs? and to what extent? A machine or a piece of equipment is adaptable if it does not lose efficiency when there are changes in the *quantity produced* of a given commodity. The concept of flexibility implies the capacity to maintain a high degree of efficiency even when there are changes in the *qualitative characteristics* of the products. From this point of view *efficacy*, in the sense of an appropriate response to the market, becomes important. In some circumstances it is not only necessary to minimize the cost per unit, but it is also important to produce those goods or services which are appropriate for the time, the place, and the manner in which they can respond to market demand. The concepts of adaptability and production flexibility will be discussed more thoroughly in chapter 12.

Section E is concerned with demand – that is to say, the quantitative and qualitative orientations of the markets of the different production elements involved in each intermediate stage. Information on demand cannot be derived from the matrix of functions of time of the production elements, but information about demand is useful in identifying the relationships between changes in techniques of the different intermediate stages, and the evolution of the markets of outputs.

Lastly, section F deals with the quality of semi-finished goods in relation to the production process method of execution, measured by the average percentage of defective products which occur during the production process. Obviously many process innovations aim to reduce the percentage of defective products. For example, in some activities the application of microelectronics to the monitoring of production makes it possible to measure the frequency of interruptions of the process for each machine. Maintenance operations can then be concentrated on the machines most often interrupted, thus considerably reducing the amount of waste and idle times, and increasing productivity.

In order to verify the applicability of the matrix of production elements and its suitability for empirical analysis, in chapter 9 some numerical examples are considered, referring to certain case studies on production units.

9 Towards empirical implementation: some case studies

9.1 Preliminary methodological considerations

In the introductory chapter on scope and outline of the book I emphasized that one of the main aims is to present an analytical scheme which can be used for the applied research of production processes and the transformations undergone by production units and industrial sectors. The first step in assessing the scheme's suitability for this purpose is to apply the quantitative matrix and the organizational scheme to the analysis of some case studies. This will also be useful for expository purposes, inasmuch as the numerical examples may facilitate comprehension of the model's characteristics.

As mentioned, the fund–flow model does not yet seem to have been used in empirical analysis. In applied studies the effects of technical progress have been examined mainly through the estimates of the *production function*, or through data on *R&D expenses* and *patents*, or through *interviews* with firms.

Empirical studies, based on econometric estimates of the *production function*, often assume mathematical properties of functions that do not fit the characteristics of the techniques which are relevant for evaluating the economic effects of technical change.[1] Furthermore, these studies consist in a purely quantitative representation of the production process, ignoring the effects of the relationships between the time profile of the production process and the organization of labour on the size of the production unit. This representation therefore has to be 'supplemented' by means of other analytical tools.

As far as *expenses in R&D* and *number of patents* are concerned, the use of these two variables in applied research, as a measure of innovative

---

[1] References to production function are in chapter 11, section 11.3, devoted to returns of scale. For convenience-assumptions that are designed merely to achieve mathematical tractability see Lawson (1987, p. 967) on the nature of knowledge in economic analysis. On this last point see also the methodological discussion in Carabelli (1988, chapter 10, and pp. 100–3, 184–6, 239).

activity and innovative output respectively, presents some analytical problems. To assume R&D as a proxy of innovative input means to neglect, in explaining innovative output, the cumulative learning-by-doing processes which are not caught by the R&D variable (Dosi, 1984, p. 90). Moreover, R&D expenditure is likely to underestimate the innovative contributions of small firms, which sometimes innovate on an 'informal' basis. Patents are a measure of inventive output rather than innovative success, and patenting underestimates the innovation output of big firms, which appear to show a lower propensity to patent (Freeman 1974, pp. 53ff.; Kamien and Schwartz 1982, ch. 3; Dosi 1984, pp. 90, 1988, p. 1151; Dasgupta 1986, pp. 522, 541; Griliches, Pakes, and Hall 1987; Leoni 1989).

In the matrices of production elements the characteristics of the production process are inferred directly from firms' accounting data regarding the single elementary processes. Clearly the advantage of this method of investigation, compared to the usual interviews on innovative activity, lies in the fact that the effects of innovations, rather than being described through the necessarily *subjective judgements* of the executive interviewed,[2] can be evaluated on the basis of an analytical scheme constructed from a limited number of figures regarding the production processes. Once the historical series of matrices is available it may be interesting to compare the opinions expressed in the interviews with the results that emerge from matrices over several years.

Moreover, the matrix of production elements allows the time profile of processes to be considered. The need to deal with temporal and organizational, as well as quantitative, aspects obviously depends on the aims of the analysis. In some circumstances, for analytical or expository reasons, it may be opportune to concentrate on the study of quantities alone. It should be noted, however, that the temporary isolation of quantitative aspects for analytical or expository purposes, within a model which also takes account of the interrelationships of the quantities with temporal and organizational aspects, is something quite different from the *implicit a priori exclusion* of any relation between quantities and the time profile and organization of the production processes. Moreover, in many cases the examination of quantities alone is not enough. It is clear that in studying the effects of technical change it is impossible to isolate the quantitative aspects of the temporal, organizational and qualitative dimensions of production processes. Therefore the following empirical application, like the analytical scheme from which it is derived, extends

---

[2] Despite the limitation just mentioned, in some cases the interview remains an indispensable research tool. In these notes the interviews with firms have been used to supplement the information given in the tables.

the field of investigation beyond the range of traditional microeconomic analysis.

In the case studies, the production units examined engage in differentiated production, with a very wide range of goods. Therefore a representative commodity of the product mix must be chosen. In this connection it should be noted that the level of aggregation in our analysis is necessarily lower than that of normal manufacturing accounting. Such accounting would in fact require, on the one hand, a matrix to be calculated for each different type of product, and on the other hand, all the inputs to be counted, including those I have omitted from the empirical examples because they are not important for the present study.

The cooperation and interest displayed by the firms have ensured a high degree of reliability of the data given in the tables in the Appendix to this chapter. The case studies presented here constitute a numerical example, based on real data from certain production units, regarding the capacity of the quantitative matrix and the organizational scheme to provide an analytical representation of the production process. In other words, they may allow us to ascertain the 'explanatory and descriptive' potentialities of the proposed scheme. Obviously only the formation of a historical series will make it possible to bring out the transformations of these processes over time. Owing to problems of reliability I have not included data for previous years, for which the firms could not produce exact figures. A 'reconstruction' of such figures by those in charge of production would have involved wide margins of error, and hence would be of little use for the purposes of the analysis.

The comparison between matrices referring to successive periods may give information on changes undergone by industrial sectors, if the sample of production units is enlarged enough to make it statistically representative. From this point of view the proposed methodology is a useful instrument for collecting statistical information on the transformations undergone by production processes. These transformations may involve different levels of analysis: the production unit, the firm, the group of collaborating firms, the industrial sector, the economic system, or a certain number of important sectors of activity. The study of efficiency of individual firms, within the analysis of the organization and efficiency of the sector to which they belong, is one of the main themes of industrial economics.

With technical change, however, it is not enough to study the economic effects within each sector because some new technologies have a very wide field of application and involve important compensatory effects, so that a decrease in input requirement for one sector may correspond to an increased input requirement in another sector. These compensatory effects may be very important in explaining changes in demand for labour. Clearly, only an *inter-sectoral study*, based on input–output tables, would make it possible to evaluate phenomena of compensation between different sectors of activity. Very interesting in this connection is the analysis of Leontief and Duchin (1986) in which the authors – using a dynamic input–output model – estimate the direct and indirect effects of introducing computer-based equipment on the future output and input levels throughout all sectors of the economy, assuming different future rates of application of new technology.[3] Given the importance of qualitative elements in the demand for labour, inter-sectoral analysis has to be related to statistical data on input requirements broken down according to occupation and the other main indicators of labour demand (sex, age, educational level). These data are supplied at microeconomic level by the 'organizational scheme'.

In conclusion, the proposed model has been conceived as a scheme of the production process which is open to organizational, temporal and qualitative factors, and suitable for collecting data on changes undergone by industrial sectors. I consider this model to be a useful tool both for describing production processes (and the changes they undergo) as well as for making business decisions (regarding new production techniques), under specific hypotheses on agents' behaviour and market structure.[4]

9.2   The textile industry

I have chosen case studies from the textile sector for several different reasons. Firstly, this sector lends itself easily and conveniently to exposition. It is characterized by a fairly linear *filière* and 'mature' technology, the comprehension of which does not require complex and specialized technical knowledge. In addition, the decomposability of the overall production process into many intermediate stages permits a full application of the method presented in the preceding pages. Lastly, sub-contractors are often involved in the production of both yarns and woven fabrics, so that the proposed method can be applied not only to the study

---

[3] Leontief and Duchin (1986) consider almost 100 industries from 1963 to 2000, and they examine in particular the effects of technical change on the manufacturing industry, office work, education and health sectors. See also Leontief et al. (1953, chapter 2) and Leontief (1966, chapter 19). For an analytical treatment and some methodological considerations on the implementation of input–output models in studying technical change see Giannini (1981), and Torriero (1989). On the relationship between sectoral interdependence and the time profiles of production processes cf. Tani (1988), Baldone (1989), Oda (1990).

[4] Hence this scheme may be added to a range of instruments already available such as those derived from operations research and activities analysis (linear programming). In this connection see Dorfman (1953, p. 797) and the Introduction to Manne's book, significantly entitled *Economic Analysis for Business Decisions* (1961). Activities analysis has been used also in descriptive studies of the production process, for example, Manne and Markowitz, eds. (1963, part 4).

of the relations between one intermediate stage and another within a production unit, but also to the study co-operation between different production units which perform different intermediate stages of a single elementary process within the same production *filière*.

A second order of reasons for choosing the textile sector lies in its particular position within the production *filière*, with respect to innovative activities. As is well known, and as also appears from our case studies, this sector tends to acquire technologies from other sectors; hence according to Pavitt's definition it is a 'suppliers–dominated' sector (Pavitt, pp. 356ff.). In fact the textile sector adopts innovations from the textile machinery and electronic sectors, whereas radical changes in the product have been rather limited in recent years. In some intermediate stages organizational innovations and technical changes leading to improvements in the quality of the product have been quite important.

In the textile industry the application of microelectronics has a dual nature: on the one hand, it is a radical innovation, based on a completely different technology, which may involve the automation of certain phases or the fusion into one phase of several formerly separate operations, with considerable modifications in the organization of the work; on the other hand, it permits incremental improvements in existing plant, based on traditional technologies, through the progressive introduction of sensors, automatic devices, control apparatus etc. Continuous gains in productivity are thus obtained without substantial modifications to the production cycle.

Finally, the textile sector is interesting because of the particular influence of innovation upon trends in the international division of labour. In the course of the 1970s the textile sector was thought to be in decline – antiquated and technologically stagnant. In many areas a progressive loss of competitiveness among industrialized countries in favour of developing countries had been forecast. The trends of the 1980s have partly contradicted these pessimistic predictions. In fact, in some industrialized countries, the restructuring processes have led to a recovery of competitiveness. This is especially true where there is a great need to influence and follow the evolution of markets where qualitative aspects and the speed of response of production units are fundamental (cf. Rullani and Zanfei 1988a). Indeed, the adoption of computer-based technology and organizational innovations in the textile industry may play a decisive part in recovering competitiveness in countries with relatively high labour costs. Thus, the textile sector today represents an interesting field for analysing the economic effects of transformations of production processes.

9.3   Some remarks on the results of the case studies

In the following pages we shall analyse three Italian production units: two spinning plants (cases A and B) and one vertically integrated unit that carries out the whole *filière* from spinning to finishing of the fabric (case C).[5] All three cases involve firms active for many years, although the production unit examined in case B was recently installed, having been added to the other units which had been operating in the same firm for some time. The case studies taken into consideration concern three different situations:

(A) a non-decomposable production process performed by a sub-contractor production unit belonging to a monoplant firm;
(B) a non-decomposable production process performed by a production unit belonging to an independent firm with five other production units located in the same area;
(C) a decomposable production process performed by an independent, vertically integrated firm with a single multi-plant production unit.

The three production units can be considered 'privileged witnesses' or 'positive examples' in the application of new production techniques. One firm (to which unit B belongs) has undergone a marked expansion in the past few years, with a substantial increase in the work force, and has shown considerable entrepreneurial and innovative capacities. In the other two (A and C) the number of employees has been essentially stable, with an improvement in the quality of the product and an increase in the quantity produced (hence an increase in productivity and efficiency).

In the Appendix, for each case study there is (a) a summary of the interview regarding the firms' main characteristics and the innovative activity undertaken in recent years, and (b) the quantitative matrix and the organizational scheme of the production process.

Given the strongly seasonal aspects of textile production, it was necessary to calculate the matrices with reference to an 'average organized elementary process' for the (solar) year of the study. The survey refers to 1987 data for cases A and C, and to 1988 data for case B (where the production unit began operating at the end of 1987). The qualitative

---

[5] The firms involved have preferred not to be identified – in any case their names and locations are not important for the purposes of this chapter: the case studies are presented purely as numerical examples. The firm to which the production unit of case B belongs is located in a different geographical area from that of units A and C, which are both in the same area. It should also be noted that there is no relationship of collaboration between the three production units here discussed.

characteristics of outputs produced by the three firms considered are not very complex; therefore, it may be sufficient for the purposes of the analysis to indicate the physical characteristics, such as kind of yarn, yarn count, width, length etc.

The interviews were based on a questionnaire concerning the general characteristics of the firm to which the production unit belongs, the type of innovations adopted in recent years, the factors underlying the innovations, the obstacles to the innovations and their main effects. In the absence of a historical series of matrices, which can be available only in the future, the interviews provide a useful source of information on the recent innovative activity of the production units under examination. The interviews offer material for reflection on the nature and complexity of technical change at microeconomic level. In the opinion of those interviewed, the economic effects of technical change cannot be reduced to simple variations in input requirements or costs: indeed cost reduction often takes second place compared to other objectives such as improvements in the quality of the product, increased adaptability (in relation to variations in the quantity produced) and flexibility (with regard to the mix of products). In some cases increased flexibility is pursued even at the cost of a reduced hourly productivity (for example, see case C). As I have mentioned, once the historical series of data contained in the quantitative matrix and the organizational scheme is available it will be possible to infer these tendencies directly by comparing the tables for successive periods.

It was assumed earlier that the input flows and fund services (machines, equipment and real estate) are paid for at the beginning of the elementary process, while labour services and output (sold by the production unit) are paid for at the end of the process. Thus for the costs of the funds represented by machines, equipment and premises I calculate an annual depreciation, whereas for goods in inventories and in progress I calculate the interest on the locked-up monetary capital corresponding to its current transformation cost. The transformation cost of goods in inventories or in progress can be inferred from the quantitative matrix itself. As indicated above, the transformation cost is obtained from the sum of flow costs, labour and machine services, while it does not include depreciation of premises, costs of parallel service processes of administration, organization, planning, marketing, distribution, and cost of stock.

For the sake of simplicity the cost of workers' services (necessary to produce one unit of goods) is obtained by multiplying the quantities by the average hourly cost. Of course, when it suits the aims of the analysis one can subdivide the units of labour according to the different occupational positions indicated in the organizational scheme (block D) and enter them in the quantitative table in that form.

The hourly cost of plant corresponds to the depreciation of one hour of use of the plant plus the costs of parallel maintenance processes. In the production units examined I found significant idle times due to mismatches of the productive capacity of individual phases or intermediate processes. Lastly, the costs of real estate consist of annual depreciation.

It will clearly emerge from examining the case studies that the cost of inventories and semi-finished goods in progress, like the cost of funds represented by machines and real estate, strongly depends on the use of those funds over time. In fact, the quantity of input flows and semi-finished goods held in inventories and in process is closely related to:

(i) The organization of the process, for example, the number of parallel processes and the particular combination of productive capacities of the different phases;

(ii) the overall duration of the process – obviously, the greater the difference between this and the net process time, the greater the quantity of goods in the warehouses;

(iii) the level of differentiation of production and the volume of production batches (this point to be discussed further in chapter 12, on flexibility);

(iv) the location of the market (for inputs as well as outputs) and associated transport costs;[6]

(v) the characteristics of the production unit. For example, examining the case studies clearly shows that production unit A, which is a sub-contractor, is able to plan its production on the basis of agreements with contractors in such a way as to significantly reduce the quantity of goods in inventories.

The case studies bring out the importance of the cost of stock for certain production processes; for example, that cost for unit C mounts to 15% of the final price. But what really matters is the size of the locked-up monetary capital: for example, for each piece of fabric sold by unit C at £372 it is around £68,000 – with a corresponding interest cost of about £58.

The number of working days per year and working hours per day differs in the three case studies, according to trade-union agreements, regulations governing working conditions and demand levels. Obviously, a greater number of days (and hours per day) means a greater number of

---

[6] For the determination of optimal inventory see, for instance, Baumol (1961, chapter 1), in which 'carrying costs' (involved in holding a warehouse) and 'delivery cost' are considered.

elementary processes carried out, and hence a lower incidence of the cost of machinery and real estate on each elementary process. From this point of view production unit B, in which production continues around the clock seven days a week, reduces idle time to a minimum, thus dividing the fixed costs by a larger number of elementary processes equal to the productive capacity of the plant.

Before going on to examine the three case studies one by one, I should say something about the difficulties involved in comparing the data given in the quantitative and organizational tables for the different production units. This comparison of the individual case studies requires great caution because of the large number of processes performed by each production unit and then the different types of products involved. Even within the same output (for example, worsted of medium quality), the input requirements may vary greatly according to different yarn counts (thickness, weight etc.).[7] With multi-production, quantities of inputs may vary substantially from one product to another, and, in some cases, it is not easy to calculate certain input requirements for each type of product. Consequently, it is useful to choose a commodity 'representative' of the mix of outputs of the production unit (i.e. with average characteristics) so that the average input requirement of the multi-production will be as close as possible to the actual requirement for the commodity in question.

Moreover the elementary technical unit of plant varies from one production unit to another. The size of the technical elementary unit of the plant affects the number of parallel elementary processes and the net process time or gross machine time. Though the net process time or gross machine time may vary from one production unit to another, depending on the characteristics of the elementary technical unit, the average costs shown in the quantitative and temporal matrix are nevertheless comparable for the different production units.

The calculation of depreciation of fixed capital (machines and premises) is another area where caution is required when making comparisons. As noted in chapter 8, within the quantitative matrix the hourly cost of services of equipment used is calculated on the basis of technical depreciation reflecting the expected life of the machines in terms of the number of elementary processes executed. This calculation is straight-forward if the production unit is new and the machines are all the same age (production unit B), but it becomes very complicated when the capital goods are of different vintages (production unit A and C). For the sake of simplicity, in the case studies I have considered the hourly cost of the plant

---

[7] For example, in case B we have considered a consumption of 2,600 Kwh per kg. for the production of a yarn count of 12 Ne, while a yarn count of 6 Ne would consume 1,500 Kwh.

and premises, calculated by the firms on the basis of the annual average depreciation in relation to the number of hours worked per year. Therefore, it is worthwhile repeating that the hourly cost of fixed capital *is strongly influenced by the production organization* and in particular it is related to the degree of equipment utilization. Moreover, depreciation naturally includes the interest rate on the monetary capital invested. The particular conditions of the financial markets create perceptible differences in interest rates applied by the different production units. This is reflected not only in the calculation of fixed capital depreciation, but also in calculating the cost of various inventories.

Finally, following the theoretical scheme presented in the preceding chapters, maintenance costs should be considered as costs of parallel intermediate stages. Because of the difficulties of separating these costs from those of the other intermediate stages, in order to simplify, I have considered maintenance costs as a percentage of the hourly cost of plant services, amounting to about 2% of depreciation (according to firms' estimates). However, in this way the cost of maintenance is underestimated because production units only consider services which are supplied by outside firms and hence invoiced. In fact it is very difficult to evaluate the cost of maintenance services provided by production unit employees who also carry out direct productive activities within the elementary process in question. Thus the cost of maintenance services provided by employees ends up being included as production labour cost.

In these notes the costs of administration and organization, marketing and distribution, and minor costs, are calculated as a portion of the mark-up on direct costs. Nevertheless, as already emphasized, there are no analytical difficulties in including parallel processes of administration and organization, marketing and distribution in the quantitative matrix and the organizational scheme, when these can be considered intermediate stages and hence can be represented along with the industrial processes within the same analytical scheme. In the cases studied industrial costs are clearly prevalent. However, in some cases industrial processes may be less important than the 'service' intermediate stages involved in planning, organization, marketing and administration. In these cases, which are more and more frequent, it is clear that the cost of such processes can no longer be considered a 'residue' computable as a part of the mark-up. The proposed scheme lends itself to an analysis which includes the evaluation of flows and funds involved in producing these services.

It has been verified that in the textile sector an important part of the transaction costs, along with transport charges (which in any case are generally paid by the subcontractor), involves the knowledge of the quality of the product. For example, the need to control the quality of the product is given as a principal reason for vertical integration between spinning and weaving operations. It has been argued that using outside firms in some cases would not permit full knowledge of the true characteristics of the yarn, and then this might compromise the quality of the goods obtained from the following intermediate stage. In this case, the integrated producer, having full knowledge of the qualitative character-istics of the yarn and cloth, can often get better results at lower cost.

As far as the quality of the semi-finished goods is concerned the percentage of defective product (point F, Table 8.2) has not been given because the three production units consider this insignificant.

Let us now go on to examine one by one the principal elements which emerge from the case studies. We begin with the simplest case study, in which the production process is not decomposable.

9.4   Case A

This production unit belongs to a single establishment firm which produces high-quality yarns covering a very broad mix of products. Spinning is a production process comprising various phases, but it is not decomposable according to the definition given at the beginning of chapter 7. In fact the semi-finished product which emerges from the different phases does not have an independent existence outside the process and, hence, cannot exit from the process without further transformations.

The firm operates as a subcontractor, with very stable collaborative relationships with its client firms. This condition enables it to produce a wide range of woollen yarns through a simple organizational structure. From the interview it emerged that the innovations introduced were of an 'incremental' type and consisted essentially of increasing the speed and reliability of the production process, with positive results for productivity and quality. The main declared purpose of these technical changes was to improve the quality; in terms of its effect on the organization of production and on occupational levels its aim was a reduction in the number of unskilled employees, mostly women (cf. Table A2).

Table A1 shows the quantity of input flows and funds services necessary to produce one economically indivisible unit of output. For simplicity I shall consider only eight production elements: the outflow, consisting of spun woollen yarn, the intermediate outflow from the transport process performed by a secondary subcontractor, the inflow of energy, the inflow of wool, belonging to the contractor, the services provided by workers, plant and establishment, the quantity of semi-finished products in inventories and in progress. It should be noted that the subcontractor bears only the cost of industrial transformation, plus transport costs, while the contractor bears, among other costs (such as marketing, distribution etc.) the cost of the main inflow, the wool, and the cost of related inventories.

The production is carried out by two plants working in parallel, each of which has 3,500 spindles. The structure of the single production lines is a delta: after passing through the phases of mixing, ironing and finishing, the wool is divided between a very large number of spindles. Thus each of the two lines consisting of 3,500 spindles constitutes an 'economically indivisible plant', while the 'elementary technical unit' is the single spindle. The level of use of the productive capacity of the whole production unit thus corresponds to the number of spindles in action.

The 'gross machine time' or 'net process time' is sixteen hours, including set-up, loading and maintenance interruptions. That is the time required to produce 1 kg of yarn on one spindle. Table A1, in fact, tells us that to produce 1 kg of yarn requires 16 hours of the services of one spindle of the 7,000 of the whole production unit. If the production unit could be considered technically indivisible, the 'net process time' would be about 8 seconds of the services of the whole production unit (16 hours divided by 7,000 kg).

Unlike the machines, not all the workers operate in parallel: some of them in fact work on both lines. Hence the quantity of labour necessary to produce 1 kg of goods is given by the total number of hours of the single elementary process, divided by the number of kg produced in parallel (43 workers present for the 16 hours of the elementary process, in three 6-hour shifts each). This gives a total number of hours which, divided by the number of kg produced during the elementary process, gives us a labour requirement of about 2 minutes per kg (cf. Table A1, point C1). The same method is used to calculate the quantities of wool and yarn held in warehouses and in progress, and the area in square metres required for the establishment. The quantities of goods in the warehouses are rather limited because the production unit works to order as a subcontractor and thus is able to programme the flows of raw materials and semi-finished products.

Let us now go on to examine the organizational scheme in detail (Table A2). The production unit in question belongs to a subcontractor which produces everything in-house (Table A2, section A). The 'process time' includes 24 hours of technical inventory. If we consider also the organizational inventory we have the 'duration' of the elementary process, which is fifteen days. This 'duration' corresponds to the 'response time', as the agreements with the client firms permit long-term programming of production batches (section B).

Section C of the organizational scheme shows the distribution of employees according to qualification, sex, age, education, specialization and employee/machine relationship. This brings out, among other things, the high concentration of women among unskilled workers. The second part of section C includes the distribution of jobs according to tasks, occupational positions and the corresponding skills. The content of tasks is valued according to the amount of time devoted to the different jobs. The total working time of each level of qualification is therefore distributed among different jobs, such as: (1) loading and unloading of machines, transport from machine to machine or from intermediate stage to intermediate stage; (2) the transformation of input flows; (3) organization; (4) maintenance work; and (5) innovative activity. Finally, in the organizational scheme we consider five different aspects which together characterize the skills attributed to the different occupational positions: (i) the complexity of the activity performed and the specialization possessed, expressed by the average time required for training inside and outside the production unit; (ii) polyvalence, i.e. the capacity to perform several jobs and functions; (iii) autonomy and control/self-control; (iv) degree of interaction with other workers inside and outside the intermediate stage; (v) flexibility, defined as the capacity to adapt readily and adequately to unforeseen changes of the production process. Each of these five components of skills is assigned a rating from one to five (1 = very low, 2 = low, 3 = average, 4 = high, 5 = very high).

With regard to the plant (section D), the bottleneck is in the productive capacities of the first three phases (mixing, ironing and finishing) so that the productive capacity of the spindles is underused by about 12%. In fact, spindles work 16 hours instead of 18. Set-up, loading and maintenance breaks, which are included in utilization time, amount to about 5% of this time for the first three phases and to about 8% for the spinning phase.

Finally, the firm declares that it applies a mark-up on industrial costs of about 30% of the price. This percentage is confirmed by the data which emerge from the quantitative matrix.

9.5   Case B

The firm to which production unit B belongs specializes in the production of cotton yarns. In the past ten years it has developed considerably, with the construction of four new production units located in the same area (growing from two production units in 1974 to four in 1986 and six in 1988). The firm is run by a family (four brothers and their sons). The strong points of the firm lie in a considerable knowledge of the techniques used (the firm began as a textile machinery workshop) and in a market entrepreneurial dynamism. During the 1970s innovations were concentrated mainly on the introduction of an open-end system, which brought changes in the production process and in the product. The adoption of open-end spinning rotors involved: (i) high volumes of production; (ii) saving of space and energy; (iii) use of low-quality raw materials; (iv) recycling of waste materials; and (v) a different final product (denim). In the 1980s innovations were linked with the introduction of micro-electronics, which permitted: (a) greater control of quality; (b) greater adaptability and flexibility of plant; and (c) gains in productivity. In particular, the increases in productivity were obtained through: the automation of certain phases of the process, the reduction of idle time of plant and time for set-up and loading, and the fusion of some phases of the production process. In the course of the 1980s both the available technologies and the evolution of the market have led to an increase in the quality of the product.

From the reply to question 2.1, regarding the type of innovation, the importance of improvements in product quality emerges clearly during the 1980s, compared to the preceding decade when the accent was mainly on increases in productivity following the introduction of a new product (denim). The importance of the qualitative improvements is mentioned several times in the replies to the questionnaire, in connection with the reasons motivating the innovations and with their effects (points 3.3 and 5.1). Finally, it is interesting to note that the main difficulty encountered by the firm in carrying out its innovative strategy arose from problems of information regarding the new technologies, and from the fact that an innovation cannot be fully known and understood until it is actually applied to the production process (point 4.1).

Little more than half the production of the spinning production unit is sold in its crude state; the remaining part is passed on to a subcontractor that specializes in dyeing and finishing. The use of subcontractors, with which permanent collaborative relations are established, is justified by the fact that this allows greater flexibility of production, and in some cases lower costs.

The *elementary technical unit* of the spinning unit is one of the 9 machines with 192 heads. Thus the net process time corresponds to the time necessary to produce 1 kg of open-end yarn on one of the 9 machines. The spinning unit is characterized by a high degree of utilization of fixed-capital funds (machines and premises) thanks to a production process working continuously 24 hours out of 24 for 7 days a week. This naturally leads to very low unit costs. The incidence of breaks within the process (such as set-up, loading and maintenance) is also very low, about 3% of the 'utilization time'. The machinery, all recently installed (the end of 1987), contributes as well to the efficiency of the production unit in question. The mark-up on transformation costs is about 20 % of the price.

9.6   Case C

Case C involves a firm with a single integrated production unit, for which four intermediate stages have been examined (spinning, weaving, dyeing and finishing). From these, the weaving intermediate stage has been considered in some detail. The firm provided interesting information about the nature of the innovations adopted during the past four years, and their main consequences for production and employment levels, skills and jobs.

The innovative activity of recent years has been based essentially upon the 'embodied technical change' through the acquisition of new machinery. There have been six main innovations, of which five were radical and one incremental. The radical innovations involved the introduction of: (a) a spinning machine (Repco) with a technology completely different from the traditional ring; (b) an automatic healder; (c) computerised perforation of the cards of the looms; (d) instrumental colour mixing by means of a personal computer; and (e) a new automated packing line. The incremental innovation involved some modifications to the stenter, which brought a noticeable increase in speed as well as a saving of energy.

These changes involved an increase in productivity and in production as a whole. The total number of employees remained substantially constant. Only in the case of two innovations out of six did the labour requirement fall by a few units (9 fewer employees overall for the introduction of a new spinning machine and an automatic packing line). All the innovations led to changes in jobs performed, often involving a reduction in the physical force required and the need to learn to use computer-based equipment. In two cases out of six the working shifts were also modified (by the introduction of a new spinning machine and automatic healder). All in all, the innovations led to an increase in the volume of production with an essentially stable number of employees. The most important changes concerned the qualitative composition of the labour force more than its absolute numbers. In most cases, in fact, the change in the content of the work meant that the demand for labour was oriented towards more qualified or at least better trained personnel. This aspect has favoured the taking on of school leavers.

The calculation of data for the quantitative matrix and the organizational scheme was considerably simplified by the excellent manufacturing accounting system used by the firm (each piece of fabric is accompanied by a 'costing card' showing the unit costs of the main industrial inputs).

In the quantitative-temporal matrix (Table C1), the output of one intermediate stage, which become inputs of the following intermediate stage, undergo a progressive contraction because of shrinkage (from 28.5 to 28 kg. of wool, from 59.6 to 54 metres per length). The spinning plant consists of 24 fronts of 250 spindles. Each front is an elementary technical unit. In the organizational scheme (Table C2) the quantities of product emerging from one intermediate stage do not correspond with the quantities of product that go into the next intermediate stage. This is due to the presence of externally subcontracted productions, towards which part of the semi-finished outputs are destined, and from which part of the intermediate inputs come. The organizational scheme focuses in particular on the intermediate weaving stage. During this sub-process, there are long idle times in the early production phases (the machines are used from 9 to 16 hours for 24 hours of loom use). Thus an increase in the productive capacity of the last phase by a rise in the number of looms would lead to more efficient use of the funds employed in the three earlier phases of the same sub-process (firing, healder, warping-mill). The production unit works 220 days per year. Set-up and loading breaks are considerable during the first three phases, with a maximum of 50 % of utilization time during the second phase, while these breaks are about 5 % for looms. The hourly cost of the funds represented by machinery and by an establishment's premises has been measured on the basis of the annual depreciation calculated by the firm (on the basis of an interest rate of 18 %). Finally, the firm states that it applies a mark-up on transformation costs of 30 % of price. This percentage is confirmed by the data which emerge from the quantitative matrix.

Appendix: Interviews and tables: case studies A, B, and C

A9.1   Production unit A

1   General characteristics of the firm

1.1   Legal form, type of business and number of production units
Single production unit making woollen yarn in subcontracting. The firm is run by a proprietor-entrepreneur.

1.2   Type of product
High-quality fibre worsted yarn.

1.3   Production process
From worsted wool to yarn on the spindle.

1.4   Sales, quantity produced and exported
The production is about 1.3 million kilos of yarn per year, making a turnover of about £1 million (1987). The turnover may seem quite low, but it should be underlined it is calculated only on the transformation process, excluding the cost of wool, whose incidence on the final price is very high and which belongs to the contractor.

1.5   Number of employees
43 employees.

1.6   Pricing
Mark-up on the industrial costs is about the 30% of the price.

1.7   Structure of market and relations with other production units
A very large number of producers, of varying sizes. Low barriers to entry. Steady collaboration agreements with contractors.

2   Type of innovations

2.1   Innovations of product, process, services or organization
Innovation in process: instrumentation for production control, monitoring of spindles; this allows an improvement in quality.

2.2   Time of innovations
About one year.

3   Factors underlying innovations

3.1   Origin of innovations
The main source of acquisition of new technology is through the acquisition of capital goods.

3.2   Source of financial resources necessary for innovations
50% leasing, 50% self-financing.

3.3   Reasons which induced the firm to introduce innovations
Improvement of quality.

3.4   Elements which favoured the introduction of innovations
Technical opportunities offered by the textile machinery sector and consultants specialized in the automation of the processes.

4   Obstacles

4.1   Main difficulties encountered in carrying out the innovative strategy
No important difficulties.

5   Effects of innovations

5.1   Effects on techniques and production
Improvement in the quality of the product.

5.2   Changes in organization and employment
Reduction in employees at the unskilled level.

Table A1 *Quantitative-temporal matrix of an elementary non-decomposable process performed by a sub-contractor production unit: 1987 (quantities for the production of 1 kg of high quality wool yarn, yarn count 20,000 Mt/kg, 'process time' 40 H)*

		Spinning	Price unit cost	Total elementary process
A	*Output flows and external intermediate stages*:			
A1	Transport (sec. sub-contr. proc.)	01:30:00 H	0.007 £/kg	0.01 £
A2	Spinning internal process	1 kg	0.82 £/kg	0.82 £
B	*Input flows*			
B1	Energy input	−0.52 Kwh	0.06 £/Kwh	−0.03 £
B2	Wool input	−1.04 kg	0.00[a]	0.00
C	*Funds*			
C1	Spinning workers	00:01:58 H[b]	7.86 £/H	−0.26 £
C2	Spinning plant	16:00:00 H[c]	0.01 £/H*	−0.16 £*
C3	Wool warehouse[d]	22.4 kg	0.000[a]	0.00
C4	Spinning area (0.71 m^2)	16:00:00 H	0.004 £/H*	−0.07 £*

* Estimated data, which does not come directly from the firm's accounts.
[a] The wool input belongs to the contractor firm, the cost of wool input is about 4·80 £/kg, while the cost of wool warehouse is about 0.004 £/kg.
[b] 00:01:58 H equal to 1.96 minutes.
[c] 16:00:00 H equal to 16 H/spindle.
[d] And in progress.

A9.2   Production unit B

1   General characteristics of the firm

1.1   Legal form, type of business and number of production units
The production unit in question belongs to a firm producing cotton yarns, controlled by a holding company which owns 98 % of the capital. The firm began in 1958 as a mechanical workshop which was transformed into a spinning plant in 1960. The owner-entrepreneurs are four brothers, plus their sons. The number of production units has increased from four, in 1986, to six, in 1988.

Table A2 *Organizational scheme of an elementary non-decomposable process performed by a sub-contractor production unit: 1987 (1 kg of high quality wool yarn, yarn count 20,000 Mt/kg)*

Spinning

A Output

A1 Daily production   7,000 kg

B Time

B1 Net process time[a]   16:00:00 H
B2 Process time   40:00:00 H
B3 Working time   —
B4 Duration   15 dd*
B5 Response time   15 dd*

C Workers

C1 (who)

Workers number per shift, sex, age, education

Occupations	shifts	sex M	F	age 14-24	25-49	50-64	education[b] PS	JHS	HS	UN
foreman	—[c]	1	0	0	1	0	0	0	1	0
assistant foreman	—	2	0	0	1	1	0	2	0	0
worker (unskilled)	—	4	32	20	16	0	22	14	0	0
warehouse man	—	3	0	1	2	0	3	0	0	0
electrician	—	1	0	0	1	0	0	1	0	0
Total	43W 3S 6H 6D/We[d]	11	32	21	21	1	25	17	1	0

C2 (how)

% average time for each job per task

Jobs	m.loading %	transf. %	organ. %	maintenance %	innovation %
Occupations					
foreman	0	0	70	20	10
assistant foreman	0	30	50	20	0
worker (unskilled)	20	80	0	0	0
warehouse man	90	0	10	0	0
electrician	0	0	0	100	0

Skill degree from 1 to 5*[e]

Skill		special.	polyval.	autonomy	interact.	flexibil.
Occupations						
foreman	—	4	3	4	5	5
assistant foreman	—	3	3	3	4	4
worker (unskilled)	—	2	3	2	1	2
warehouse man	—	3	2	3	3	3
electrician	—	4	4	4	3	4

C3 (where)
Employee/machine ratio
(direct and undirect work)   167 spindles/man (60% preparing, 40% spinning)

D Plants

Number per type, time and degree (speed) of utilization (hours per day[f] and days per year), set-up & loading, maintenance times, idle times (hours per day)

	No	Speed	Ut.Time	S&Ltime	Maintenance	Idle Time
mixing machine	2	—	18H/D 220D/Y	00:22:00*	00:33:00*	06:00:00
intersecting	8	—	18H/D 220D/Y	00:22:00*	00:33:00*	06:00:00
finishing machine	4	—	18H/D 220D/Y	00:22:00*	00:33:00*	06:00:00
spindle	7,000	437kg/H	16H/D 220D/Y	00:50:00*	00:30:00*	08:00:00[g]

D2 Adaptability
(% var. on production capacity)   5%

D3 Flexibility
(minimum batch)   2,000 kg

E Output demand
E1 Quantitative variation   smaller batches
E2 Qualitative variation   increasing quality

* See note to Table A1.
[a] Net process time for producing 1 kg of yarn on a spindle.
[b] PS = primary school, JHS = junior high school, HS = high school, UN = university degree.
[c] The dash indicates the case where the data are missing because they were not provided by the production unit and could not be estimated.
[d] 43 workers, 3 shifts, 6 hours per day, 6 days per week.
[e] 1 = very low, 2 = low, 3 = medium, 4 = high, 5 = very high.
[f] Set-up, loading and maintenance times are included in utilization time (H/D).
[g] 7000 spindles, 437 kilos per hour of speed, used 16 hours per day and 220 days per year, 50 minutes of set-up and loading time, 30 minutes of maintenance time and 8 hours of idle time.

1.2 Type of product
Pure 100% cotton yarn in a vast range of types and qualities.

1.3 Production processes
(a) open-end (2 production units);
(b) worsted spinning, conventional ring type (3 production units);
(c) finishing, packing and shipping (1 production unit).

1.4 Sales, quantity produced and exported
The 1988 turnover amounted to about £23 million; 30% of the yarn is sent to the final market. One-third of the production is exported.

1.5 Number of employees (of the 6 production units) on 31 December 1986

directors	7
administrative employees	20
technical employees	6
foremen	30
workers	159
total	222

1.6 Pricing
Prices of inputs and outputs are determined by the world market. International cotton prices are influenced by climate, limited information and agents' expectations.

1.7 Structure of market and relations with other production units
Low entry barriers. The work of dyeing and finishing is performed by subcontractors, under agreements providing for quality control. The firm buys from subcontractors 'because they allow greater elasticity in the volumes of production and in some cases lower costs'. The firm has also conducted joint ventures with foreign firms (currently there is one with an East European country, involving the installation of plant and the provision of indigo for jeans).

2 Type of innovations

2.1 Innovations of product, process, services or organization
(a) Innovations in the process have been obtained through the installation of new machines or modifications to old equipment.

(b) The process innovations have led to innovations in the product. In the 1970s a new product (denim) was introduced. In the 1980s the quality of the yarn has been increased.

(c) The process innovations have also led to organizational changes.

2.2 Time of innovations
About eighteen months from planning to operation.

3 Factors underlying innovations

3.1 Origin of innovations
The firm has close relations with firms in the textile machinery sector, which construct custom-made equipment to meet the specific requirements of the production unit. Specialized firms are used for the introduction of electronic apparatus and the operations of controlling and maintaining it. Only occasionally does the firm register patents or trade marks.

3.2 Source of financial resources necessary for innovations
The investment sources have been self-financing.

3.3 Reasons which induced the firm to introduce innovations
The innovations were imposed by the characteristics of the market in which the firm operates; one significant factor is the continual demand by the client for an input of better quality yarn, arising partly from the adoption of new weaving techniques. The entry into the sector of countries with low labour costs has forced the industrialized countries to reduce process times and to improve quality of the product.

3.4 Elements which favoured the introduction of innovations
(a) Characteristics of the suppliers of innovation technologies: willingness to offer custom-designed products.

(b) Internal characteristics of the firm: considerable capacity for self-financing; technical ability at managerial level, with innovative traditions; small size; change in the firm's market position (with the cessation of subcontracting work) requiring a change in the product mix and the acquisition of a commercial structure, using in-house resources.

(c) Characteristics of the environment: opportunities offered by permitting the introduction of Sunday shifts; higher qualification of labour

Table B1 *Quantitative–temporal matrix of an elementary non-decomposable process performed by a production unit: 1988 (quantities for the production of 1.02 kg of open-end undyed cotton yarn, yarn count 12 Ne, 'process time' 24:01:15 H)*

		Spinning	Price unit cost	Total elementary process
A	*Output flows*			
A1	Spinning output	1.02 kg^a	1.59 £/kg	1.62 £
B	*Input flows*			
B1	Energy input	−2.64 Kwh	0.03 £/Kwh	−0.09 £
B2	Cotton input	−1.12 kg	0.77 £/kg	−0.87 £
B3	Water input	−0.10 m³	0.03 £/m³	−0.003 £
C	*Funds*			
C1	Spinning workers	−00:00:28 H^b	7.95 £/H	−0.06 £
C2	Spinning plant	−00:01:15 H*	13.64 £/H	−0.28 £
C3	Cotton warehouse	−67 kg*	0.0004 £/kg*	−0.03 £*
C4	Undyed yarn warehouse^c	−30 kg*	0.001 £/kg*	−0.02 £*
C5	Spinning area (555 m²)	−00:01:15 H	1.75 £/H	−0.05 £

* See Table A1.
^{a} 1.02 kg of undyed yarn for producing 1 kg of dyed yarn; the dyeing process is performed by a sub-contractor firm.
^{b} 00:00:28 H equal to 0.47 minutes.
^{c} And in progress yarn.

supply (now, even secondary-school leavers work at machines), easing of the firm's debt position in years of high inflation.

4   Obstacles

4.1   Main difficulties encountered in carrying out the innovative strategy
Problems of 'knowledge' of innovation, which cannot be complete before its direct application.

5   Effects of innovations

5.1   Effects of techniques and production
(a) Effects on the products: improvement in quality of the product; change in appearance of the product.

(b) Effects on processes: merging of different intermediate stages; reduced adaptability of plant; use of lower quality raw materials (open-end case); reduction in the high levels of noise and dust, reduction of process times, increase in productivity through elimination of idle times and manipulation times; improvement in quality of the product (for example, through control of the effective speed of the machines); increase in operating speed (in the case of open-end spinning); saving in space (innovations of the 1970s); saving on unit costs of energy (use of shifts in 'off-peak' hours). An innovation now in progress will provide automatic conning loading and unloading, which by merging these phases and reducing movement and manipulation will doublt productivity. The introduction of microelectronics in the various phases of the process will also allow a lower degree of rigidity in the scale of operations.

5.2   Changes in organization and employment

The innovation tends to reduce the labour requirement (for the same output) and to raise the level of qualification of the employees, who are required to perform more flexible roles to carry out more complex tasks. The new technologies require organizational changes: the high cost of investment necessitates continuous working shifts. The firm's policy has aimed at training existing staff, which has a very low turnover.

A9.3   Production unit C

1   General characteristics of the firm

1.1   Legal form, type of business and number of production units

The production unit of case C belongs to a firm producing yarns and woven fabrics, with a single factory built in 1970. The firm, which has been operating for more than a century, carries out the complete cycle, making considerable use of sub-contractors for almost all the intermediate stages in the cycle and for some minor or accessory operations.

1.2   Type of product

The firm produces three basic types of product:
(a) fabrics for clothing produced with shuttle looms (using spun yarns of wool, cotton, linen and synthetic fibres according to variations in market demand);
(b) knit fabrics produced on circular looms using very different fibres;

Table B2 *Organizational scheme of an elementary non-decomposable process performed by a production unit: 1988 (open-end undyed cotton yarn, yarn count 12 Ne)*

		Spinning
A	*Output*	
A1	Daily internal production	13,000 kg
A2	Daily selling	7,000 kg^a
B	*Time*	
B1	Net process time	00:01:15 H^b
B2	Process time	24:01:15 H
B3	Working time	—^{c}
B4	Duration	15 D*
B5	Response time	18 D*
B6	Gross duration	90 D*

C Workers

C1 (who)

Workers number per shifts, sex, age, education

Occupations	shifts	sex		age			education^a			
		M	F	14-24	25-49	50-64	PS	JHS	HS	UN
foreman	1W 1S 8H 5D/We^e	1	0	0	1	0	0	1	0	0
assistant foreman	5W 3S 8H 5D/We	5	0	0	5	0	0	5	0	0
worker (unskilled)	15W 3S 8H 4D/We	15	0	0	15	0	0	15	0	0
Total	21W 3S 8H 4D/We	21	0	0	21	0	0	21	0	0

C2 (how)

% average time for each job per task

Jobs	m.loading %	transf. %	organ. %	maintenance %	innovation %
Occupations					
foreman	0	0	60	30	10
assistant foreman	5	5	30	60	0
worker (unskilled)	55	40	0	5	0

Skill degree from 1 to 5*[a]

Skill	special.	polyval.	autonomy	interact.	flexibil.
Occupations					
foreman	5	5	4	4	4
assistant foreman	3	4	3	3	3
worker (unskilled)	2	3	1	3	1
C3 (where) Employee/machine ratio (direct and undirect work)	—	—	—		

D *Plants*

D1 Number per type, time and degree (speed) of utilization (hours per day[f] and days per year), set-up & loading, maintenance times, idle times (hours per day)

	N.	Speed[g]	Ut.time	S&L time	Maintenance	Idle time
spinning machine (each 192 heads)	9	60 r/min	24H/D 334D/Y	00:36:00	00:12:00	00:00:00[h]

D2 Adaptability (% var. on production capacity) 20%

D3 Flexibility (minimum batch) 700 kg

E *Output demand*

E1 Quantitative variation increasing

E2 Qualitative variation —

* See Table A1.
[a] 7000 kg is the daily production sold undyed, the remaining 6000 kg is the daily production dyed by a subcontractor firm.
[b] Net process time for producing 1.02 K on 1 out of 9 machines.
[c] See Table A2, note c.
[d] See notes b, e in Table A2.
[e] See Table A2, note d.
[f] Set-up, loading and maintenance times are included in utilization time (H/D).
[g] In thousands rotations per minute.
[h] See Table A2, note g.

(c) knitting yarns (of different compositions), sold to knitwear manu-
facturers working mainly with flat looms.

1.3   Production processes
(a) Worsted spinning; (b) warping; (c) weaving on shuttle looms; (d)
knitting on circular looms; (e) dyeing of tops, skeins and fabric pieces; (f)
finishing.

1.4   Sales, quantity produced and exported
The sales for 1987 amounted to about £30 million, about a third of which
was from exports. The quantities produced were as follows: (a) fabric
woven on shuttle looms, 3,000,000 metres; (b) knit fabric 500,000 metres;
(c) knitting yarn 1,450,000 kg.

1.5   Number of employees on 31 December 1987
directors   5
clerical staff   52
foremen   28
manual workers   233
total   318

1.6   Pricing
Application of a mark-up on the direct 'industrial cost'. 70% of the final
price covers costs of labour, raw materials and depreciation. The
remaining 30% covers the gross margins, administration and management
expenses, sales commission and interest.

1.7   Structure of market and relations with other production units
A few large firms and a great number of small ones. Each product has its
own market with particular characteristics. Relations of collaboration
with sub-contractors.

2   Type of innovations

2.1   Innovations of product, process, services or organization
The innovations have mainly involved the production processes. Nevertheless, new types of cloth have also been tried. Process innovations, such
as the introduction of the automatic healders, have led to a change in the
product. The processes affected by innovations are: (a) spinning

(introduction of Repco spinning); (b) weaving (introduction of the automatic healders and perforation of loom cards by personal computer), finishing (modifications of Stenter); (d) dyeing (automated reading and classification of colours); (e) services (automated packing systems).

2.2 Time of innovations
The delivery times for new machines vary from 6 to 12 months. Running-in time varies depending on the type of innovation; in the most complex cases around two years have passed from the moment of decision to innovate to the moment of full production.

3 Factors underlying innovations

3.1 Origin of innovations
The innovations are introduced through the purchase of new machines, furnished by the textile machinery sector. The production unit has experimented with yarns of certain new characteristics. There is no R&D department within the firm, only a technical and logistic office.

3.2 Source of financial resources necessary for innovations
Self-financing, bank financing, leasing.

3.3 Reasons which induced the firm to introduce innovations
The innovations were imposed by the characteristics of the market in which the firm operates. Technological innovation is the way to obtain the following objectives (in order of importance):
(1) increased productivity through saving of process time and hence lower unit cost; (2) saving of space, (3) simplification of working methods and rationalization of operations; (4) qualitative improvement of the product and greater variety of products; (5) creation of products with new characteristics; (6) easier managerial control.

3.4 Elements which favoured the introduction of innovations
(a) Characteristics of suppliers (reliability of equipment supplied, quality of after-sales service, availability of assistance at technical level);

Table C1 *Quantitative-temporal matrix of an elementary decomposable process performed by an integrated production unit: 1987 (quantities for the production of a piece of worsted wool, average yarn count, length 54mt, width 150cm, g/mt 440, 'process time' 66:32:30 H)*

Intermediate stages	Spinning	Weaving	Dyeing	Finishing	Total elementary process	Price unit cost	Price total cost
A **Output flow**							
A1 Spinning output	28.0 kg	−28.0 kg			0	—[a]	—
A2 Weaving output		59.6 Mt[b]	−59.6 MT		0	—	—
A3 Dyeing output			56.6 Mt	−56.6 Mt	0	—	—
A4 Finishing output				54.0 Mt	54 Mt	6.89 £/Mt	372.01 £
B **Input flow**							
B1 Energy input	−71.4 Kwh	−20 Kwh	−9.2 Kwh	−20 Kwh	−120.6 Kwh	0.06 £/Kwh	−6.73 £
B2 Wool input	−28.5 kg				−28.5 kg	4.77 £/kg	−136.02 £
B3 Colour input				−1.75 kg	−1.75 kg	18.58 £/kg	−32.60 £
C **Funds**							
C1 Spinning workers	−02:48:00 H				−2.8 H	8.02 £/H	−22.46 £
C2 Weaving workers		−03:30:00 H			−3.5 H	8.80 £/H	−30.80 £
C3 Warping workers		−59.6 Mt[b]			−59.6 Mt	0.07 £/Mt[c]	−4.28 £
C4 Dyeing workers			−00:24:00 H		−0.4 H	7.54 £/H	−3.02 £

Item		Allocation	Quantity	Rate	Amount
C5	Finishing workers	−01:48:00 H	−1.8 H	8.15 £/H	−14.67 £
C6	Spinning plant	−2:30:00 H	−2.5 H	1.81 £/H	−4.50 £
C7	Weaving plant	−10:00:00 H	−10.0 H	0.75 £/H	−7.50 £
C8	Dyeing plant	−06:00:00 H	−6.0 H	0.09 £/H	−0.54 £
C9	Finishing plant	−02:30:00 H	−2.5 H	0.71 £/H	−1.78 £
C10	Wool warehouse[a]	−1,710 kg*	−1,710 kg*	0.004 £/kg	−6.68 £*
C11	Yarn warehouse[a]	−2,548 kg*	−2,548 kg*	0.005 £/kg	−12.39 £*
C12	Pieces warehouse[a]	−76 Pc*	−76 Pc*	0.17 £/Pz	−12.82 £*
C13	Dyed pieces warehouse[a]	−58 Pc*	−58 Pc*	0.21 £/Pz	−12.26 £*
C14	Finished pieces warehouse[a]	−59 Pc*	−59 Pc*	0.23 £/Pz	−13.46 £*
C15	Spinning area (362 m²)	−02:30:00 H	−2.5 H	3.69 £/H	−9.21 £
C16	Weaving area (81 m²)	−10:00:0 H	−10.0 H	0.56 £/H	−5.60 £
C17	Dyeing area (82 m²)	−06:00:00 H	−6.0 H	1.48 £/H	−8.91 £
C18	Finishing area (166 m²)	−02:30:00 H	−2.5 H	1.72 £/H	−4.30 £

* See Table A1.

[a] See Table A2, note c.

[b] For this cloth 59.6 Mt are equal to 120,000 pecks per piece.

[c] 7 pence per minute is the price of the warping operation performed in-house by a sub-contractor firm.

[d] And in progress.

(b) internal characteristics of the firm (availability of capital, supervisory staff and managerial ability.

4   Obstacles

4.1   Main difficulties encountered in carrying out the innovative strategy
The greatest difficulties arise from re-training of personnel and the re-organization of working shifts.

5   Effects of innovations

5.1   Effects on techniques and production
The introduction of Repco spinning led to a doubling of production per worker. The adoption of the automatic healders brought an increase in flexibility thanks to the possibility of increasing the product mix by increasing the number of resettings of the looms. The perforation of the loom cards by computer permits a reduction of almost 10 % in the net machines times, as well as permitting a greater flexibility in the preparation of collections. The modifications to the stenter have led to a 30 % increase in productivity and to a considerable saving of energy. The instrumental and automatic colour mixing permits an objective control of quality, with qualitatively better and more economical colour recipes, optimizing the use of dyes. The new packing systems have brought a marked reduction in physical effort; moreover the quality of the packing has improved.

5.2   Changes in organization and employment
The adoption of Repco spinning made it necessary to introduce three 6-hour shifts for 6 days a week (as against the two 8-hour shifts for 5 days with the rings), and the hiring of young workers (more dexterity and speed of response are required). In this department there has been a reduction of 7 out of 40 workers.

The introduction of the automatic healders has led to a change in shifts (formerly 2 shifts from 6 am to 2 pm hours and from 3 pm to 10 pm, now one shift from 8 am to 12 pm and 1 pm to 5 pm). The phase which required the greatest dexterity is now executed by the machine. The number of workers has fallen from 5 to 3.

The perforation of loom card by personal computer, modifications to the stenter and instrumental recipe formulation have not had significant effects on the organization of these processes and there have been no changes in the number of workers. The reorganization of the packing

Table C2 (cont.)

Intermediate stages	Spinning	Weaving										Dyeing	Finishing	Total process elementary
			sex		age			education[b]						
			M	F	14-24	25-49	50-64	PS	JHS	HS	UN			

C Workers
C1 (who)

	Spinning	Weaving	M	F	14-24	25-49	50-64	PS	JHS	HS	UN	Dyeing	Finishing	Total
Workers number per shifts, sex, age, educ.	shifts	shifts										shifts	shifts	
Occupations														
foreman	—	1W 1S 8H 5D/We[c]	1	0	0	0	1	0	0	1	0	—	—	
assistant foreman	—	4W 2S 8H 5D/We	4	0	0	4	0	3	0	1	0	—	—	
worker (skilled)	—	21W 3S 8H 5D/We 34W 2S 8H 5D/We	42	13	5	39	11	45	10	0	0	—	—	
worker (unskilled)	—	1W 1S 8H 5D/We — — —	1	0	0	1	0	1	0	0	0	—	—	
Total	70W 2S 8H 5D/We	61W	48	13	5	44	12	49	10	2	0	6W 2S 8H 5D/We	50W 2S 8H 5D/We	187W

C2 (how)

	m.loading %	transf. %	organ. %	maintenance %	innovation %
% average time for each job per task					
Jobs					
Occupations					
foreman	0	0	90	0	10
assistant foreman	10	0	50	40	0
worker (skilled)	20	80	0	0	0
worker (unskilled)	100[d]	0	0	0	0

	special.	polyval.	autonomy	interact.	flexibil.
Skill degree from 1 to 5*[b]					
Skill					
Occupations					
foreman	5	3	4	5	5
assistant foreman	4	3	3	4	3
worker (skilled)	4	2	2	2	2
worker (unskilled)	1	1	1	1	1

C3 (where) Employee/machine ratio (direct and undirect work): —

Table C2 *Organizational scheme of an elementary decomposable process performed by an integrated production unit:
1987 (worsted wool, average yarn count, length 54 mt, width 150 cm, g/mt 440)*

Intermediate stages	Spinning	Weaving	Dyeing	Finishing	Total process elementary
A *Output*					
A1 Daily internal production	4,440 kg	13,921,000 Pk	100 Pc	231 Pc	231 Pc
A2 Daily external production	—[a]	13,800,000 Pk	—	—	—
A3 Daily selling	—	27,721,000 Pk	—.	—	—
B *Time*					
B1 Net process time	00:02:30 H	10:00:00 H	06:00:00 H	02:30:00 H	21:00:00 H
B2 Process time	48:02:30 H	10:00:00 H	06:00:00 H	02:30:00 H	66:32:30 H
B3 Working time	—	—	—	—	—
B4 Duration	30 dd	15 dd	7 dd	8 dd	60 dd
B5 Response time	—	—	—	—	60/90 dd
B6 Gross duration	90 dd	15 dd	7 dd	8 dd	120 dd

D *Plants*

D1 Number per type, time and degree (speed) of utilization (hours per day[e] and days per year), set-up & loading, maintenance times, idle times (hours per day)

	No	No.		Speed	Ut. Time	S&L time	Maint.	Idle time	No	No
Spinning	24 fronts × 250 spindles									
Weaving										
fizing		1	—		9H/D 220D/Y	01:48:00	00:27:00	15:00:00[g]		
healders		1	—		16H/D 220D/Y	08:00:00	00:48:00	08:00:00		
warping-mill		5	—		16H/D 220D/Y	05:36:00	00:48:00	08:00:00		
loom		54	—		24H/D 220D/Y	01:12:00	01:12:00	00:00:00		
dyeing								—	—	—
finishing								—	—	—
D2 Adaptability[f] (% var. on production capacity)							—		—	—
D3 Flexibility (minimum batch)	1,000 K						1 Pc		—	—

E *Output demand*

		No	No
E1 Quantitative variation			decreasing trend
E2 Qualitative variation			increasing quality

[a] See Table A2, note c
[b] See Table A2, notes b and e
[c] See Table A2, note d
[d] The unskilled worker performs only cleaning jobs.
[e] See Table A2, note f.
[f] Adaptability is obtained by varying the quantity given to sub-contractor firms.
[g] See Table A2, note g

systems has not brought any organizational problems, although the workers have had to learn to use the computers. There has been a significant reduction in physical effort. Of the three packing machines installed only one has brought about a loss of jobs. Overall the number of packing workers has dropped from 13 to 11.

Part 3

Economies of scale, economies of scope and production flexibility

Part 3 is devoted to examining two particular cases of technical change: varying the *dimension of scale* and the degree of *flexibility*. These two aspects of technical change can be examined by comparing: different techniques at different moments in time (time series analysis); or different techniques at a given moment in time (cross-section analysis).

The complementarity, indivisibility and irreversibility properties, used within the fund–flow model expounded earlier, do not hinder analysis as happens within some other economic theoretical representations. There is therefore no need to remove these properties through special initial axioms, or to consider them implicitly irrelevant for the purposes of analysing the phenomena in question. On the contrary, taking organizational aspects into account and discussing the concepts of complementarity, indivisibility (of processes and elements) and irreversibility (of time) are essential to making a coherent analysis of the problems involved in changing to techniques with a different *dimension of scale* or with a different level of *production flexibility*. Such a coherent analysis is indispensable to a precise definition, understanding and description of these phenomena.

The analytical representation of the process can be seen both as a scheme of relations between the economic variables of production, open to changes in 'environment' and 'institutional' conditions, as well as a method for empirical research. I will now discuss the theoretical implications of the proposed methodology and assess its possible empirical applications, leaving to further studies the actual implementation of the model in empirical analyses of the economic effects of changing production techniques.

As emphasized earlier, the link between the theoretical scheme and empirical research is very close. In fact the capacity of empirical observation to grasp the economic effects of technical change depends on the adequacy of the theoretical scheme on which these empirical observations are (implicitly or explicitly) based. Evidently, the definition itself of the concepts in question assumes different meanings and features, depending on the theoretical scheme used. For example, it has been shown that if just the quantitative aspects of production are taken into account in the theoretical scheme, technical change appears simply as a factor which reduces inputs in relation to outputs. Naturally technical change cannot be reduced to pure variations in quantity, in the same way as the study of a production process requires temporal, organizational and qualitative aspects to be examined in addition to the relationship between the quantities of production elements. This influence of the theoretical scheme on the perception of the economic phenomenon in question naturally applies not only to the notion of technical change, but also to the particular aspects which the technical change can assume, such as the two aspects discussed in Part 3 dealing with changing the scale dimension or changing the degree of production flexibility (linked to the variety and variability of the product mix).

The subjects of returns of scale and flexibility have very different positions in the history of economic analysis. The phenomenon of scale returns has been studied since the time of Adam Smith. The economists during that period and the following decades who witnessed the first industrial revolution could not be unaware of the importance of increasing returns in manufacturing linked to the widening of the market and the adoption of new manufacturing techniques, nor of the problems related to a possible loss of efficiency in agricultural and extraction industries due to the intrinsic limits of natural resources.[1] The second theme of production flexibility has been arousing interest in recent times, particularly with increased market instability and the spread of computer-based technology. During the last decade a lively debate has developed on the trends in many industrial areas and many developed market economies towards the establishment of the flexible specialization model. Unfortunately, because of the myriad meanings which the term flexible evokes, a universally acceptable taxonomy has not yet been reached in economic literature. An attempt will be made here to contribute to the search for a precise taxonomy of the phenomena related to production flexibility and based on the fund–flow analytical scheme proposed in Part 2. Moreover, as will be seen, this scheme may provide a suitable analytical representation of the production process for examining the problems raised by writings on flexible specialization.

For the sake of simplicity, the problem of changing scale dimension and that of varying the degree of flexibility will be dealt with separately. Indeed, these two problems can be isolated analytically since, as will be

---

[1] As is well known, according to the classics, the need to cultivate new land or to exploit new ore deposits involved a tendency towards decreasing returns in marginal production units.

seen later, contrary to some widely held beliefs, production flexibility is largely independent of the size of firm (or production unit).

Chapter 11 deals with changes in techniques which have a different scale dimension, and therefore with the problem of possible scale returns. The fund–flow model proves most useful in analysing efficiency variations as the scale dimension changes, principally because indivisibility (of goods and processes) is an indispensable element in formulating a precise definition of returns of scale, and in comprehending their underlying causes. Unfortunately the relationship between indivisibility and increasing returns has not always been discussed appropriately and consistently in economic literature. This has led to misunderstandings which have dragged on for many years. Secondly, the complementary relationship between the various production processes and elements discussed in Chapter 6 contributes to determining the size of an enterprise. Therefore it is a key factor in assessing the size–efficiency ratio of a production unit (or enterprise). Thirdly, the decomposition properties of the production process, examined in chapter 7, allow the relationship between scale dimension and efficiency to be analysed in terms of the different 'microeconomic units' used and the different operational levels where the intermediate stages take place. In fact, economies of scale work simultaneously at different operational levels (such as elementary technical unit, plant, production unit, firm, group of firms) and affect the individual intermediate stages to different degrees, so that unit costs in relation to quantities produced at the various operational levels and intermediate stages are interdependent. For instance, because of bottlenecks in productive capacity (due to indivisible production elements), a scale increase at an intermediate stage may create a better balance of processes and reduce productive capacity wastage at other intermediate stages or operational levels. Fourthly, taking account of the production process time profile, particularly the production speed, together with the number of parallel processes carried out, enables a precise definition of productive capacity to be obtained. Lastly, the fund–flow model is a fruitful analytical tool for collecting statistics on costs related to differently sized production units, as an alternative to the production function approach. In conclusion, it seems that very interesting points will also emerge as to the possibilities of using the fund–flow model both in theoretical discussion and to supplement the analytical methodologies currently adopted for measuring economies of scale.

Chapter 12 is devoted to comparing techniques with different degrees of production flexibility. The fund–flow model shows how production flexibility can be obtained by changing either the production organization or the technology adopted. In addition it enables the various industrial organizational models to be more clearly defined in terms of specific characteristics of production units. For example, the time profile for using various fund elements is essential in differentiating between artisan and industrial activity. Furthermore, the fund–flow model employing a quantitative–temporal matrix and an organizational scheme, proves useful in identifying the economic effects of introducing new information technology which increases production flexibility. It is known that this technology tends to considerably reduce production process duration and set-up times in particular. The production time profile (duration of process, response times etc.), the overall idle times and the size of the minimum efficient batch (contained in the quantitative matrix and organizational scheme) are all useful elements to be considered in assessing the efficiency and efficacy of processes in relation to production flexibility.

Finally, comparing several 'quantitative–temporal matrices' and 'organizational schemes', of the same production unit at different times, allows quantitative and qualitative input variations and the differences in production times to be grasped at a microeconomic level. With particular regard to the labour market, an 'organizational scheme', giving the number of employees per job, skill and occupational level, can be useful in identifying possible job displacement phenomena and changes in skill requirements and labour force composition, due to the introduction of flexible technology or to any changes in techniques.

11   Economies of scale

This chapter deals with the theoretical problems connected with variations in efficiency resulting from changes in the scale of production. Costs are influenced by many forces and it is very difficult to isolate the effect of scale dimension upon unit costs from all the other factors. First of all, costs are influenced by technical change. Often there is a close interdependence between technical change and economies of scale, because an increase in dimensions may favour the adoption of new techniques, just as the introduction of new techniques may allow an increase in the scale of production. As we have seen, technical change affects not only costs (i.e. efficiency), but also the ability to respond to the needs of markets (efficacy). Efficiency and efficacy together contribute to the competitiveness of a production unit. However, there is no predetermined relationship between dimension of scale and efficacy, since in the same industrial sector we may have production units or firms with high ability to respond to markets needs, but with very different dimensions of scale.

Even if we consider efficiency only in a static analytical framework (excluding technical change and production efficacy for the moment), the scale dimension is certainly not the only factor which affects costs. This point was highlighted by E. A. G. Robinson (1931, p. 155) in his pioneering work on industrial structure. For instance, efficiency depends upon capital endowment, the characteristics of entrepreneurship, technical training, market characteristics, the life of each product, the total cumulative output over time, organizational aspects, and the degree of utilization of machines and plants in relation to the time profile of production processes. All these factors change from firm to firm and in relation to the specific institutional environment. Hence the problem of determining the 'optimum size' of a production unit or a firm is not univocally predetermined. And the notion itself of 'optimum size' for a production unit or a firm, based only on the simple relation between dimension of scale and unit costs, is strongly misleading. In fact, as stressed by Georgescu-Roegen (1964):

the optimum size of an economic organization is not a technical problem like that of the optimum size of a plant. The optimum size of organizations involves comparisons of quality, efficiency, therefore, belongs to the qualitative residual of the analysis of a productive process exclusively by the production function (p. 296)

As mentioned, the organizational and qualitative aspects of production are indispensable elements in formulating a precise definition of returns of scale. They are also very useful in discussing the relationship between economies of scale and degree of adaptability (second section). The third section covers the different methods used to measure static and dynamic economies of scale. The fourth section is devoted to the importance of the unit of analysis adopted in considering economies of scale. It will be seen that the latter act at different operational levels which correspond to different microeconomic units. The fifth section examines the relationship between economies of scale and technical change. After the concluding remarks, an Appendix has been added discussing the essential points in the long debate on the underlying causes of economies and diseconomies of scale.

11.1   Returns of scale, complementarity and indivisibility

Returns of scale are generally defined as a relationship between an equiproportional increase in all inputs and the resultant increase in output.[1] A change in the scale of production, which leads to a variation of all inputs *in the same proportion*, is conceivable. However, as highlighted by Adam Smith, an increase in the quantity of inputs permits a reorganization of production that changes the relative requirements and hence their combination. Thus, the relations of complementarity among the different inputs tend to change in response to different dimensions of scale.[2]

---

[1] This definition is widely accepted in many textbooks and is usually illustrated by referring to a map of isoquants: there is an *equiproportional increase* in both inputs (x and y), if the level of output grows along the path of expansion represented by a straight line from the origin which intersects the various isoquants corresponding to the different levels of output. See, for instance, Samuelson (1948, pp. 34ff.), Baumol (1961, pp. 272–3).

[2] Therefore, it may seem misleading to define – as, for example, in Samuelson's famous textbook – increasing returns of scale as a more than proportional increase in output when there is an increase of 'all factors at the same time and by the same proportion', and, on the other hand, a few lines below, to attribute increasing returns to increased specialization and changes in production techniques involving a more efficient and more complex organization of production, 'a fairly elaborate productive organization' (Samuelson, 1948, pp. 34–7 *passim*). In fact, these are changes which alter the proportions among inputs (if not the inputs themselves).

Production elements tend to be combined, *at each given moment* and *for each given scale of production*, according to specific relations of complementarity, which allow a fairly narrow substitution range (chapter 4, sections 4.2, 4.3). Complementarity relations are determined by economic conditions (such as relative prices), the respective chemical–physical and technical characteristics, the knowledge possessed by members of the production unit, prevailing rules and habitual practices, and specific characteristics of the product. On the other hand, at any given moment, a different technical combination of production elements leads in many cases to a *qualitative change in the product* which makes the new combination no longer comparable with the old one. This is true for all commodities that can be made either industrially or by craft production, for example a suit, a table, a piece of furniture or the binding of a book. In this case a commodity produced using automatic labour-saving devices which yield a standardized product is a different commodity (with a different market and a different price) from the commodity produced using simple tools because the techniques of production affect the intrinsic qualities of the commodity produced, the number of variants of a product (according to the customer's specification) and the response time.

Of course this does not mean that a change in relative prices has no influence on the proportions in which inputs are used. If for each given dimension of scale there exist well defined relations of complementarity between the inputs, a change in relative prices may induce a series of technical changes leading to new relations of complementarity. For example, a change in relative prices may encourage experimentation with new technologies or new materials, or it may stimulate changes in standards which establish new complementary relations among inputs. These changes take time. A variation in relative prices will not generally lead to an immediate replacement of more costly inputs by inputs whose price has fallen in relative terms. Moreover, such technical changes are for the most part irreversible. Therefore they must be excluded from static equilibrium analysis.

Any given complementary relationship among inputs is a result of the particular development path of the production unit involved. As already mentioned, this development path is cumulative, irreversible and specific to the individual production unit. For each given dimension of scale reached by the production unit, there is a certain corresponding stage of development of the agent's 'concrete knowledge' regarding the use of specific machines and equipment. If this is true, there are not very many alternative techniques that can be chosen as in a blueprint, corresponding to different dimensions of scale. On the contrary, it is worth repeating that techniques develop gradually (chapter 2, section 2.2 and chapter 3, section

3.4). Summing up, a change in the relations between inputs generally comes about as a result of changes in 'fundamental conditions' such as relative prices, available technologies, demand conditions, product standards imposed by retailers, institutional environment, and the characteristics of the available inputs. These basic conditions are closely interrelated.

If different relations of complementarity among inputs prevail the main economic problem of production is choosing the dimension of scale of different production processes or intermediate stages (within and outside the production unit). This choice must take account of their different productive capacities and of the amount of internal and external transaction costs. In other words, the fundamental function of the entrepreneur is the investment choice, which involves the necessity of matching the productive capacities of the different operational levels and intermediate stages, taking account of transaction costs, within the evolution of markets, technological, institutional and environmental conditions.

To come back to the notion of increasing returns of scale, if complementarity relations tend to be rather rigid for each scale of production, and to change when the scale increases, it is useful to distinguish between increasing returns of scale with constant relations of complementarity and increasing returns with variable relations of complementarity. In this second case, as dimension of scale increases, the average productivity of individual production elements will tend to rise, but the rate of change will differ from one element to another, because the average physical productivities of the various inputs increase differently. This can easily be clarified by an example. If the scale dimension of manufacturing a fabric increases, it may be supposed that the quantity of yarn increases in proportion to the output, so we shall not have returns of scale corresponding to the use of that element;[3] but the quantity of labour, space, stocks and energy will increase less than proportionately with respect to output, so that returns of scale may be *considerable* with regard to energy consumption, *average* with regard to the labour requirement, and *low* with regard to stocks and space occupied. Finally, there will be *considerable* returns of scale with regard to the inputs necessary for the sample-book.

Let us now consider the debated problem of the relationship between increasing returns of scale and indivisibility. Increasing returns of scale imply indivisibility of processes, although indivisibility of processes does

---

[3] For simplicity, in this example we exclude the hypothesis that larger plant permits the installation of equipment which reduces waste.

not necessarily imply increasing returns of scale.[4] Increasing returns, and hence the indivisibility of processes, may result from a larger scale of organization of *divisible* production elements, if the increase in scale leads to a reduced input requirement per unit of product. In fact, processes may be indivisible even in the presence of divisible production elements. Therefore, the assertion, often found in economic literature, that in the final analysis increasing returns of scale always depend on indivisibility, is a tautology with reference to the indivisibility of processes, as by definition there are increasing returns of scale when the processes are indivisible; it is incorrect with reference to the indivisibility of commodities, as there can be increasing returns of scale even with divisible commodities. An unclear *distinction* between the *indivisibility of processes* and the *indivisibility of elements* perhaps lies behind the many errors of interpretation and great misunderstanding which arose between writers with different approaches during the vigorous disputes on this theme (see Kaldor 1934, 1972; Chamberlin 1948, 1949; Hahn and McLeod 1949; Georgescu-Roegen 1964; Frank 1969; Arrow and Hahn 1971, pp. 60–1).[5]

It is well known that the phenomenon of increasing returns of scale is difficult to reconcile with a theory of relative prices based on competitive equilibrium between supply and demand (see, e.g. Hahn and Matthews 1964, pp. 91ff.). In perfect competition the quantity produced by the individual firm must be small enough not to influence the market price; hence increasing returns of scale associated with large volumes of production cannot be considered (Arrow and Debreu 1954, pp. 91ff.; Hahn 1973, pp. 12ff.).[6] Moreover technical change and learning by doing, which are closely connected with the phenomenon of increasing returns of scale,[7] cannot be included in the static analysis of the short and long run. Thus, it is not surprising that the question of increasing returns of scale, although discussed by Adam Smith in the *Wealth of Nations*, has received

---

[4] A process is indivisible if it is impossible to activate processes that have the same proportions of inputs and outputs, but on a smaller scale. In terms of the traditional instrument of the production set, the property of divisibility of processes can be expressed in the following way: '$y \in Y$ implies $\lambda y \in Y$ for each scalar $\lambda \in [0, 1]$', where Y is the production set of all the vectors y, which represent – with reference to a given list of goods and services – possible production processes in a given situation. The set Y is thus a subset of R^n, which indicates the set of the $n \cdot$ tuple of real numbers (cf. Tani, 1986, pp. 16, 26, 50).

[5] For a review of the literature on the problem see Morroni (1985). On the relation between indivisibility and decreasing returns see below, Appendix, p. 158 in which the factors involved in increasing returns and economies of scale are examined.

[6] As is well known, in the presence of increasing returns of scale the production set is not convex (assuming the possibility of inaction – i.e. if $0 \in Z$). On this point see chapter 3, section 3.2, in particular n. 7.

[7] In fact an increase in size favours the adoption of new techniques, just as the introduction of new techniques often allows an increase in the scale of production.

little attention from economists (with a few exceptions such as Karl Marx and Alfred Marshall) until fairly recent times, when the theories of oligopoly based on the analysis of Joe S. Bain and Paolo Sylos Labini (Bain 1956; Sylos Labini 1956), and the theories of economic growth derived from John Maynard Keynes[8] have provided an analytical context capable of dealing with that phenomenon. As Alfred Marshall realized, increasing returns can find a place only in the context of a dynamic analysis and with reference to a market which is not perfectly competitive (Marshall 1890, pp. 238–9, 379–82).[9]

In conclusion, *increasing returns of scale* are closely connected with a number of factors, which are considered within the fund–flow scheme: (i) the indivisibility and complementary nature of the production processes and the individual elements of production; (ii) conditions of separability of the different intermediate stages comprising an elementary process; (iii) the duration of the production process; (iv) the specific organizational systems adopted (in relation to the particular characteristics of the development path taken by each individual production unit).

11.2   Economies of scale, productive capacity and adaptability

The notion of *returns of scale* has an essentially technical nature because it is independent of any assumptions about the prices of inputs and output.[10] If prices are given, there is an inverse relationship between returns of scale and total average costs, so that increasing returns of scale and (total average) costs can be taken as equivalent.

On the other hand, the notion of *economies of scale* is used with reference to a situation in which there may be *variation in the prices* of inputs in relation to the quantities acquired (for example consider pecuniary economies examined in the Appendix to this chapter). In fact economies of scale occur when a larger dimension of scale of a specific microeconomic unit leads to a lower total average cost of the product

---

[8] The connection between increasing returns of scale and economic growth, present in some classical economists, is highlighted in Nicholas Kaldor's works, where it is enriched by contributions of Keynesian analysis on the relation between investments and income. Kaldor considers economic growth as the result of interaction between increases in demand induced by increases in supply, and increases in supply generated in response to increases in demand. The increasing returns of scale which he believes are obtainable mainly in the manufacturing sector enter and amplify this cumulative process. The greater the tendency to use additional income to acquire industrial products whose production benefits from increasing returns of scale the more rapid will be the process of growth (see Kaldor, 1972).

[9] On the notion of increasing returns to scale in Marshall cf. Loasby (1988, p. 7).

[10] In excluding changes in relative prices for theoretical convenience, we should not forget, of course, that the choice concerning the dimension of scale, and hence returns of scale, may be affected by change in relative prices.

obtained from it. The opposite phenomenon is called diseconomies of scale. According to this definition, it has been observed that 'the concept of economies of scale includes all the phenomena in which an increase in size brings advantages in terms of cost' (Tani, 1986, pp. 82–5). If the hypothesis that prices of inputs are taken as given is abandoned, prices of inputs may vary in relation to the demand expressed by the individual production unit, and thus the assumption of a perfectly competitive market for the inputs must be relinquished.

With regard to the scale dimension there is no common unit of measurement for firms, plants and pieces of equipment with different characteristics; hence their dimension of scale must be expressed by an indirect index: the productive capacity of a given microeconomic unit in relation to a product or a 'family of diversified products'.[11]

The productive capacity of a microeconomic unit is defined as the level of output (or range of outputs) in which the various elements are used in the most technically advantageous combination, according to a given organizational structure and the complementary relations established by technology, economic and institutional conditions (i.e. market conditions, 'laws', standards and agreements regulating the use of production elements). In other words, productive capacity relates to the specific level of equipment utilization allowed by environmental conditions. For instance, the productive capacity of a microeconomic unit is linked to the number of hours (per day) and days (per week), in which the process operates. Obviously, a change in the rules governing work conditions may vary the shift structure and change the equipment utilization time. The productive capacity of a microeconomic unit thus corresponds to the volume of production per unit of time at the lowest unit cost, or the optimal producible quantity, in relation to given organizational and institutional conditions (on this point, see e.g. Frisch 1962, p. 287). The volume of production per unit of time is given by the number of parallel processes and the duration of those processes.[12]

The maximum productive capacity of a microeconomic unit is given by the quantity of saturation, while the minimum productive capacity is given by the quantity of activation, in relation to given production, organizational and institutional conditions. Hence the maximum and

---

[11] The number of employees or the turnover are widely used as statistical indices of the firm size, but they are not suitable for measuring the dimension of scale of a firm. For instance, it is clear that vertical integration leads to an increase in employees and turnover, and therefore in the firm size, but it does not necessarily change its dimension of scale in terms of the final output productive capacity.

[12] It is quite obvious that if, for example, machine A handles twice as many parallel processes as machine B, but at half the speed of machine B, the two machines have the same dimension of scale.

minimum productive capacities correspond to the quantities above and below which the device or operative level cannot be activated. The term 'range of productive capacities' refers to the distance between the quantity corresponding to the level of activation and that corresponding to saturation. The breadth of the range of productive capacities varies for different types of apparatus and their degrees of adaptability.

As we have seen, the concept of *adaptability* is related to variations in the quantity produced (of a given commodity). I consider a plant the more adaptable the less unit costs vary with the quantity produced.[13] In other words, the less elastic unit costs of a commodity (say x) are, with respect to variations in the quantity produced ($e_{AC_x} = dAC_x/dX \cdot X/AC_x$), the more adaptable its production is.

The technical indivisibility of machines generally implies a low adaptability level, as it causes fixed costs which in turn determine an increase in unit cost when the quantity produced decreases. As we shall see in chapter 12, greater adaptability may be pursued through particular organizational systems which tend to reduce the level of fixed costs. Obviously, in the presence of technical divisibility there would be no fixed costs and adaptability would be maximum, only if there were economic divisibility too, so that all the elements of production could be paid for according to the exact quantity used and the time strictly necessary.

11.3   Cross section analysis, time series analysis and methods of collecting data on costs

A distinction must be made between economies of scale, at a given moment in time, and economies of scale over time. The first notion of economies of scale refers to a comparison of microeconomic units with different productive capacities at a moment in time (*cross-section analysis*). The second notion refers to the development process of the productive capacity of a given production unit (*time-series analysis*). Therefore, in a cross-section analysis production processes begin at the same instant of time, while in a time-series analysis one examines production processes activated at different times.

The first methodology (based on cross-section analysis) is useful for comparing the performances of differently sized microeconomic units, involved in the production of a single commodity (or of very similar

[13] However, where demand is highly variable a given optimum quantity cannot be defined. In this case the probability distribution within a certain range of production must be considered. In conditions of uncertainty the entrepreneur will tend to choose the plant that allows him a combination of production levels which, on the basis of the probability distribution relative to levels of demand, permits him to minimize the total costs accumulated for a given period of time.

commodities), and hence it may serve as a basis for analysing the efficiency of a given industrial structure. This methodology allows the comparison of different production processes resulting from past investment choices and learning processes, which are considered only in terms of their final effect on efficiency levels.

On the other hand, the time-series analysis considers the evolution of an individual microeconomic unit size over time. By this method it is possible to ascertain the effects of unit costs of an increase in the microeconomic unit, due to investment activity. It is not easy, however, to isolate the effects of changes in the dimension of scale on efficiency, from the effects of technical change, learning processes, and in general of all variations in forces which affect production. Hence, the time series analysis seems more suitable as a method for evaluating the whole effects of technical change, among which economies of scale often play an important role.

Following the time series analysis, a change in the dimension of scale will thus be indicated as a shift from one scale of production to another.[14] For simplicity I consider three different ways in which an increase in the scale of production can take place:

(i) by *substituting* a new microeconomic unit of greater productive capacity for the old one;[15]

(ii) by *multiplying* the number of microeconomic units (e.g., acquiring a certain number of machines exactly like the first);[16]

(iii) by *juxtaposition*, adding a new (different) microeconomic unit to the existing one.

An example may serve to clarify the differences between these three ways of enlarging the scale. If we consider an elementary technical unit

[14] In exercises on comparative statics it is usual to speak of a 'shift' along an isoquant or along the expansion paths belonging to a map of isoquants. In this case the term 'shift' is quite misleading, because in static comparative analysis there is no place for processes of shifting (which must obviously occur in historical time). In fact in static analysis all the points that belong to the isoquants and the corresponding expansion paths constitute possible alternative equilibrium points, but not development paths along which to move. If we were to admit the passage of time, which allows shifting from one position to another, the map of isoquants would undergo a modification (owing to learning processes and improvements to machinery) which would induce not a simple shift along the old curves, but a series of 'leaps' onto the new curves as these gradually took shape as a result of the changes. On this point see J. Robinson (1980a, p. 87), and chapter 3, section 3.4 in part I.

[15] Substitution here implies an increase in productive capacity. By contrast, in the traditional microeconomic literature substitution generally refers to the comparison of two different combinations of inputs belonging to the same isoquant of production, and hence the substitution occurs when the volume of production remains the same.

[16] It should be noted that if increasing returns of scale are obtained by simply multiplying the number of inputs, such increasing returns cannot arise from technical factors alone; organizational aspects must also play a part.

such as a bread oven, the scale can be increased either by replacing the elementary technical unit with an oven of larger 'dimensions', or by multiplying the elementary unit, acquiring a certain number of identical ovens, or by setting up a new different oven next to the old one.[17]

The basic point is that these three modes apply not only to equipment, as in the above example, but also to plants, production units and firms. Clearly economies of scale can be obtained by substituting, multiplying or juxtaposing machines within one plant, plants within one production unit, production units within one firm, or firms within one group.

As far as the problem of measuring economies of scale is concerned, the main current methodologies are: statistical cost analysis or engineering estimates.[18]

The first methodology (the cost analysis) is in general based on the cost functions, with the usual strict assumptions about market structure and mathematical proprieties of production functions.[19] Some interpretation problems arise because the production costs level is linked, not only to dimensions of scale, but also to several other factors, such as: the entrepreneurial capacity, industrial relations, the training and specialization level of employees, the age of fixed capital and depreciation accounting system, inputs prices and output mix, the percentage of capacity utilization and the organization of production, the cumulative volume produced, the characteristics of financial markets and the institutional environment.[20] It is very difficult, if not impossible, to isolate

---

[17] Most textbooks on microeconomics illustrate only this particular system (multiplication of identical units) for increasing the scale of production. In fact the formulation of increasing returns through a three-dimensional map of isoquants places the quantity produced (situated on the axis perpendicular to the plane) in relation to the quantities of only two homogeneous inputs (situated on the plane). With reference to the static notion of economies of scale all three methods (substitution, multiplication and juxtaposition) can be represented in analytical terms by comparing different production sets.

[18] In some studies economies of scale are estimated also using census data. On the severe limitations of this approach see Pratten (1988, pp. 26–7). Stigler (1958) proposed a method, called survivor test, in order to measure economies of scale. This method has been applied in several empirical studies (among others, Saving 1962, and Rees 1973). As pointed out by many authors, the survivor test involves serious methodological problems. On ambiguities of its results see, for instance, Shepherd (1967, pp. 113ff), Scherer (1980, pp. 92–3), Pratten (1988, p. 30). The empirical measurement of economies of scale, however, is outside the scope of this study; on this point see the recent review paper by Pratten (1988). Cf. Scherer (1980).

[19] The literature on the subject is immense, see for instance the following review studies: Wiles (1956), Solow (1957), Johnston (1960), Walters (1963), Scherer (1980). For a recent clear introductory book on production functions and their implementation see Heathfield and Wibe (1987). See also: Haltmaier (1984), who measures technological change using activity analysis models, and Betancourt (1986) where the duration of operations and capital utilization are examined formulating cost functions on the basis of duality approach.

[20] As emerged in chapter 9, the cost comparability of different production units may be impaired also by differences in cost accounting conventions (cf. Scherer, 1980, p. 93).

all these factors from the effect of scale dimension upon average costs of production units, to which the microeconomic units under consideration belong. On the other hand, as we shall see, one advantage of the method of estimating economies of scale by comparisons of costs is that it permits not only technical economies of scale to be considered, but also economies of scale in non-industrial intermediate stages such as R&D, administration, selling, marketing, etc. The matrix of production elements, discussed in previous chapters, can provide a methodological basis for collecting statistics on costs related to differently sized production units. It allows indivisibility and technical complementarities, which are important causes in determining economies of scale, to be considered. Moreover, in ascertaining the extent of economies of scale, the fund–flow model can take account not only of intermediate industrial stages but also intermediate stages which belong to other operative levels, such as administration, organization, selling and marketing. Finally, this model does not use firm's budget data, which may present different accounting systems, but it employs a standard methodology for all the microeconomic units in question. This avoids problems of comparability linked with differences in cost accounting conventions.

Engineering estimates consist in assembling data 'from managers, engineers, economists and accountants of the cost of operating at different scales of production' (Pratten, 1988, pp. 28–9). This method is widely considered the most reliable source of information on the cost–scale question at plant level. The main advantage of the engineering approach is that, if the estimates are correct, it is possible to isolate some determinants of costs such as the relative prices, market constraints, transport costs and different fixed capital vintages (*ibid*).[21] However, its weakness is that engineering estimates are based on evaluations by managers and executives, which are subject to a margin of error. In particular, it must be recognized that there is the risk that executives and managers of firms with a large market share might tend to justify its size by overestimating economies at plant level.[22] This kind of overestimation may come about by including (in the measurement of scale economies at plant level) economies which are made on other operational levels, such as economies of scale in R&D, administration, organization, selling, distribution. Consequently, the estimate of the minimum efficient scale (at plant level) may be close to the plant's actual productive capacity.

Cost analysis, based on fund–flow methodology expounded above, and engineering estimates may complement each other. Firstly, it would be useful to check the reliability of cost analysis data, on plant level, by

---

[21] There is a vast literature on engineering estimates of economies of scale. Cf., among others, Bain (1956), Haldi and Whitcomb (1967), Pratten (1971), Weiss (1976).
[22] I am indebted to Augusto Ninni for this point.

comparing engineering estimates. Secondly, cost analysis can give information on non-industrial processes, while engineering estimates provide data at plant level.

11.4   Microeconomic units and operational levels

Economies of scale are often discussed with reference to the firm, which is implicitly identified with a single plant consisting of one or more homogeneous pieces of equipment. But if we abandon this assumption and consider the case where in the same firm there are several production units, several plants, several indivisible elements of production with different productive capacities, then failure to take account of the operational level at which economies of scale take effect may generate substantial problems of interpretation. This is because economies of scale may assume very different forms according to whether they concern the elementary technical unit, the plant, the production unit, or the group of firms linked by relations of collaboration. Each of these microeconomic units corresponds to what I define as an 'operational level'.[23] Problems of interpretation, arising from a dearth of reference to the operative level at which economies of scale work, have led to endless debates between economists of different tendencies.[24]

Analysing economies of scale is difficult because they often work contemporaneously on several operational levels. For example, if a microeconomic unit is replaced by another of greater productive capacity, one may obtain (technical) economies of scale related to the new microeconomic unit at the operational level where the substitution takes place, but also economies related to the plant organization (hence at a higher operational level), and pecuniary economies at the operational level of the firm if the greater scale dimension brings an increase in market power (on the factors underlying economies of scale see the Appendix to this chapter p. 158). Furthermore, since the production process is often decomposable into different intermediate stages with necessarily inter-connected productive capacities, changing the scale of a single intermediate stage will also favour changes in the scale of other intermediate stages at different operational levels.

An increase in scale brought about by the expansion of a single intermediate stage or a certain operational level may lead to reductions in

[23] The importance of different operational levels has been considered, for instance, by E. A. G. Robinson (1931, p. 25) and Silberston (1972, p. 373).

[24] In this respect, Archibugi (1988) writes: 'One has the impression that the microeconomic unit of measure considered by theoreticians of flexible specialization, by neo-Schumpeterians and by post-Keynesians is not at all the same: in fact for the first group it means the plant, for the second it is the firm (in the Anglo-Saxon sense), and for the third it is the financial group. And until the different schools talk about the same unit of measure the debate between them will be like a dialogue between deaf people.' (p. 87)

unit costs in other intermediate stages or operational levels. A firm can increase the dimension of scale at a given level or in a given intermediate stage in order to obtain economies of scale at other operational levels, or to better utilize funds belonging to other intermediate stages. In other words, the firm can increase the dimension of scale of a plant, say, even without obtaining economies of scale at plant level, if this increase in size leads to reduced costs in another intermediate stage, or to providing economies of scale at another operational level. For example, if we suppose that in a given sector there are significant economies of scale in *distribution*, the firms in that sector will tend to increase their production, even without achieving economies of scale in production, simply in order to reach the threshold which allows them to enjoy the economies of scale in distribution, and hence to realize further economies of scale at the level of the firm, the group or network of firms.[25] Therefore, an increased production capacity may involve economies from two different aspects: a technical aspect at plant level, and an organizational aspect, at firm level (Teece, 1980).

We have seen that bottlenecks in productive capacity can be created in the presence of indivisible elements of production. These bottlenecks often lead to the sub-optimal use of the productive capacities of some devices or machines. A scale increase in an intermediate stage may thus create a better balance of processes and reduce the waste of productive capacity in other intermediate stages or operational levels. Hence, in all the cases mentioned above it is not enough to evaluate economies of scale at the level of the single plant; the relations between the dimensions of scale of the different related intermediate stages must be analysed (on this point, see E. A. G. Robinson 1931, p. 25).

In essence, increasing the dimension of scale at a particular operational level may trigger a series of changes in input requirements, and possible production reorganization at other operational levels or in other related intermediate stages. However, this reciprocal influence between operational levels and intermediate stages is not necessarily always positive. In fact it is conceivable that an increase in the dimension of scale at a certain operational level might involve increases and reductions in costs at other operational levels (or intermediate stages). Hence a change that may represent an economy of scale at a certain operational level may lead to

[25] This approach to economies of scale is based on the consideration of the links among different activities (or sub-processes). Moss expresses a similar view in the following terms: 'A backward linkage is a technological relationship between one production activity which is being expanded (or perhaps contracted) and the production processes which provide its inputs. A forward linkage is a technological relationship whereby the outputs from...expanding production activities can enter other production activities as inputs' (1981, pp. 60–1). The origin of the concepts of backward and forward linkages is in Hirschman (1958, p. 100).

a diseconomy of scale at another operational level or in another intermediate stage. What counts, therefore, is the net overall result of a change in the scale of production for the firm.

The fund–flow model can handle this double relationship resulting from an increase in scale: (i) the 'vertical' links between different operational levels, and (ii) the 'horizontal' links between different intermediate stages. Hence it is possible to deal with the problem of separability of the different intermediate stages without assuming, as Stigler (1951) does, the hypothesis of *independence* among costs in different intermediate stages, which must be assumed in traditional analysis based on static curves of average and marginal costs.[26]

11.5   Economies of scale and technological change

The *minimum efficient scale* (MES) or the *minimum optimum scale* (MOS) is defined as the scale at which unit costs cease to fall.[27] Technical change leads not only to a change in the minimum efficient scale (MES), but often also to the expansion of what we may call the *range of scale* of a family of technical units used in producing a given commodity. An expansion of the range of scale is obtained by lowering the minimum scale and/or raising the maximum scale which is technically possible for that family of technical units.

In recent years lowering the minimum technical scale has taken place often thanks to the application of new technologies. However, still, in cases where the minimum technical scale of a piece of equipment or a machine (i.e. its minimum productive capacity) is unchanged (or even increased), new technologies may be compatible with lesser dimensions in production unit (or firm) overall scale. The reasons for a lowering in the

---

[26] The basic idea developed in Stigler (1951) is present in A. E. G. Robinson (1931): 'There is no reason to suppose that all the different functions of management and of manufacture will reach their optimum size at one and the same total output of the product. The problem, therefore, arises of reconciling the different optimum sizes of different parts of the same organisation' (p. 94).

[27] Pratten proposes the following definition of the minimum efficient scale for empirical research purposes: 'the minimum scale above which any possible doubling in scale would reduce total unit costs by less than five per cent'...(1971, p. 56; 1988, p. 6). Numerous empirical studies on economies of scale (Florence, 1953; Bain, 1956; Johnston, 1958 and 1960; Pratten, 1971; Dean, 1976), though they differ in the methodologies adopted and in the statistical sources they use (see Walters, 1963; Gold, 1981), seem to agree as to the presence of economies of scale in most of the industries examined. In particular, on the basis of the data given by Pratten (1971, pp. 269–77) on forty-four sectors belonging to twenty-five different British industries, the minimum efficient scale for a single plant corresponds in seven cases to 100% and more of the whole production of the United Kingdom, and in 10 other cases it is over 25%. Of course, the share of MES production on total production depends on the extension of market. As argued by Scherer (1980, p. 98), how high concentration must be to secure production efficiency depends upon the balance between production techniques and market size.

overall dimensional threshold of firms in implementing new technologies lie mainly in the decrease of their price and in space occupied, as well as in the progressive simplification of their use, in terms of a reduction of training times inside and outside the production unit. The decrease in machine prices determines in some cases a lowering of the financial burden, which makes possible a sub-optimal utilization of the new machines by small production units. The spread of computers or equipment based on microelectronics in small firms and even in families is a very significant example of this tendency of the entry threshold to drop.

At the same time, technological change creates a tendency to increase the dimensions of the maximum technical scale attainable by raising the productive capacity of the machines through increasing the number of parallel processes and/or the speed of the individual elementary processes. There are numerous examples of such increases in the maximum scale: they have occurred in most means of transport (ships, especially tankers, lorries, trains, etc.), thanks to increases in volume and speed; and in computers thanks to increases in memory size and calculation speed, and the possibility of running several programmes at once.

Computer-based technology may favour both small and large-scale enterprises, depending on the technical solutions adopted in response to environmental conditions. In this sense some innovation may be 'centripetal' or 'centrifugal' according to the economic conditions in which they are applied. Hence, in an environmental situation favourable to the development of the small firm, centrifugal characteristics mainly will be exploited. While, in a context where large dimensions are an essential condition for competitiveness, firms will take advantage of the centripetal characteristics of the available techniques.[28]

When an increase in size involves the introduction of a new piece of equipment, there is a progressive improvement in the use of the new machines, due to learning processes. This means a constant, if slight, increase in productivity. From this point of view, as has been brought out by Alchian (1959) and Arrow (1962a), cost is a function not only of the volume of production per unit of time, but also of the total volume of production planned and actually realized (accumulated volume).

11.6   Concluding remarks

Three points that are worth recapitulating have emerged in the course of the analysis carried out in this chapter.

---

[28] The distinction between 'centrifugal' and 'centripetal' technologies was introduced by Blair (1972, chapter 6).

Traditional microeconomics textbooks have accustomed us to thinking in terms of *substitutability* of homogeneous and divisible inputs, for a given productive scale, and in terms of the new *proportional increase* of all the inputs if the productive scale changes (returns of scale). However, the complementary relations between inputs are rather rigid in any given dimension of scale and usually change when the scale of production increases. In fact, a variation in proportion between inputs occurs either because an increase in production reduces the spare capacity of inputs (within a given productive scale), or because the complementary relationship changes when the volume of production moves to a different scale. In the first case, there is an increase in the degree of utilization of a microeconomic unit, such as a piece of equipment or a plant; the second case involves a move to microeconomic units with a greater productive capacity. In other words one should distinguish between increasing returns involving a single given microeconomic unit, owing to its more efficient use, and increasing returns of scale, which arise from changing to a more efficient microeconomic unit. The former depend on reducing levels of sub-optimality, that is to say, on bringing the quantity actually produced nearer to the optimal productive capacity of the microeconomic unit in question. Such a reduction may come about through the reduction of idle times. In the second case, the increase in the volume of production, and the associated possible increase in efficiency, involves a change in scale dimension, linked to the use of equipment with a larger productive capacity. Therefore proportions among inputs mainly change together with changes in the volume of production.

The second point is that economies of scale have the particular characteristic of acting at different operational levels and of affecting individual intermediate stages to different degrees, so that unit costs in relation to the quantities produced at the various operational levels and intermediate stages are interdependent. Hence the balance of quantities produced, according to different productive capacities of the various microeconomic units, must be considered. For the purposes of an empirical analysis of scale economies, therefore, the methodology presented in Part 2 should be applied to all different intermediate stages at different operational levels, including both industrial transformation, as well as non-industrial processes such as organizational and administrative intermediate stages.

Finally, the third point which emerges – not only in this chapter but throughout the analysis so far – is that efficiency, and hence costs, cannot be attributed to one single variable, the size of the scale of production. The effect of economies of scale on average total costs and on the size of firms is certainly important, but I cannot help agreeing with E. A. G. Robinson that 'many economists tend to overrate the importance of scale' and to underrate the importance of any factors other than the size of firms. 'I regard it as a sad consequence of the habit of drawing exaggeratedly steep two-dimensional cost curves, relating costs exclusively to quantities', he writes (1931, p. 155). In reality, the efficiency and efficacy of production, which together determine the competitiveness of a firm, are linked not only with its size but also with factors which can sometimes offset the effects of size on production costs. Among these are the factors I mentioned at the beginning of this chapter: capital endowment, the characteristics of entrepreneurship, technical training, market characteristics, regulations affecting employment, tax legislation, mechanisms for the spread and adoption of new technologies, the life of each product, cumulated output over time, organizational aspects and the time profile of production processes. All these factors change in relation to different institutional environments.

Appendix: factors underlying economies of scale and diseconomies of scale

A11.1 Economies of scale

Four different groups of factors may be mentioned, which combine to produce economies of scale: technical factors, statistical factors, organizational and distributional factors, and factors deriving from an increase in market power.

I Technical factors

Among the *technical factors* which cause economies of scale we can identify those related to the three-dimensionality of space, to heat dissipation, or to the presence of intermediate stages or production elements which exist in fixed quantities regardless of the scale adopted.

(i) *Economies of increased dimensions.* Increasing the size of machines often makes it possible to reduce the costs (per unit of product) involved in the construction and management of plants. These economies derive from the three-dimensionality of space – that is to say, the fact that in the case of containers (cisterns, tubes, ovens) the cost increases approximately in proportion to the surface area of the walls, while the productive capacity increases in proportion to the volume (for example, a twofold increase in the diameter of a boiler gives a fourfold increase in productive capacity) (see E. A. G. Robinson 1931, pp. 22–3; Scherer 1980, pp. 82–3; Pratten 1988, p. 10). In some productions an increase in plant size reduces not only the investment cost per unit of product, but also the unit costs of the operation, thanks to the reduction in heat loss obtained by lowering the surface/volume ratio of the plants.

Economies of increased dimensions arise not from the *indivisibility of production elements*, but from the three-dimensionality of space, which in itself has nothing to do with indivisibility. In fact it is possible to construct containers (tubes, cisterns, ovens) over a continuous range of increasing dimensions. This has been brought out explicitly by Kaldor (1972, p. 93), who has changed his position on relations between increasing returns and indivisibility which he expressed in his article of 1934.

158

Koopmans had formerly advanced the opposite thesis. Examining the 'interesting exchange of opinions between Nicholas Kaldor (1934) and E. H. Chamberlin (1949) on the problem of whether increasing returns of scale are wholly or necessarily due to indivisibility', he in fact observes:

I have not found one example of increasing returns to scale in which there is not some indivisible commodity in the surrounding circumstances. The oft-quoted case of a pipeline whose diameter is continuously variable can be seen as a case of choosing between alternative pieces of capital equipment, differing in diameter, used to carry oil from Tulsa to Chicago, say. No matter what diameter is selected, one entire pipeline of the requisite length is needed to render this service. Half the length of line does not carry half the flow of oil from Tulsa to Chicago. (Koopmans, 1957, p. 152, n. 3).

One might easily object, however, that increasing returns in the case of the oil pipeline mentioned are due to the change in diameter over the same length, as the length of the oil pipeline is of course not influenced by the change in the dimension of scale. Now, as we have just mentioned, changing to a different diameter involves no element of indivisibility, since oil pipelines can in principle be made in a continuous range of diameters. Thus Koopmans here seems to confuse the presence of indivisibility (each oil pipe is an indivisible element) with the cause of economies of scale (the three-dimensionality of space). In the case of all sort of containers, using the simple terms of static cost curves, indivisibility of production elements may thus be responsible for a decrease in direct unit costs (up to a certain point) of a simple indivisible plant (if the plant is divisible, direct unit costs are constant), but not for a decrease in the (long-run) total unit cost obtained by going from one indivisible plant to another. Then, we can say that indivisibility of production elements would determine the *form* of the (short-run) direct unit cost curves rather than their *relative position* within a long-run diagram formed by several individual plant curves.[29]

(ii) *Economies of threshold dimensions.* By economies of threshold dimensions I mean the reduction of total unit costs arising from the presence of indivisible intermediate stages which remain constant for all possible scale dimensions in the overall process of production. In fact the technical characteristics of many production processes require some intermediate stages whose dimensions are (wholly or partly) independent of the production scale of the overall production process to which they belong. A frequently mentioned example of an intermediate stage with minimum activation threshold (which is the same for all dimensions of scale) is the production of a first copy of a book (for proofreading) or a prototype for later production of a serial model. In such cases the

---

[29] The difference between economies of plant and economies of scale is brought out clearly, for example, by Chamberlin (1948 and 1949), Georgescu-Roegen (1964), and Kaldor (1972).

economies of scale derive from the fact that as the overall productive capacity increases these fixed costs are divided among an ever larger number of units produced.

(iii) *Economies of superior techniques.* An increase in scale dimensions often means that techniques giving increases in productivity can be used. For instance, as scale is increased, automatic machinery may be used instead of manually operated machinery (Pratten, 1988, p. 12). This also applies to information technology being used in production and administration processes. The role of the new information technology is discussed in chapter 12.

II   Statistical factors

By statistical factors I mean the possibility of reducing any type of stocks and reserves (for instance raw materials, machine spare parts, circulating capital) by increasing the overall quantities involved in production. These economies are called *economies of massed reserves or resources* (see E. A. G. Robinson, 1931, pp. 26–7). As is well known, according to the theorem of the central limit (or the law of large numbers) the gap between the sample average and the universe average narrows when the sample becomes larger. Now the greater the number of resources involved the smaller, in proportion, is the quantity of inventory necessary to provide for possible unforeseen circumstances. For instance, an increase in the number of machines of the same type, used in the same enterprise, gives a saving in the number of spare parts that must be stocked to repair possible faults. Similarly, an increase in the quantity produced and sold involves a less than proportional increase in the inventories. It is a fact well known that an inventory should increase only in proportion to the square root of the quantity produced and sold. In other words, if sales of an item double, the inventory should not be doubled – it should be increased to much less than 200 per cent of its original amount (Baumol, 1961, p. 10).

Moreover, as Pratten rightly observes, a 'large company's ability to spread risk may enable it to take greater risk. Large concerns have a greater opportunity for experimenting with new methods and introducing new products without jeopardising the future of the business if particular methods or products are unsuccessful' (Pratten, 1988, p. 12).

In conclusion, the indivisibility of *production elements* cannot be considered the cause of statistical economies. There are many cases in which economies of massed reserves exist in the presence of perfectly divisible inputs (such as grain or cement).

III   Organizational and distribution factors

Organizational, managerial, selling and *distribution economies* arise from all the cooperative advantages of team production, from a greater specialization of funds, and a better use of indivisible resources. These economies of scale concern both the organization of directly productive intermediate stages, including the various production services such as promotion, marketing,[30] research and development (see C. Freeman 1974; Kamien and Schwartz 1982; Scherer 1984; Pratten 1988), distribution and sales etc. In Part 1 we examined the advantages in terms of productivity, and hence in terms of costs, of an increase in the scale dimension which allows a reorganization of production elements within the same intermediate stage and a greater specialization of those elements. We have seen that the scale increase of one intermediate stage may lead not only to economies of scale within that intermediate stage, but also to production increases by other intermediate stages, which may bring about further economies of scale or merely a reduction in sub-optimal levels of production. In the latter case, when the quantity actually produced comes closer to the (optimum) productive capacity economies of plant can be exploited in addition to economies of scale in the strict sense.

From the point of view of organizational economies, it must be noted that the entrepreneur or executive staff's capacity to coordinate can be amplified as the company grows by adopting different control systems and allocating many administrative and organizational tasks to specialist staff. On organizational and administrative economies, Scherer argues that with an increased size of firm, staff functions are designed to supply decision-making information to the chief executive, communication is simplified and accelerated by technological innovations, techniques of cost accounting and budgetary control are brought to a high state of perfection, and ways are devised to make large organizations manageable through decentralizing operating authority and financial responsibility to product line or territorial division (Scherer, 1980, p. 86; cf. Penrose, 1959). In short, growth in the firm's size also increases the division of labour in organizational and administrative sub-processes.

IV   Economies through control of markets

Lastly, there are economies achievable *through increased power over the markets of inputs and output*. All other things being equal, an increase in the dimensions of scale of a firm or group of firms, in relation to the scale of the industry, increases its market power with regard to both inputs and

[30] On the relations between promotion, marketing and economies of scale see Scherer (1980 pp. 108ff.).

output. In fact a firm that uses more resources can enjoy advantages arising from the purchasing conditions of raw materials and intermediate goods (*pecuniary economies*). Similarly a large firm can obtain substantial advantages in raising capital. At the same time, a rise in productive capacity may increase the element of discretion in fixing the output price.[31]

A11.2   Diseconomies of scale

As mentioned before, *increasing returns of scale* derive from the possibility of augmenting the inputs in optimal proportions to the various dimensions of scale. *Decreasing returns of scale*, on the other hand, occur when there is some restriction that prevents some elements of production from increasing in optimal proportions.[32]

We have seen that the need to harmonize the productive capacities of machines, plants and intermediate stages in production units implies an increase according to the lowest common multiple of the different productive capacities. Thus, development of a production unit takes place in leaps rather than along a continuum of increasing dimensions of scale. At any given moment the technical unit, such as a piece of equipment, a machine or a continuously operating plant, has a maximum projectable dimension of scale. Beyond that point technical problems are created which would involve a rise in costs, thus making it inadvisable to increase the dimensions of scale. Hence, technical economies of scale may operate up to this dimensional maximum, beyond which it is necessary to duplicate the plant (Pratten, 1988, p. 16). Therefore, technical problems which arise above a certain dimension appear to be a 'limitation on the source of economies of scale, rather than a source of diseconomies' (*ibid.*).

The impossibility of increasing such elements creates 'disproportions' that reduce the efficiency of production. This holds good not only for physical inputs but also for labour services, and in particular for organizational activities. Organizational diseconomies, in fact, arise if organizational inputs cannot grow as they need to in order to enjoy economies of scale. In other words, organizational diseconomies can come into existence only if one assumes that the organizational capacity is given.[33] In this study, however, we assume that organizational capacity

---

[31] Of course, firm's pricing policy depends not only on its relative size. For example, recent literature on contestable markets has emphasised the importance of sunk costs and entry conditions in determining the equilibrium price. See Baumol (1982), and Baumol, Panzar, Willig (1982).

[32] The analytical difference between increasing and decreasing returns of scale was highlighted by Sraffa in his 1925 and 1926 articles.

[33] It is well-known that the hypothesis of a given organizational capacity for the individual firm, but not for the industry as whole, is needed to obtain – even in the long run – decreasing returns at firm level.

may increase with the size of the enterprise, by the employment of specialized personnel and more efficient organizational and control schemes. One cannot but share Pratten's observation that the 'competitiveness of some giant companies such as IBM, Toyota, Boeing, Siemens, etc. shows that the problems of managing very large organizations and motivating employees of large organizations are surmountable' (1988, p. 112). The development of a firm's size involves, in fact, the application of new technological opportunities and new organizational systems designed to avoid disproportions between production elements and mismatches among their productive and organizational capacities, which might cancel out the positive effects of returns of scale on the productivity of those elements.

In short, increasing returns of scale act as an incentive to a firm's development, whereas decreasing returns of scale, *at any given moment*, tend to limit its development. However, technical change tends to extend these limits to growth, which explains why in the past few decades we have seen a considerable increase in the maximum size of numerous families of machines or devices, plants and means of transport (for example, chemical plants, aeroplanes, oil tankers, computers, etc.). Technical change and reformulating organizational models often aim to stretch these limits in order to exploit increasing returns.

Decreasing returns of scale involve a drop in the average *physical productivity* of individual inputs; hence, when scale dimension increases so does the total average cost (with unchanged prices of inputs). As far as dimensions of scale are concerned, they may be linked not only to a fall in physical productivity but also to a rise in input prices. In fact, restraints on the increase of some elements of production may lead to an excess of demand over the supply of these elements, and this may make their prices rise (*pecuniary diseconomies*). An example of pecuniary diseconomies consists in the increasing difficulty in finding workers whose skills are similar to the production unit's job requirement. In this case the production unit must face a wage increase, for certain skills, as the labour demand rises in the production unit area. To summarise, *diseconomies of scale* may be due either to a technical factor (decreasing returns of scale) or to an economic one (rising prices of inputs accompanying an increase in size).[34]

Finally, the cost of delivering output to customers may counteract economies of scale at individual plant level. In fact, as observed by Scherer: 'If more output is produced in a plant, more must be sold. To sell

---

[34] As mentioned in section 4.3 (chapter 4), economies and diseconomies of scale resulting from changes in input prices are incompatible with the hypothesis of *ceteris paribus*, essential to a partial equilibrium analysis.

more, it may be necessary to reach out to more distant customers. This in turn can lead to increased transportation costs per unit sold' (1980, p. 88). Obviously, for bulky, low-value commodities 'like sand or beer bottles unit transportation costs rise relatively rapidly with distance shipped. For compact, high-value items like transistors and machine tools, they rise slowly' (*ibid.*). A very common way of reducing the incidence of transportation costs and of exploiting economies of scale at firm level (organizational, financial, administrative, and selling economies) is to distribute production units geographically so that transport costs and technical economies (at plant or production unit level) offset each other.

12 Flexible production systems and economies of scope

Flexibility expresses the capacity for adjustment to variations in external conditions, in other words, it is the ability to learn from experience and change plans over time.[1] The greater the uncertainty, the greater, of course, is the need for flexibility. In fact, flexibility is required if environmental conditions change rapidly and if there is a low degree of predictability with regard to the direction and magnitude of changes. 'True uncertainty' depends on the inability, or impossibility, of considering all future contingencies and their probability distribution.[2] If there is a low degree of predictability, agents' choices are taken in a situation of 'bounded rationality'. In short, in the presence of uncertainty, flexible action tends to reduce the degree of irreversibility of economic decisions, so as to better react should something unforeseen or unforeseeable occur.[3]

In the following pages I shall devote particular attention to one aspect of flexibility which has aroused increasing interest in recent years: flexibility of production processes. Production flexibility permits output

[1] On different meanings of flexibility see: Stigler (1939) who discusses flexibility in the context of static decision-making; Marschak and Nelson (1962) where flexibility makes subsequent actions less costly or preserves more choices; Koopmans (1964) on flexibility of future preference; Jones and Ostroy (1984) who consider flexibility in relation to the probability distributions of payoffs over time in a sequential decision context. See also the interesting discussions in Merkhofer (1975), Piore (1980a and 1980b), OECD (1986), Mills (1986), Vercelli (1986), Boyer and Wolleb, eds. (1986), Rubery, Tarling and Wilkinson (1987), Cohendet and Llerena (1988), Lanzara (1988), Del Monte and Esposito (1989), Amendola et al. (1990), Boje (1990).

[2] On 'true uncertainty' and probability, see Keynes (1921, chapter 6; 1936, pp. 148, 152, 168, 316; 1937, pp. 112–14), F. H. Knight (1921), Carabelli (1988, pp. 47, 58–9, 199, 212–22).

[3] As observed by Jones and Ostroy: 'The more variable are a decision-maker's beliefs, the more flexible is the position he will choose … One position is more flexible than another if it leaves available a larger set of future positions at any given level of cost. … flexible options are attractive … because they are good stores of options' (1984, pp. 13ff.). These authors provide a formalization of these concepts in a sequential decision context; on this point see also Vercelli (1986, p. 133). For a discussion on the relationship in Keynes between uncertainty, irreversible time and the analysis of decisions to invest in terms of expectations, see Carabelli (1988, p. 216).

flows to be regulated following the evolution of market conditions. As will become clear, production flexibility is not an exclusive prerogative of either small or large firms (or production units). It is even independent of the technology adopted, as it may be achieved through the flexible organization of rigid equipment or production units.

In industrial countries, during the 1970s, increasing uncertainty – due to greater economic instability and the saturation of some important markets, which have progressively become substitution markets – led to an increased need for production flexibility. This in turn led to a rise in complexity, to which firms reacted in two different ways. On the one hand, they tried to adapt their organizational systems, and on the other, they began to exploit the technological opportunities offered by computer-based technology. This technology has reduced flexibility costs, especially through drastic reductions in set-up times, in the quantity of goods in progress held in inventories, and hence in the overall duration of the production process.

Many of the new flexible systems using computer-based technology involve such a high investment per operator that they have to run for twenty-four hours a day. This means that increased attention must be given to the length and distribution of idle times of machines, the regulation of working hours and, in particular, the structure of shifts. Finally, the introduction of computer-controlled technology implies a profound change in the quality of inputs and outputs, as well as in skill requirements and in the content of tasks and jobs.

In conclusion, organizational and technical innovations aiming to increase flexibility lead to a change in those elements of production which are mostly excluded from analyses based on estimating the production functions. The lack of an appropriate production process model is particularly evident in the theoretical treatment of the flexibility phenomenon. In the following pages, an analytical description of the production process, based on a fund–flow model, will throw considerable light on some important problems involving flexible systems of production.

In the next two sections the different meanings of the term flexibility in the economic literature will be discussed briefly, with particular reference to production flexibility. Then the link between uncertainty and flexibility will be examined. Lastly, in sections 12.4 and 12.5, production flexibility will be analysed, taking account first of the organizational aspects and then of the technical ones. Including both organizational and technical aspects in the analysis of production flexibility means that important recent trends of the industrial structure and market forms of industrialized countries can be taken into account.

12.1 Different concepts of flexibility

Various notions of flexibility appear in the economic literature and there is still not a definitive taxonomy concerning flexibility in economics. Some of these definitions are closely interdependent; others oppose or exclude each other because they are concerned with non-homogeneous analytical contexts. Before proceeding to the main subject of this chapter – the analysis of the causes and effects of applying *flexible methods of production* – it is worth looking at the interconnections and possible differences between the main concepts of flexibility used in the economic literature. It will be seen that some of these definitions are quite different from the notion of flexibility used in the present analysis.

The term flexibility can be used with reference to a number of factors, such as:

(a) The organization of a firm (or group of firms) and the technical characteristics of its (or their) production elements (production flexibility).
(b) Conditions of the *labour market*. This involves:
    Functional flexibility, i.e. the ability to adjust workers' skills within the firm. It implies internal mobility across tasks, changing job assignment, improved job design, flexible job boundaries, training and retraining.
    Numerical flexibility that involves the modification of the number of employees (external numerical flexibility), or changes in the number of working hours per employee (internal numerical flexibility).
    Dualistic flexibility, due to the presence of a dualism between strong and weak segments of the labour market.
    Wage flexibility in relation to the labour market conditions.
(c) *Market* conditions affecting *raw materials* and *semifinished goods*; this kind of flexibility refers both to the sensitivity of inputs prices to market conditions, and the ability of the intermediate commodities suppliers to respond to variations in the inputs markets caused by changes in final commodities markets (raw materials and semi-finished goods market flexibility).

Because of the diversity of meanings and concepts of flexibility there is a risk of 'semantic slippage' which could complicate its analysis and create some misunderstandings. As noted at the beginning of this chapter, in some cases the various notions of flexibility are closely linked and in others they may be opposed because of the different assumptions involved in the analysis.

Production flexibility expresses the capacity for adjustment to variations in external conditions; hence it is an essentially dynamic concept. Flexibility in production processes may refer both to the capacity to change processes and goods produced, i.e. to the innovative capacity (strategic flexibility), and to the organizational and technical characteristics of a given process in the absence of technical change (operational flexibility).[4] In other words, *strategic flexibility* implies the ability to change production processes, production elements endowment and the qualities of outputs in relation to changes in environmental conditions. On the other hand, what I term *operational flexibility* is related to the possibility of varying the quantities produced within a given mix, using a given productive structure.

Strategic flexibility is often considered an index of innovative capacity. The latter, however, is a wider concept: innovative capacity, unlike flexibility, does not simply react to changes in the environment. It includes changes which create new needs, which anticipate the evolution of the market. On the other hand, operational flexibility does not presuppose technical change, but it may nevertheless favour the introduction of new processes and new goods, and hence of strategic flexibility.

According to the circumstances change can be dealt with either through a flexible structure or by changing the existing structure. Strategic flexibility involves a change in production processes or products, but not necessarily a change in the degree of operational flexibility of the firm or production unit. In short, even if innovation increases the flexibility of the production structure at the macroeconomic level, it does not (necessarily) increase the operational flexibility of the production unit in which the innovation is introduced. For instance, the notion of technological flexibility adopted by Vercelli (1986) concerns the flexibility of the production structure as a whole, including strategic flexibility and operational flexibility.[5]

Operational flexibility concerns both the organizational structure and the technique used; hence it includes both organizational flexibility and technical flexibility. The former refers to the capability to organize rigid

---

[4] Strategic flexibility is also called dynamic or long-run flexibility, while the concept of operational flexibility is similar, in many respects, to the definition of static or short-run flexibility applied by Cohendet and Llerena (1988), cf. Del Monte and Esposito (1989).

[5] Still broader is the concept of 'flexible specialization' introduced by Piore and Sabel. By 'flexible specialization' they mean a model of organization of firms and markets based on the development of small firms with high flexibility and a propensity for innovation, specialized labour and collaboration between firms (Piore and Sabel, 1984, p. 17; Sabel and Zeitlin 1982). See also Storper (1989). For a critical discussion on 'flexible specialization', see Minsky (1985), Murray (1987), Landes (1987), Williams et al. (1987), Hyman (1988), Archibugi (1988), Amin (1989a).

microeconomic units in a flexible way, in order to guarantee variability in the mix of outputs; the latter refers to characteristics of individual machines, i.e. the capacity of produce different goods with the same funds. No deterministic relationship exists between technical flexibility and organizational flexibility in the sense that technical flexibility does not require organizational flexibility, because it is conceivable that polyvalent machines or plants may be utilized within a rigid organizational structure. Conversely, a production unit can achieve a degree of organizational flexibility, through the combination and organization of inflexible (highly standardized mono-use) machines. Likewise, a firm can secure organizational flexibility by arranging the activity of several mono-product units (or even firms).

There are of course many connections between strategic flexibility and labour market flexibility, as a change in production processes may require an adaptation of skills (functional flexibility), and an adjustment of the number of operators (numerical flexibility). On the other hand, variations in the labour market may induce changes in the qualitative and quantitative composition of the labour force and in the organization of production processes.

Production flexibility entails workers being subjected to turbulence and changes in productive activity, since it implies workers are actively involved in the production process and rapidly adapting their own skills to changes in products and processes. In many situations the demand for greater functional flexibility is met by compensation mechanisms that make changes more acceptable to workers and to society. Thus it happens that *some forms of flexibility are counterbalanced by forms of rigidity*. Functional flexibility may be accompanied by a low numerical flexibility, so that functional flexibility is compensated (and limited) by the stability of the worker–firm links. For example, this is the case in the large Japanese firms where there is a high degree of functional and internal numerical flexibility, but little external numerical flexibility (employees are said to have 'a job for life'), with a strong dualistic flexibility in the labour market.[6] Moreover, in some contexts the workers direct involvement may be achieved or simply encouraged by forms of participation, co-management and co-operation which can result in a reduction of external numerical flexibility. In still other situations strategic and operational flexibility can be obtained through external numerical flexibility, within the context of a social system that guarantees a network of protection, such as unemployment benefits and opportunities for retraining. This

---

[6] On compensation mechanisms between flexibilities and rigidities see Salvati (1988, pp. 80ff.), cf. Dore (1986).

reduces the costs of external mobility and hence facilitates movement from one firm to another. In this case, external numerical flexibility (in relation to variations in firm production levels) is obtained in a way that conflicts with the assumption of perfect competition. In fact, external mobility, encouraged by forms of insurance or welfare provisions which protect workers against the risk of losing their income (unemployment subsidies), undoubtedly limits the competitiveness of the labour market.

There are marked contrasts between authors on the subject of *wage flexibility*.[7] It is well known that different theoretical assumptions on returns of scale and market conditions lead to opposing conclusions on this issue.[8] On the other hand, econometric studies have shown that there seems to be no *strong* relationship between wages and employment (see Reichlin 1986; OECD 1986; Summers and Wadhwani 1987; Zenezini 1989).

As far as flexibility of inputs markets is concerned, it is well known that in conditions of perfect competition, an excess of supply over demand for a given commodity leads to a reduction in the price of that commodity which tends to eliminate the excess. In this connection it should be noted that the assumption of flexibility of inputs markets and the assumption of strategic and organizational flexibility refer to diverse market structures. In fact, flexibility of prices in inputs markets requires conditions of perfect competition, whereas the notion of strategic and organizational flexibility, with reference to a range of products, presupposes product differentiation and low predictability of market evolution, and thus implicitly involves market structures which are not perfectly competitive.

It should be stressed that each specific context features a combination of rigidities and flexibilities that vary from one situation to another and from one historical moment to another. What has been said so far about the relations between the different concepts of flexibility validates the thesis proposed in Part 1 regarding the need to consider the organization of production processes as the outcome of a combination of several elements whose characteristics may take very different and specific forms in different types of firms. In fact, in market economies different organizational systems can live side by side, and each organization system reflects not only the institutional environment in which the firm operates and which is formed by a set of conditions concerning: financial structure,

---

[7] Wage flexibility may be defined as follows: 'Nominal wage rates are flexible if they rise pretty promptly and rapidly when there is excess demand for labor, and fall pretty promptly and rapidly when there is excess supply for labor' (Hahn and Solow, 1985, p. 1).

[8] On this point Hahn and Solow (1985) observe that 'there are perfectly reasonable circumstances, with a heavy dose of increasing returns to scale, in which equilibria with higher employment have higher real wage rates. In such economies even real-wage flexibility may create more problems than it solves' (p. 1).

economic policies, social security system, industrial relations and market characteristics. Moreover, for any given environmental context, there is a subjective element of managerial choice which contributes to determine the specificity of each firm. This is not to deny, however that, depending on the evolution of environmental factors, one organizational system may, in a given economic system or geographical area and at a given moment, be identified as the prevalent one or as the one with the greatest potential for development. For instance, it is easy to predict a strong development of flexible organizational systems and technologies in industrial countries. Sections 12.3 and 12.5 below are devoted to examining reasons that explain the growing need for flexibility and to some considerations on the impact of computer-based technology.

It is worth stressing in concluding this section that even flexible organizational systems and technology are characterized by a blend of flexibilities and rigidities, determined by the influence of the evolution of institutional and social factors.

12.2   Adaptability, operational flexibility and economies of scope

Flexibility in production systems is the ability to adjust production to meet different customer needs, and, in particular, the capacity to change the mix of products according to market evolution. This change may refer to the quantities or to the qualities of output mix. As already indicated, strategic flexibility may involve changes in product quality, while operational flexibility involves only quantitative change within a given mix of outputs. Thus, strategic flexibility implies the possibility of modifying plants in order to change the productive capacity of single production lines (alterability) and the quality of the mix of products (convertibility). In a changing environment a certain degree of strategic flexibility may be achieved, for instance, by buying less durable equipment (see Rosenberg 1976c, p. 109).

Operational flexibility (in relation to a quantitative change in the output mix) should not be confused with adaptability; the latter in fact refers only to variations in the quantity produced of a single commodity. Generally the economic literature on production flexibility does not consider variations in the product mix and concentrates only on adaptability, basically dealing with exercises in comparative statics for different degrees of adaptability attributed to different production structures (see, e.g. Stigler 1939, pp. 110ff.; Marschak and Nelson 1962; Mills 1986). We saw in chapter 11 (section 11.2) that a mono-product plant is more adaptable the less its unit costs vary with the quantity produced – i.e. the lower unit cost elasticity is in relation to the volume of production. It is generally assumed that there is a trade-off between adaptability and efficiency. Since greater adaptability makes plant more approximately efficient over a large range of output, it reduces efficiency at the optimum technical output level.[9] If there is a trade-off between production flexibility and efficiency, the firm's choice, regarding which plant and organizational system to adopt, depends on the level of flexibility required by environmental conditions in relation to flexibility costs.

The indivisibility of production elements and 'sunk-cost irreversibility' of investment in capital goods generally imply a low adaptability level. Hence, firms pursue adaptability by increasing plant divisibility and by reducing its fixed cost. In short, adaptability may be obtained by:

(i) numerical flexibility;
(ii) functional flexibility;
(iii) hiring of equipment;
(iv) keeping inventories that serve to compensate for quantitative fluctuations in demand;
(v) keeping in-house old machines and equipment, which are already fully amortized, and which are brought back into use only when the demand is particularly high;
(vi) employing sub-contractors, so that variability of demand is largely transferred to suppliers.

Adaptability in the output quantity may concern different operational levels, and then the technical characteristics of equipment or the organization of the firm. In fact, as argued above, a firm can have an adaptable production using adaptable funds or organizing rigid machines in a 'flexible way'.

Operational flexibility (in the mix of outputs) depends on the degree of *adaptability* in the single processes of the commodities produced. In fact, operational flexibility lies in the possibility of changing the quantities of various outputs, increasing the production of some commodities while at the same time reducing the amount of other commodities produced in the same range.

Product differentiation involves a cost when it leads to a loss of economies of scale inherent in standardized productions. Basically,

[9] In the Stigler (1939) analysis the trade-off between adaptability (flexibility, in his terminology) and efficiency is expressed by the slope and position of *short-period* average cost curves: the unit cost curve of a more adaptable plant is flatter, but with the minimum point higher, than the unit cost curve of a less adaptable plant. According to the different hypotheses about the probability distribution of the quantity demanded, the firm can determine its 'optimal plant' in relation to the expected range of output. Cf. Marschak and Nelson (1962, pp. 42ff.), Mills (1986), Del Monte and Esposito (1989, pp. 9–11), Cohendet and Llerena (1988, pp. 252–3).

differentiated production will be more costly than standardized production when the loss of economies of scale is greater than the economies of scope that can be obtained when the different processes are carried on within the same firm or production unit. There are economies of scope when it is less costly to 'combine' the productions of two or more commodities than to perform them 'separately'.[10] We have economies of scope if it is possible to economize on some shareable production elements or intermediate stages by saturating their productive capacities. Generally only the combination of different production lines within one firm is considered, but the economies of scope may operate at different operational levels. In fact, there are economies of scope at the following levels.

Firm level, where it is less costly to combine two different production units, which produce different commodities within one firm, than to produce the same commodities in different firms. For instance, a firm's know-how applied in some intermediate stages, such as administration, marketing, organization, etc., can find a variety of product applications (on this point, see Teece 1980, pp. 226, 231).

Production unit level, where it is less costly to combine two or more plants producing different commodities in one production unit than to produce the same commodities in different production units (within the same firm).

Plant level where it is less costly to produce two or more commodities by means of one plant than to produce them by means of two or more separate plants (within the same production unit).

Finally, at *product line* level, when it is less costly to produce two or more commodities on one production line than on more than one production lines (within the same plant).

In economic literature flexibility is often linked with the existence of economies of scope. It should be noted, however, that economies of scope make multi-production within a single microeconomic unit desirable,[11] *but they do not determine* its degree of flexibility. This is determined by the adaptability of the production processes of single items. On the other hand, it is possible to produce a vast range of outputs in a flexible way, without enjoying economies of scope. In fact, a wide product mix may be obtained by using sub-contractors rather than producing all the

---

[10] Panzar and Willig (1981, p. 268). Given two output vectors y_1 and y_2, we have economies of scope if we can assume the following relation between the cost functions:

$$C(y_1 y_2) \leqslant C(y_1, 0) + C(0, y_2).$$

See also Teece (1980, pp. 225ff.). On production diversification see Grant (1988).

[11] For the distinction between multi-production and joint production see above, chapter 6, section 6.3.

commodities in-house. We have seen that sub-contracting reduces fixed costs and hence increases the adaptability of the processes.

Cutting down set-up times for switching machines from one process to another is a key element in reducing the cost of producing differentiated goods with the same equipment. In fact, decreasing set-up times makes it possible to produce a wide range of products in small batches (i.e. short production runs), without keeping large inventories; this reduces flexibility costs. On the relationship between flexibility and the length of machine set-up times, see Appendix A12.1 at the end of this chapter. Greatest flexibility is obtained when the same degree of economies of scale, for the overall output range, can be enjoyed in producing single-unit lots (i.e. one-of-a-kind) as in producing a single homogeneous product. In conclusion, a substantial reduction in set-up times may allow economies of scope and economies of scale to be exploited at the same time (on this point, see Bailey and Friedlaender 1982, p. 1026; cf. Del Monte and Esposito 1989, p. 23).

The next section will deal with factors which have led to the increased need for production flexibility.

12.3   Market differentiation and economic instability

During the 1950s and the 1960s the economic development of industrialized countries had been based on stability and a highly standardized demand, ready availability of unskilled labour, and technical changes allowing large economies of scale, through the application of rigid automation in the production process.

Until the end of the 1960s automation was 'more or less synonymous with mechanization'. The progressive introduction of automatic machines led to a reduction in the number of workers undertaking physical manual operations with machines, and to marked increases in productivity (ECE 1986).[12] This type of automation is called rigid automation because it is based on the use of product-specific machines with a high level of rigidity. Rigid automation developed especially in sectors with mass production, standardized products and significant economies of scale. Although rigid automation does not necessarily involve the adoption of non-flexible organizational models, the mechanization of production processes has been accompanied by the increasing diffusion of Tayloristic organizational models.

Tayloristic models consist in a rigid organization for the mass production of standardized goods through the use of special-purpose (or

---

[12] This research report contains a broad and thorough review of recent trends in flexible automation.

product-specific) machines and unskilled workers. As mentioned in chapter 3, for these models, a good organization is one in which functions, tasks, jobs, organizational structures, procedures and processes are specified as fully as possible, and interconnected through a pre-ordained plan, in order to ensure maximum overall efficiency. Tayloristic mechanistic organizational models correspond to a specific production context characterized by an environment with a high degree of predictability and stability, and by standardized final consumer goods. These models represent the production process as clockwork, rather than as an organism. The primary goal is efficiency, understood only as maximization of the quantity produced at a given cost. Rigid automation enables substantial economies of scale, so that the reduction of unit costs is mainly connected with expansion of the scale of production.

Postwar industrial development has been characterized, at least up to the late 1960s, by the increasing market power of large (or giant) firms and by the presence of a dualistic industrial structure (within many sectors) between: (a) large monopolistic or oligopolistic firms which have enjoyed large economies of scale, rapid technical change, high division of labour, and which therefore have accounted for a considerable increase in the industrial output; and (b) a fringe of small firms[13] with considerable capacities for adapting to the demand for intermediate goods expressed by large firms, or to the demand for strongly differentiated goods, services and local markets.[14] In short, the first two decades after the second world war were characterized by mass production and corporate development at microeconomic level, and by what were labelled Keynesian policies, at macroeconomic level (Vercelli 1988, p. 105; Minsky 1985; Blackburn, Coombs, Green 1985; Boyer 1988, pp. 84ff.).[15]

During the 1970s these conditions were progressively reversed. Market

---

[13] There are different classification criteria and statistical definitions of small firms (see Storey, 1982, p. 6, cf. Vercelli 1988, p. 110). The prevailing criterion is to consider small every firm with less than 200 employees.

[14] On the dichotomy in the structures of enterprises see Piore (1980b, pp. 55 and ff.); cf. Sylos Labini (1956), Marris (1964), Averitt (1968).

[15] 'To apply "Fordism" in the productive process and "Keynesianism" to macroeconomic regulation'... permitted, after the second world war, first an extraordinary recovery and then an unprecedented boom founded on the rocketing growth of mass consumption (the long waves theorists would label it as the recovery and boom of the fourth Kondratief)' (Vercelli, 1988). On this point see also Duijn (1983). On the other hand, Minsky has stressed the importance of the 'lesson of Keynes, Kalecki, and today's post-Keynesians about how the mass of profits in a capitalist economy is rigged by policy'. In essence, according to Minsky, 'there is a wide spectrum of possible Keynesian policies that determine aggregate profits and the way these profits are then distributed among firms' (1985, pp. 61, 64).

structure and production organization were influenced by a number of factors which raised uncertainty.[16] Among these factors one can mention:

(a) Instability of demand, saturation of some important markets and production differentiation.
(b) Remarkable increases in raw materials prices and wages, and in general changes in relative prices of inputs and outputs due to inflation.
(c) Floating exchange rates and recurrent financial disturbances.
(d) Labour unrest. In particular, variations in expectations regarding levels of skill and job satisfaction. The educational level of the labour supply rose and there was an increasing rejection of repetitive jobs.
(e) Increased competitiveness of developing countries in mass production.
(f) Finally, the diffusion of computer-based technology. This factor became increasingly important since the late 1970s and the 1980s. New technology sharply reduces the cost of production flexibility (this point will be developed in section 12.4).

All these changes have certainly induced many enterprises operating in industrialized countries to seek greater organizational and technical flexibility.

The saturation of many mass markets, which have increasingly become substitution markets, and the related evolution of consumption models, are leading to the spread of more and more differentiated and personalized commodities with a larger service component. Consequently many firms have become more 'market oriented' and their competitiveness is based more and more on flexibility in evolving in response to changes in market conditions. By contrast, during the 1950s and the 1960s increased competitiveness was mainly due to the possibility of expanding the production of standardized goods so as to enjoy the significant economies of scale arising from increased size and from the (rigid) automation of processes.

The need to produce differentiated goods may also derive from reasons of international competitiveness. In fact, standardized production, based on rigid automation technologies, has become less and less competitive in industrialized countries as it spreads among developing countries, which often have considerably lower direct costs. In these mature sectors international competitiveness is maintained only in those market segments where the differentiation of the product is essential, and where the products have a high service content.

---

[16] For a thorough analysis of these factors see Piore and Sabel (1984), Boyer (1988), Barca and Magnani (1989).

In short, intensifying competition, due to economic instability and market differentiation, has led to the development of flexible production systems. The accent has shifted from expansion to differentiation. In other words, it is becoming increasingly essential to develop productive structures which are flexible in terms of their capacity to respond to the evolution and growing differentiation of consumer models. Not only efficiency (in terms of input requirements), but also efficacy (in terms of matching market needs) have become an increasingly important aspect of competitiveness for many firms.

12.4   Flexibility without flexible technology

The emphasis usually placed on computer-based technology, and on the opportunities it provides for making production processes flexible, may often induce people to forget that flexibility can arise from the way the elements of production are organized regardless of the technology used. In fact, flexibility in production is first and foremost an economic phenomenon, which may even be *independent of the technology adopted* (see below, section 12.5).

From this point of view there are many analogies with the economic significance of the change from handicraft to factory production in Britain at the end of the eighteenth and beginning of the nineteenth century. The analysis carried out in Part 1 has shown that factory production was born historically as a modification of the way handicraft production was organized. To put it very briefly, the expansion of the market led to an increase in the quantity produced, which in turn allowed the reorganization of production for greater productivity through an increase in the division of labour and a reduction in idle times of funds (machines and plant), regardless of the technology used. The new organization then favoured the introduction of new machines which meanwhile had become available, and which would have been absolutely uneconomic if used in the old organization.

The new machines progressively replaced workers in many operations thanks to the introduction of automatic devices, and thus led to radical organizational changes. The widening of the market offered the chance to organize different inputs so as to increase the division of labour and reduce idle times. The new organization facilitated the introduction of new technologies, though it did not presuppose them. It follows that, as we have seen, the introduction of the factory system (and the abandonment of handicraft production) represented an economic rather than a technical innovation, because the increased productivity it created did not depend on changes in technology.

A very similar process of *reciprocal causation* – between changes in market conditions, modifications in the organization of production, and the introduction of new equipment which in turn exert an influence on market conditions and the organization of production units – seems to occur also in a change from rigid industrial production to flexible industrial production. In fact, changes in market conditions have induced numerous firms to seek greater productive flexibility; in many cases this flexibility has been obtained even before the advent of new information technology, through the adoption of various organizational models and production structures able to adapt to a differentiated and rapidly evolving market.

A certain degree of operational flexibility is obtainable by increasing the adaptability of single production lines, without recourse to computer-based technology. In this case, operational flexibility is mainly achieved through:

(i) in-house organizational systems, such as:
multi-production by juxtaposing many production units within the same firm and or several product lines within the same production unit;
just-in-time production;
(ii) agreements between 'specialized' firms (groups or constellations of independent firms, subcontracting, etc.).

In other words, flexibility can be increased, while still using rigid technologies, by combining individual, rigid productions and organizing them in a flexible way. With rigid automation technology, agreements between independent firms and in-house multi-production involve simply the sum of specialized elements that produce the different goods. A wide range of goods can be achieved in all these cases by using specialized machines, plants or production units to manufacture a given commodity. Therefore, flexibility depends on the extent and cost of adaptability in different processes.

Thus, the growing need for flexibility has led to the development of flexible forms of production linked with an increase in the number of small production units (or firms). This development has occurred in different ways depending on the environmental contexts and historical phases; they have involved both small not very innovative firms which are dependent on large firms, and small independent innovative firms which are often involved in a dense network of relations with other small firms, consultants and industrial promotion agencies. In fact in a climate of uncertainty and rapidly changing technical conditions, small firms are able to provide the required flexibility. This has led people to speak of a renaissance of the small firm and a revival of innovative Schumpeterian entrepreneurship.[17] When we consider this evolutionary tendency, we must distinguish, however, these different types of small firms:

(i) traditional artisan (or craft production);
(ii) dependent firms;
(iii) independent firms.

The category of small independent firms may in turn be divided into those using simple and traditional technology, on the one hand, and high-technology firms on the other (Brusco and Sabel 1981, pp. 99ff.; cf. Vercelli 1988, pp. 110ff.).[18] But not all small high-technology firms are innovative. In fact, as has been observed, there is a group of small independent firms which 'exploit the residual viability of high-tech products in an advanced stage of their life-cycle'. These firms belong to what is called 'interstitial independent high-tech sector' (Vercelli 1988).[19] While the demand for these products may be falling slowly, 'residual markets ensure a good level of business for such small-scale producers. Indeed, in a sense, this declining market protects such firms from the competition of larger producers' (Oakey 1984). Generally firms of this type do not require R&D activities, nor a high level of production flexibility. But there is another type of small, independent, high-technology firm which exploits 'the first phases of the life cycles of innovative products. We will call these firms new technology-based small firms (NTBSs)' (Vercelli 1988, p. 112; Rothwell and Zegveld 1982, pp. 35ff.; Oakey 1984; Oakey et al. 1988), to adopt an increasingly popular terminology. NTBSs have to invest in R&D and do need a high degree of organizational and technical flexibility.

Not only decentralization but also the just-in-time method of production can be seen as a production philosophy aimed at achieving a certain degree of flexibility while still using non-flexible technology. In fact just-in-time production began as an attempt to organize rigid equipment in a flexible way, by making agreements with supplier firms, so as to drastically reduce the quantity of goods lying in warehouses and in intermediate inventories.

---

[17] For a useful critical discussion on the debate about the renaissance of small firms see Piore and Sabel (1984), Vercelli (1988), Phillimore (1989). On the role of small firms on innovative processes, see also: Rothwell and Zegveld (1982), Oakey (1984), Oakey et al. (1988), Vercelli (1986), Curran, Stanworth, Watkins (eds.) (1986, vol. II).

[18] The most frequently adopted indicators of high-technology activities are the proportion of scientists, professional engineers and technicians in the labour force, and/or R&D intensity (ratio of R&D expenditure to revenue). For a discussion of the definition of high-technology activities see Aydalot and Keeble (eds.) (1988, chapter 1), Keeble (1988, pp. 70ff.).

[19] Oakey labels this group of firms as 'long product life cycle' based firms (1984, p. 143).

The just-in-time model was tested by Toyota in car production at the beginning of the 1960s, on a differentiated line of models built of common and standardized components. The philosophy of just-in-time production could be summed up as the smallest possible quantity (of production elements) at the latest possible time. Just-in-time is a system whereby materials are bought and components are built only at the moment when they are to be used, without any intervening storage period (further information on just-in-time is to be found in Appendix B at the end of this chapter). With just-in-time models a certain level of flexibility is obtained, on the one hand, by trying to reduce set-up times, and, on the other hand, producing small batches with the Kanban system. The Kanban system allows semi-finished parts to be adjusted according to variations in the product mix, using special order cards which are passed from one centre of operations or 'work cell', to the one that precedes it in the production chain. What happens in essence is that various orders come from the market and pass successively back through the different 'work cells' of the production cycle to the suppliers of intermediate goods and raw materials (the pull system). This system favours flexibility, at least within the limits imposed by set-up times; in fact, production is oriented towards the types of products most demanded by the final consumer (see Appendix A12.2). But the just-in-time system aims first of all to reduce stocks; in fact a completely rigid just-in-time production, with no inventories and no product differentiation, is entirely conceivable. Flexibility is obtainable from just-in-time production only if the set-up times can be reduced.

The just-in-time production model is not applicable to all operations. In fact it requires a particular set of technical and organizational environmental conditions. For example, suppliers must be near at hand, because long delivery times would make it advisable to have large reserve stocks despite the costs of locked-up semi-finished products. Another important condition is a stable demand; sudden changes can create a crisis for a production system with no reserves. Lastly, there should be no bottlenecks in the flow of production, which means actually that the productive capacity must be well proportioned along the various intermediate stages.

The diffusion of computer-based technology helps to remove some constraints on the spread of the just-in-time production model. In fact new technology – by cutting down set-up times and providing an information network from final consumers to the suppliers of materials and semi-finished goods (through the different production units which go to make up the *filière*) – reduces the volume of the minimum economic batch and hence the need for intermediate inventories.

To sum up, on the one hand, adopting flexible organizational systems facilitates the application of information technology, on the other, the development of this new technology makes radical organizational changes possible. As will be seen in the next section, which is devoted to a brief examination of the main economic effects of the spread of flexible technology, computer-based technology has not only provided considerable opportunities for the development of small innovative firms, but has made it possible to overcome the trade-off between economies of scope and economies of scale. This means that large size has become compatible with flexibility of production.

12.5   The impact of computer-based technology

The main property of computer-based technology is the *automation of information processes*, between people, but also between machines. This has several important consequences.

(a) Increased flexibility and efficiency of organizational processes by reducing the specificity and complexity of information management.
(b) Changes not only in the *quantity* of inputs in relation to output, but especially in their *quality*. In particular, with regard to the labour market, skill requirements and work patterns (shifts, hours of work etc.) undergo a drastic change. In many industrialized countries, the growth of service employment leads to a displacement of the demand for labour from traditional industrial occupations to new service occupations even within the manufacturing sector itself.
(c) Increased (technical) flexibility of equipment through cutting down the duration of the production process, response time, and set-up times (hence reduced quantities of goods held in warehouses and reduced working capital).

(a)   Automation of organizational and administrative processes

The management of information and organizational roles in firms is based on routines specific to each firm, which have developed over time. As we have noted in the section on the nature of technical change (chapter 2, section 2.2), this combination of routines and specific jobs is the fruit of the particular firm's evolutionary process (or development path), which gives it its individual character. Increased uncertainty leads to an increased need for information and knowledge within each firm and relationships between firms engaged in differentiated activities. An increased need for information may involve added management and organization costs which tend to reduce the competitive advantages that may arise from flexibility. From this point of view the development of information technology and its application to production organization makes it possible to collect and manage a large amount of information in real time. It also leads to an increasing degree of separation of administrative and managerial processes from employees' specific tasks and capacities.

The processes involved in information and organization are tending more and more to standardize their own output. Information technology leads to the automation of organizational work, reducing its costs and increasing its potentialities. As observed by Rullani (1988), with the advent of microprocessor technology information processes are codified and expressed in symbolic form, through codes and languages. 'These codes and languages, as formalized knowledge, can be transferred and replanned; they have the characteristics of reproducibility typical of industrial artifacts. Then organization itself becomes reproducible in all its relationships expressible through codes and languages' (pp. 96–8).

The firm, as a whole, then becomes a continuous flow system of activities, information, evaluations and decisions (Perez, 1985, pp. 453–4). On the one hand, there is a growth of service content in industrial production, and on the other hand these service functions are increasingly automated. To put it very briefly, conditions of uncertainty lead to an increase in flexibility, which in turn brings an enormous increase in the complexity of information management and coordination of different activities. The importance of computer-based technology is that it simplifies the management of information and the coordination of activities. Lastly, it should be noted that production flexibility is also sought through the development of complementary strategic and operative relations with other firms. Through a telematic network a firm can acquire its semi-finished goods and production services and thus enrich its own products mix.

The automation of organizational and administrative processes does not have a univocal influence on the size of firms. In fact, the greater ease of managing complex information may encourage the formation of networks of small firms with collaborative contacts, and a division of labour based on the differentiation of intermediate stages and functions. On the other hand, it may favour the expansion of large firms which coordinate numerous production units.

(b)   *Overcoming the trade-off between economies of scope and economies of scale*

The second aspect of the effects of computer-based technology concerns the increase of *technical flexibility*, due to the reduction of set-up times. In fact, as stressed above, the possibility of controlling and coordinating the actions of machines permits an enormous reduction in set-up times. This makes it possible to produce a range of differentiated goods by using one line to produce a succession of different products, reducing the need to keep organizational inventories. Thanks to information technology a high degree of flexibility can thus be obtained while still maintaining the typical advantages of industrial production: the economies of scale (on the overall range of output). Before the advent of computer-based technology, when economies of scope were opposed to those of scale,[20] differentiated production required two or more lines operating in parallel, or else very long set-up times, with large quantities of semi-finished goods in inventories. Thanks to the spread of information technology industrial production acquired some of the elements typical of traditional artisan production (high flexibility and trade specialization). This has been effectively brought out by the literature on flexible specialization.[21] Alongside these similarities, however, there are two important differences between artisan production and flexible industrial production. It was argued, in Part I (chapters 4 and 6), that artisan production has three basic characteristics: high flexibility, long idle times for tools, and long training times for workers (high specialization). The long idle times for tools are due to the fact that the craftsman moves from one operation to the other, using his tools one at a time. The more operations performed by one craftsman, the longer the idle times of the tools will be. Generally the craftsman's tools are simple and the incidence of idle times on total unit costs is relatively low. The great advantage of handicraft production is its flexibility, which allows very small batches or indeed single units to be produced. The importance of this advantage is such that in many activities handicraft has never been completely supplanted by cheaper industrial production, but has survived alongside it. On the other hand, the industrial production, based on the factory system, allows the excess of productive capacity of equipment to be reduced, in particular, the idle times of single machines and tools. Therefore, the difference between artisan and industrial production lies in the fact that the latter, unlike the former, permits a reduction in idle times, and allows economies of scale. In short, new technology provides the opportunity of enjoying the advantages of artisans (or handicraft) production, in terms of flexibility, and at the same time the advantages of industrial production, in terms of shortening funds' idle times and exploiting economies of scale.

The possibility of reconciling economies of scope with those of scale means that even large production units can enjoy high levels of flexibility in the product mix. For example, consider the recent evolution of the

[20] On the relationship between the evolution of technological paradigms and the nature of flexibility–scale trade-off, see Dosi (1988, pp. 1153–5).

[21] The recent spread in market economies of the 'model of flexible specialization' is seen by Piore and Sabel as a return to the model of artisan production: '[Flexible specialization] leads back to those craft methods of production that lost out at the first industrial divide' (Piore and Sabel, 1984, pp. 6, 17–8, 124).

automobile sector and the clock industry, where new technology allows economies of scale and production flexibility at same time.[22] Hence the very common assertion that with the information technology economies of scope tend to prevail over economies of scale is not accurate. If anything the contrary is true: information technology tends to link economies of scope with economies of scale. This leads to the spread of a new model of industrial organization for firms and markets: *large-scale flexible production*. In fact, 'on-line' linkages between markets and producers, and flexible technology, allow 'custom made' production in large establishments (Perez, 1985, p. 461, n. 23).

According to different sectors and economic environments, large-scale flexible production may coexist with other forms of production and market organization: small-scale flexible industrial production, industrial production based on rigid technologies and flexible organizational systems, mass production and traditional artisan production. The prevalence of one form of production over another in a geographical area or sector of activity depends, as argued above, on the interaction of a great many elements. It should be emphasized that there is no one way causal flow going from institutional conditions to industrial organization, to the structure of markets, to the running of firms and, finally, to their performance. On the contrary, all these elements are mutually interdependent.

Hence, I cannot but share the conclusion reached by Del Monte and Esposito that 'it is not possible to make flexibility requirements correspond to a specific industrial organizational model' (1989, p. 1). In particular, while there is no doubt that conditions of uncertainty demand greater flexibility, there is no univocal relationship between the pursuit of greater flexibility and the size of production units or firms. In fact, in some cases new technology allows a high degree of flexibility in large-scale production, while in other cases it favours the economic potential of small firms or production units. This determines the presence of different technical and organizational structures and the coexistence of firms of greatly different size and function within the same industry (on this point, see Rosenberg and Birdzell 1986, chapter 6).

Moreover, just as traditional artisan production was not ousted by the rise of mass production in the last century, it seems likely that flexible industrial production (on a large or small scale) will not mean a complete decline in mass production – at least while there exist markets where highly standardized goods predominate together with a demand elastic to prices, and where the production process uses non-flexible techniques

---

[22] On clock industry it is worth noting that, as mentioned by Landes (1987, pp. 24–5), computer-based flexible technology has contributed to the disappearance of artisan production (see also Archibugi, 1988).

(rigid and specialized plant) to permit substantial economies of scale. In some industries the coexistence of mass production lines and flexible production lines, addressed to different market niches, is even conceivable within the same firm (or production unit).

The extreme differentiation and pervasiveness of computer-based technology means that it can be applied in many sectors of activity, and in enterprises of very different sizes. As observed in chapter 11, new technology based on microelectronics may reduce the minimum investment cost required. This lowering of the entry barriers, which allows new firms access, is essential, but is not sufficient for the formation and development of a large number of small flexible specialized firms. Other determining factors are: the characteristics of financial markets and financial availability, the spread of entrepreneurial abilities, trade-union regulations and industrial relations, central and local governments industrial policies, and laws on taxation and social security contributions.[23] Like any investment choice, the adoption of flexible production models obviously depends on the behaviour of macroeconomic variables, the examination of which is beyond the scope of this study.

Very often, the introduction of 'flexible automation production systems' in small and medium companies still faces considerable difficulties. In particular the diffusion of computer-integrated manufacturing (CIM) or computer-aided manufacturing (CAM) (for definitions see Appendix 12.3, p. 193) involve several main problems.

(a) Higher investment cost per employee than old technologies based on rigid automation.[24]
(b) The need to produce a large total volume of differentiated product in order to benefit from the economies of scale allowed by flexible equipment.
(c) In-house technical expertise.
(d) Resistance to modifying the existing organization and distribution of skills.
(e) The technical difficulty in making software used in different areas compatible.

The spread of computer-based technology within firms usually begins

---

[23] For instance, the impact of 'regional institutions' on the spread of flexible specialization is stressed by Piore and Sabel (1984, pp. 264–5); while on the role of financial structure and credit institutions, see Minsky (1982, 1985), Storey (1982, chapter 8), Piatier (1984, pp. 205ff.), Williams et al. (1987, p. 424), Vercelli (1988), Reid and Jacobsen (1988).
[24] Northcott and Walling, reporting the results of thorough empirical research on the impact of microelectronics in British industry, observe that more than one-fifth of the user factories have experienced economic difficulties due to high development costs (particularly for product application), and lack of finance for development (1988, p. 11). On this theme see also Williams et al. (1987, pp. 431–4), Vickery and Campbell (1989, pp. 125ff.).

with 'islands of automation' with very little interconnection between them. In other words, the implementation of computer-based technology in each area follows its own path and its own logic, with no overall standard of communication (see Sorge *et al.* 1983; ECE 1986, pp. 24ff., 45ff.; Gaibisso *et al.* 1987; Edquist and Jacobsson 1988; Francis and Grootings, eds. 1989). The search for a common language permitting communication between different areas of automation may prove technically difficult, and hence economically burdensome. At the present stage of software development this difficulty may discourage the planning and realization of computer-integrated manufacturing (CIM). Thus, at the beginning of the 1990s, computer-integrated manufacturing (CIM) still constitutes a possible tendency that represents what may be the factory of the future in some sectors.

The application of information technology within firms through islands of automation and the coexistence of a variety of organizational and technical solutions correspond to the nature of the technical change described in chapter 2. The capacities of the people working in a firm develop gradually with the introduction of new techniques, according to the way in which these new techniques are translated into practical knowledge. All these capacities, which have evolved through the history of the firm, together determine the specific nature of the firm itself. The choice of new technical solutions depends on the opportunities which the new technologies provide for solving the problems that come up from time to time (problem solving). This creates an interaction between the development of technological opportunities, linked to computerized manufacturing techniques, and the evolution of flexible organizational structures.

In conclusion, the spread of computer-based technology is influenced by the specific characteristics of different environmental contexts, so there is not always a univocal relationship between size and the technology used. In fact in some cases this technology allows a high degree of flexibility in large-scale production, while in other cases it favours the economic potentialities of small firms or production units. On the other hand, it is worth repeating that the relationship between technology and size is not conditioned only by technical questions, but also by a series of economic factors whose influence differs enormously from one sector of activity to another.

(c)   *Decreased process duration and changes in work patterns*

We have seen that an important effect of flexible production systems, based on the use of microelectronic technology, is to reduce the overall duration of the elementary process by increasing the speed of machines and by cutting down the quantity of goods held in warehouses and also set-up times.[25] Tighter inventory control by advanced manufacturing technology allows a further reduction in goods lying in warehouses, and consequently, the whole 'duration' of the production process.

The 'duration' of the production process has a double nature: it can be seen on the one hand as a sort of input, objectified in the quantity of stocks and goods in process, and on the other as a contributory factor in determining the quality of the goods.

Reducing the 'duration' of the process means cutting down the quantity of semi-finished goods in the warehouse and in process, but it may not proportionally decrease the quantities of other production elements used – for example raw materials (and all limitational flows), and the services of labour and fixed capital. Therefore the quantity of inputs normally used in estimating production functions cannot be considered a good approximation of the duration of the process. Hence, when we consider changes in techniques, we must distinguish, as in chapter 7, at least three main forms: 'time-saving', 'organizational inventory-saving' and 'inputs-saving technical change'.

With regard to the second aspect – the 'duration' of the production process as a qualitative element of output – the influence of the process 'duration' on the product quality can be understood in two different ways. In the first place the process 'duration' frequently determines the 'response times', and the latter are generally included among the qualitative characteristics of the product. 'Duration' also affects the degree of strategic flexibility in qualitative changes of the product mix. In fact the shorter the production process 'duration', the easier it is to vary the output qualitative characteristics in relation to market changes. For example the CAD/CAM can drastically reduce the time required for planning, design and production of a given product.

In certain industrial sectors that are strongly influenced by fashion (where the evolution of design plays a crucial role in orienting demand), as well as in service sectors, the overall process 'duration' and 'response times' are particularly important in determining the efficacy and efficiency of a production unit. Hence they have a decisive influence on its competitiveness.

'Flexible automation production systems' usually require high investment per operator, which makes it indispensable to keep the plants running twenty-four hours a day. Therefore the production process tends

---

[25] Some empirical analyses show that introducing computer-based technology leads to a substantial increase in the degree of use of machines; cf. ECE (1986, pp. 2–3), Leontief and Duchin (1986, p. 46), Duke and Brand (1981, p. 31). The reduction in production process 'duration', allowed by 'new assembly line' systems, is stressed also by Coriot who considers in his analysis the savings in production time (1981, p. 42).

to be organized according to principles similar to those in the continuous-process industries, such as the iron, steel, chemical and paper industries (ECE, 1986, p. 135). With increased capital intensity, idle times must be reduced through flexible utilization of working hours and shifts. Thus there are changes tending to allow a more flexible regulation of working hours.

(d)   *Employment displacement and new skills*

The advent of computer manufacturing technology has led to an accentuation of the 'creative destruction' resulting from technical change. Technical change brings changes in the composition and quality of the inputs used in the single production units. These changes are translated into changes in the demand for labour and in skill requirements.[26] This leads to an increased demand for some categories of skilled workers, and the rapid obsolescence of others. There is an increasing demand for skills characterized by polyvalence and functional flexibility (such as multi-skilled operators) – in other words those that can be applied in different jobs and be adjusted rapidly to changes (on this point, see, e.g. Stevens 1988; Phillimore 1989).

The new demand for labour is concentrated especially in occupations differing from those eliminated by the restructuring process. This phenomenon is accentuated by the fact that, in many industrialized countries, the growth of service employment leads to a displacement of the demand for labour from traditional industrial occupations to new service occupations even inside the manufacturing sector itself.

However, the economic effects and labour-market implications of computer-controlled production systems are not predetermined and, therefore, it is very difficult to reach a general conclusion about the labour-market implications of new technology. The labour effects of information technology do not depend on 'technology *per se*',[27] but they depend very much on the macro and microeconomic conditions. With

[26] Literature examining the social and labour-market implications of computer-based technology is rapidly increasing. Among the main contributions see: Rothwell and Zegveld (1979), Blattern (1981), Stoneman (1981 and 1987a, chapter 14), Cooper and Clark (1982), Bosworth (ed.) (1983), Macdonald, Lamberton, Mandeville (eds.) (1983, Part IV), Freeman and Soete (1985) (1987), Leontief and Duchin (1986), ECE (1986), Leach and Wagstaff (1986), Cyert and Mowery (eds.) (1988), OECD (1988). There is general agreement that an approach that integrates the microeconomic and macro-economic dimensions must be adopted in analysing the impact of introducing computer-based technology.

[27] In other words, technology is not the only element influencing work organization. For a discussion on this point see, for instance, Rose et al. (1986), who illustrate a case study on the introducing of new technology in British Telecom.

regard to macroeconomic conditions, the role of economic policies is essential in counteracting the effects of 'technological unemployment'. On this point, Pasinetti (1981) writes:

There is nothing in the structural evolution of technical coefficients on the one side and of per-capita demand on the other, as such, that will ensure ... the maintenance of full employment. Therefore, if full employment is to be kept through time, it will have to be actively pursued as an explicit aim of economic policy. (p. 90)

At microeconomic level, the key element is, of course, the level of competitiveness of single firms. In fact, as observed by Freeman and Soete, even those studies which are rather pessimistic about the employment effects of new technology 'usually emphasise the fact that job losses are likely to be even greater if the new technology is not accepted and diffused, because of the likely loss in international competitiveness' (1985, p. 111). In other words, it is generally agreed that if a company fails to adopt new technology, the resultant loss of competitiveness may have displacement effects of considerably higher magnitude than those caused by the technology itself (ECE, 1986, pp. 129–32).

12.6   Conclusion

A complex set of technical, organizational and institutional conditions, which combine in different ways, underlies the organizational systems chosen by firms. This is why, in the same economic system and the same historical period different industrial organizational models can coexist – for example 'traditional artisan production' (characterized by high flexibility and specialization of labour and long idle times for tools), 'mass production' (characterized by important economies of scale, rigid technologies, low flexibility, low-level qualifications in the work force), 'industrial production using non-flexible traditional technologies organized in a flexible way', 'large-scale flexible industrial production', and 'small-scale industrial production'.

The fund–flow model proposed in the preceding chapters makes it possible to consider, not only technical aspects of production, but also organizational and temporal ones. This proves very useful in studying the evolution of production methods, as it enables us to identify and define the characteristics of the different industrial organizational models. For instance, as we have seen, considering the time profile of the use of production elements is useful in order to distinguish between artisanal activity and small-scale industrial production. The structure of an industry is based on the distribution of particular types of organizational models, which in turn are linked to the production methods adopted by individual production units.[28]

The new information technology is proving to be a formidable tool for cutting flexibility costs, and thus for encouraging further development of flexible organizational systems. Hence, the potentialities offered by this technology will undoubtedly be a strong incentive to apply flexible organizational systems to both large and small firms.

We have seen that innovative processes aimed at achieving greater flexibility in manufacturing bring with them a series of changes of which the most important are the following.

(1) The automation of organizational and information processes is made possible by the application of computer-based technology, and necessary by the increase in complexity (arising from the search for flexibility of production). At the same time more and more importance (in relation to number of employees and turnover) is attached to activities which service those of pure manufacturing transformation.

(2) The application of flexible techniques and organizational systems leads to a drastic reduction in the duration of the production process, response times, and the quantity of goods lying in inventories, and goods in progress. It also reduces set-up times, which makes economies of scale compatible with economies of scope.

(3) Lastly, there is a considerable change not only in the quantity of inputs in relation to outputs, but also, and especially, in the quality of inputs and outputs. In particular, with regard to the labour market, skill requirements and work patterns (shifts, hours of work, etc.) undergo a drastic change.

Most of these changes are outside the field of analysis involved in estimating the normal function of production. By contrast, they can be studied by a fund–flow model, which may be considered as a 'fact-finding model' useful in analysing the economic effects of adopting flexible production systems (or, more generally, a new technique). It is particularly suitable for evaluating the efficiency and efficacy not only of industrial transformation processes, but also of parallel service processes (e.g. administration, organization, distribution), where aspects linked to the time structure of production and response times are key factors and important elements in the competitiveness of production units. Secondly, applying the quantitative matrix and the organizational scheme to empirical analysis may prove useful in evaluating the effects of changes in production techniques arising from the search for greater flexibility, because the quantitative matrix and the organizational scheme measure

---

[28] On the distinction between production methods (or techniques), organizational systems, industrial organization models and mode of production, see chapter 2, section 2.2.

the quantities of semi-finished goods lying in inventories and provide indications on the set-up times. We have seen that both inventories and set-up times are essential in determining the nature of the trade-off between flexibility and efficiency. Moreover, the time profile of production (duration of the process, response times etc.), total idle times and minimum efficient lot size are other elements that can provide useful indications regarding the efficiency and efficacy of the processes in relation to production flexibility. Finally, by comparing different quantitative-temporal matrices and organizational schemes for the same production unit at different times we can take account of quantitative and qualitative variations in inputs at the microeconomic level. In particular, with regard to the labour market, the organizational scheme – involving the number of employees per job, skill and occupational level – can be useful for identifying job displacement phenomena, and changes in skill require-ments and labour force composition.

Appendix: Flexibility, set-up times, just-in-time production and CIM-CAM definitions

A12.1 Relationship between production flexibility and set-up times: a numerical example

Lubben provides a clear numerical example in order to illustrate the direct relationship between flexibility and the length of machine 'set-up times' (1983, p. 87). For the sake of simplicity we are focusing only on 'set-up time' and 'net machine time' (excluding 'loading and maintenance times'). Suppose that the 'set-up time' is 1 hour and that the 'net machine time' of the elementary process is 1 minute. If the production batch is 3,000 units, the 'total machine time' will be equal to the 'set-up time' plus the 'net machine time':

total machine time = 1 hour + (1 minute per unit × 3,000 units) = 51 hours.

On the other hand if the 'set-up time' was reduced to 6 minutes, i.e. by a factor of 10, the production batch could also be reduced by a factor of 10, from 3,000 to 300 units. The reason is that if the production of 300-unit lots is repeated 10 times, the 'total machine time' and the total number of pieces would be equal to those in the original case. In other words:

total machine time = (6 minutes + [1 minute per unit × 300 units]) × 10 batches = 51 hours.

A12.2 Just-in-time production systems

The *just-in-time* philosophy has spread very slowly among Japanese firms since the 1960s. More recently, thanks also to the new flexible information technology, it has been increasingly adopted in the United States and Europe.

The Kanban system takes its name from the cards (signals) used by the work cells at a particular stage in the process to inform those at an earlier stage of the number and characteristics of the intermediate goods required for their operation (according to the specifications received from work cells still further down the chain). In many texts the Kanban system is
192

considered synonymous with the just-in-time model. But Kanban is just one way, not the only one, of applying the just-in-time organizational model; for example, the cards may be replaced by floppy discs or a computer network to inform the different work cells of the semi-finished goods required.

Work cells are groups of workers with polyvalent skills. The workers within a cell must be interchangeable. A worker should be able to move to the adjacent upstream or downstream centre in case of blockages that delay the flow of production.

According to the 'pull system', each work cell is the customer of the preceding one in the chain and the individual work cells are responsible for managing the pull of the flow of orders. Since only the final assembly can precisely know the timing and the quantity of pieces demanded, it is the final assembly line that takes the necessary pieces from the preceding phases in the necessary quantities and at the right moment for assembling the cars. The earlier phases therefore produce pieces only as required by the later phases. Each phase in turn takes the necessary semi-finished pieces or materials from the preceding processes, and so on through the whole production *filière* (Monden 1983, p. 18). In other words the 'pull production system is a demand system whereby products are produced only on the demand of the using function' (Lubben, 1988, p. 12).

An example will show how the Kanban system helps to increase flexibility: 'Suppose a customer, or the market in general, needs a different mix – more As and fewer Bs.' The market sends more A signals to the final assembly. The line sends more A signals back down the chain to sub-assembly. Sub-assembly makes more As, sending more A signals for components back down the chain (Hay, 1988, p. 108).

A12.3   Computer-integrated and computer-aided manufacturing: some definitions

Computer-integrated manufacturing (CIM) is defined as the system which manages the flow of information between and within the principal areas of the firm: planning, administration and management, and production. In other words, computer-integrated manufacturing automizes the information flow within a firm from the planning phase to the realization of the product, from the arrival of the customer's order to the delivery of the product ordered. A computer-integrated manufacturing process is one

where the material flow and the information flow are organized in a well-balanced system which produces the right amount of goods at the right time for actual demand. ... In this sense, the engineering industry, which up to now has also been called an industry for discrete manufacturing, is moving towards closed continuous processes similar to those of the process industry. (ECE, 1986, p. 5)

Computer-aided manufacturing (CAM) may involve individual numerically controlled machines, robots or flexible manufacturing systems (FMS) which are a combination of these automatic machines. In fact, the *flexible manufacturing (production) system* (FMS) is an integrated computer-controlled complex of numerically controlled machine tools, automated material and tool-handling devices and automated measuring and testing equipment that, with a minimum of manual intervention and short change-over time, can process any product belonging to certain specified families. The *flexible manufacturing unit* (FMU) is a one-machine system equipped with a multi-pallet warehouse, an automatic pallet changer or robot and an automatic tool-changing device. The *flexible manufacturing cell* (FMC) is made up of two or more FMUs. The *flexible manufacturing system* is made up of two or more FMCs connected by an automatic transportation system. The majority of FMSs are installed in metal-cutting operations (ECE, 1986, pp. 13, 45). See also Blackburn, Coombs, Green (1985, chapter 6), Bonetto (1987, pp. 84ff.).

References

ADEFI (1985), *L'Analyse de filière*, Economica, Paris.

Alchian, A. A. (1959), 'Costs and products', in M. Abramovitz et al., *The Allocation of Economic Resources*, Stamford University Press, Stamford.

Alchian, A. A. and Demsetz, H. (1972), 'Production, information costs, and economic organization', *American Economic Review*, repr. in Demstz (1988a).

Alchian, A. A. and Woodward, S. (1988), 'The firm is dead: long live the firm. A review of Oliver E. Williamson's The Economic Institutions of Capitalism', *Journal of Economic Literature*.

Amendola, M. and Gaffard, J. L. (1988), *The Innovative Choice*, Blackwell, Oxford.

Amendola, M., Ingrao, B., Piacentini, P. and Pottì, B. (1990), *L'automazione flessibile. Analisi e interpretazioni delle tendenze a livello internazionale*, F. Angeli, Milan.

Amin, A. (1989a), 'Flexible specialisation and small firms in Italy: myths and realities', *Antipode*.

(1989b), 'A model of small firm in Italy', in Goodman et al. (eds.) (1989).

Antonelli, C. (ed.) (1988), *New Information Technology and Industrial Change: The Italian Case*, Kluwer Academic Publisher, Dordrecht, The Netherlands.

(1989), 'The role of technological expectations in a mixed model of international diffusion of process innovations: the case of open-end spinning rotors', *Research Policy*.

(1990), 'Profitability and imitation in the diffusion of process innovations', *Rivista Internazionale di Scienze Sociali e Commerciali*.

Antonelli, C., Petit, P. and Tahar, G. (1989), 'La Diffusion d'une nouvelle technique: application à une innovation dans l'industrie textile', *Revue d'Economie Industrielle*.

Aoki, M. (1984), *The Co-operative Game Theory of the Firm*, Blackwell, Oxford.

Arcangeli, F., David, P. and Dosi, G. (eds.) (1991), *Frontiers of Innovation Diffusion*, Oxford University Press, Oxford, 3 vols. Forthcoming.

Archibugi, D. (1988), 'Uso e abuso della specializzazione flessibile', *Politica ed Economia*.

Arena, R., Rainelli, M. and Torre, A. (1984), *Du concept à l'analyse de filière: une tentative d'eclaircissment theorique'*, Discussion Paper, LATAPSES, Nice, Italian translation 'Dal concetto all'analisi di filiera: un tentativo di chiarimento teorico', *L'Industria* (1985).

Arrow, K. J. (1962a), 'The economic implications of learning by doing', *Review of Economic Studies*.

(1962b), 'Economic welfare and the allocation of resources for invention', in NBER, *The Rate and Direction of Inventive Activity*, Princeton University Press, Princeton.

(1971), 'The firm in the general equilibrium theory', in R. Marris and A. Wood (eds.), *The Corporate Economy: Growth, Competition, and Innovation Potential*, Macmillan, London, repr. in Arrow 1983.

(1979), 'The division of labor in the economy, the polity, and society', in G. P. O. O'Driscoll Jr (ed.), *Adam Smith and Modern Political Economy. Bicentennial Essays on the Wealth of Nations*, The Iowa State University Press, Ames, Iowa.

(1983), *General Equilibrium, Collected Papers*, vol. II, Blackwell, Oxford.

Arrow, K. J. and Debreu, G. (1954), 'Existence of an equilibrium for a competitive economy', *Econometrica*.

Arrow, K. J., Chenery, H. B., Minhas, B. S. and Solow, R. M. (1961), 'Capital–labor substitution and economic efficiency', *Review of Economics and Statistics*, repr. in Harcourt and Laing (eds.) 1971.

Arrow, K. J. and Hahn, F. H. (1971), *General Competitive Analysis*, Holden-Day, San Francisco.

Arrow, K. J. and Starrett, D. A. (1973), 'Cost- and demand-theoretical approaches to the theory of price determination', in J. R. Hicks and W. Weber (eds.), *Carl Menger and the Austrian School of Economics*, Clarendon Press, Oxford.

Ashton, T. S. (1925), 'The records of a pin manufactory 1814–21', *Economica*.

Averitt, R. (1968), *The Dual Economy*, Norton, New York.

Aydalot, P. and Keeble, D. (eds.) (1988), *High Technology Industry and Innovative Environments: The European Experience*, Routledge, London.

Babbage, C. (1832), *On the Economy of Machinery and Manufactures*, Knight, London, 2nd edition.

Bailey, E. E. and Friedlaender, A. F. (1982), 'Market structure and multiproduct industries', *Journal of Economic Literature*.

Bain, J. S. (1956), *Barriers to New Competition*, Harvard University Press, Cambridge, Mass.

Baldone, S. (1984), 'Integrazione verticale, struttura temporale dei processi produttivi e transizione fra le tecniche', *Economia Politica*.

(1989), 'Analisi interindustriale e mutamento tecnico', in Zamagni (ed.) 1989.

Baldwin, W. L. and Scott, J. T. (1987), *Market Structure and Technical Change*, Harwood Academic Publisher, Chur.

Barca, F. and Magnani, M. (1989), *L'industria fra capitale e lavoro*, Il Mulino, Bologna.

Baumol, W. J. (1961), *Economic Theory and Operations Analysis*, Prentice-Hall, Englewood Cliffs, New Jersey, 4th edition, 1977.

(1982), 'Contestable markets: an uprising on the theory of industry structure', *American Economic Review*.

Baumol, W. J., Panzar, J. C. and Willig, R. D. (1982), *Contestable Markets and the Theory of Industry Structure*, with contributions by E. E. Bailey, D. Fisher, H. C. Quirmbach, Harcourt Brace Jovanivich, San Diego, revised edition, 1988.

Beath, J., Katsoulacos, Y. and Ulph, D. (1989), 'The game-theoretic analysis of innovation: a survey', *Bulletin of Economic Research*.

Becattini, G. (1975), 'Introduzione: invito a una rilettura di Marshall', in A. Marshall and M. Paley Marshall, *Economia della produzione*, ISEDI, Milan, 1975, translated by C. Zanni and R. Zanni, *The Economics of Industry*, Macmillan, London, 1979.

(1979), 'Sectors and/or districts: some remarks on the conceptual foundations of industrial economics', in E. Goodman et al. (eds.) 1989, new version of 'Dal "settore" industriale al "distretto" industriale. Alcune considerazioni sull'unità d'indagine dell'economia industriale', *Rivista di Economia e Politica Industriale*, 1979.

Bellandi, M. (1982), 'The industrial district in Marshall', in Goodman et al. (eds.), 1989, revised version of 'Il distretto industriale in Alfred Marshall', *L'Industria*, 1982.

Bellon, B. (1984), 'La filiera di produzione', *Economia e Politica Industriale*.

Benvenuti, G. (1988), 'Tecnologia, mansioni, reticoli: un contributo alla teoria dei processi produttivi', *L'Industria*.

Berger, S. and Piore, M. J. (1980), *Dualism and Discontinuity in Industrial Societies*, Cambridge University Press, Cambridge.

Bessant, J. R. (1982), 'Influential factors in manufacturing innovation', *Research Policy*.

Betancourt, R. (1986), 'A generalization of modern production theory', *Applied Economics*.

Bianchi, P. (1984), *Divisione del lavoro e ristrutturazione industriale*, Il Mulino, Bologna.

Bianchi, R. (1974), 'Economie di scala e barriere all'entrata', *Note Economiche*.

Binswanger, H. P. et al. (1978), *Induced Innovation*, Johns Hopkins University Press, Baltimore, Maryland.

Blackburn, P., Coombs, R. and Green, K. (1985), *Technology, Economic Growth and the Labour Process*, Macmillan, London.

Blair, J. M. (1972), *Economic Concentration. Structure, Behaviour and Public Policy*, Harcourt Brace Jovanovich, New York.

Blattern, N. (1981), 'Labour displacement by technological change? A preliminary survey of the case of microelectronics', *Rivista Internazionale di Scienze Economiche e Commerciali*.

Bliss, C. J. (1975), *Capital Theory and Distribution of Income*, North-Holland, Amsterdam.

Böhm-Bawerk, E. (1889), *The Positive Theory of Capital*, Stechert, New York (1930), translated from German by W. Smart.

Boje, T. P. (1990), 'Flexibility and fragmentation in the labour market. Recent trends in the structuring of employment and industrial relations', *mimeo*, paper presented at the EAEPE 1990 Conference, Florence, 15–17 November.

Bonetto, R. (1987), *Flexible Manufacturing Systems in Practice*, North Oxford Academic, London (1988), English transl. by M. Sanders, *Les Ateliers flexibles de production*, Hermès, Paris, 1987.

Bosworth, D. L. (ed.) (1983), *The Employment Consequences of Technological Change*, Macmillan, London.

Bowles, S. (1985), 'The production process in a competitive economy: Walrasian, neo-Hobbesian, and Marxian models', *American Economic Review*.

198   References

Boyer, R. (1988), 'Technical change and the theory of "régulation"', in Dosi et al. (eds.), (1988).
Boyer, R. and Wolleb, E. (eds.) (1986), *The Search for Labour Market Flexibility. The European Economies in Transition*, Oxford University Press (1987), Oxford, English translation of *La Flexibilité du travail en Europe*, Editions La Découverte, Paris, 1986.
Braverman, H. (1974), *Labor and Monopoly Capital. The Degradation of Work in the Twentieth Century*, Monthly Review Press, New York.
Brown, L. A. (1981), *Innovation and Diffusion. A New Perspective*, Methuen, London.
Brusco, S. (1982), 'The Emilian model: productive decentralisation and social integration', *Cambridge Journal of Economics*.
(1986), 'Small firms and industrial districts: the experience of Italy', in D. Keeble and E. Wever (eds.), *New Firms and Regional Development in Europe*, Croon Helm, London.
Brusco, S. and Sabel, C. F. (1981), 'Artisan production and economic growth', in F. Wilkinson (ed.), *The Dynamics of Labour Market Segmentation*, Academy Press, London.
Burns, T. J. and Stalker, G. M. (1961), *The Management of Innovation*, Tavistock, London.
Cantalupi, M. (1986), 'Sull'estendibilità dell'approccio neo-austriaco a trattare il progresso technico: il caso dei modelli verticalmente integrati', *Il Giornale degli Economisti*.
(1989), 'Path-dependency, stilizzazioni tecnologiche e teoria della produzione', in Zamagni (ed.) (1989).
Capecchi, V. (1989), 'The informal economy and the development of flexible specialization', in Portes, A., Castells, M. and Benton, L. A. (eds.), *The Informal Economy*, The Johns Hopkins University Press, Baltimore.
Carabelli, A. M. (1988), *On Keynes's Method*, Macmillan, London.
Carter, A. P. (1970), *Structural Change in the American Economy*, Harvard University Press, Cambridge, Mass.
Chamberlin, E. H. (1948), 'Proportionality, divisibility and economies of scale', *Quarterly Journal of Economics*, repr. in Chamberlin (1957).
(1949), '"Reply" to Mr. McLeod and Mr. Hahn', *Quarterly Journal of Economics*, repr. in Chamberlin (1957).
(1957), *Towards a More General Theory of Value*, Oxford University Press, New York.
Chandler, A. D. Jr. (1977), *The Visible Hand*, Harvard University Press, Cambridge, Mass.
Chenery, H. B. (1949), 'Engineering production function', *Quarterly Journal of Economics*.
Clapham, J. H. (1913), 'Review of W. Sombart, *Luxus und Capitalism*, Leipzig, Duncker and Humblot, vols 2, 1913', *The Economic Journal*.
Clark, N. (1985), *The Political Economy of Science and Technology*, Blackwell, Oxford.
Clower, R. W. (1959), 'Stock and flow quantities: a common fallacy', *Economica*.
Coase, R. H. (1937), 'The nature of the firm', *Economica*.
Cohen, W. M. and Levinthal, D. A. (1989). 'Innovation and learning: the two faces of R&D', *The Economic Journal*, Supplement.

Cohendet, P. and Llerena, P. (1988), 'Flexibilities, complexity and integrations in production processes', in Ergas et al. (1988).

Coombs, R., Saviotti, P. and Walsh, V. (1987), *Economics and technological change*, Macmillan, London.

Cooper, C. M. and Clark, J. A. (1982), *Employment, Economics and Technology*, Wheatsheaf, Brighton.

Coriot, B. (1981), 'The restructuring of the assembly line: a new economy of time and control', *Capital and Class*.

Coutts, K., Godley, W. and Nordhaus, W. (1978), *Industrial Pricing in the U.K.*, Cambridge University Press, Cambridge.

Curran, J., Stanworth, J. and Watkins, D. (eds.) (1986), *The Survival of Small Firms*, Gower, Aldershot, 2 vols.

Cyert, R. M. and Mowery, D. C. (eds.) (1988), *The Impact of Technological Change on Employment and Economic Growth*, Ballinger Publishing Company, Cambridge, Mass.

Dardi, M. (1990), 'Il mercato nell'analisi economica contemporanea', in G. Becattini (ed.), *Il pensiero economico: temi, problemi e scuole*, UTET, Turin.

Dasgupta, P. (1986), 'The theory of technological competition', in J. E. Stiglitz and G. F. Mathewson (eds.), *New Developments in the Analysis of Market Structure*, Macmillan, London.

Dasgupta, P. and David, P. A. (1987), 'Information disclosure and the economics of science and technology', in G. Feiwel (ed.), *Arrow and the Ascent of Modern Economic Theory*, Macmillan, London.

Dasgupta, P. and Stiglitz, J. E. (1980), 'Industrial structure and the nature of innovation activity', *The Economic Journal*.

Dasgupta, P. and Stoneman, P. (eds.) (1987), *Economic Policy and Technological Performance*, Cambridge University Press, Cambridge.

David, P. A. (1975), *Technical Choice Innovation and Economic Growth*, Cambridge University Press, Cambridge.

Dean, J. (1976), *Statistical Cost Estimation*, Indiana University Press, Bloomington.

Debreu, G. (1959), *Theory of Value*, Yale University Press, New Haven.

Del Monte, A. and Esposito, F. M. (1989), *Flessibilità e teoria della organizzazione industriale*, University of Naples, Naples.

Demsetz, H. (1988a), *Organization of Economic Activity*, Volume 1, *Ownership, Control, and the Firm*, Blackwell, Oxford.

(1988b), 'The theory of the firm revisited', *Journal of Law, Economics, and Organization*, repr. in Demsetz 1988a.

De Vecchi, N. (1988), 'Schumpeterian and Austrian economics', mimeo, in O. Sullivan (ed.), *Beyond Austrian School*, Macmillan, London, 1991.

Diderot, D. and D'Alembert, J. (eds.) (1751), *Encyclopédie*, Paris.

Dore, R. (1986), *Flexible Rigidities*, The Athlone Press, London.

Dorfman, R. (1953), 'Mathematical, or "linear", programming: a nonmathematical exposition', *American Economic Review*.

Dosi, G. (1984), *Technical Change and Industrial Transformation*, Macmillan, London.

(1988), 'Sources, procedures, and microeconomic effects of innovation', *Journal of Economic Literature*.

Dosi, G., Freeman, C., Nelson, R., Silverberg, G. and Soete, L. (eds.) (1988), *Technical Change and Economic Theory*, Pinter, London.

Dosi, G. and Soete, L. (1988), 'Technical change and international trade', in Dosi et al. (eds.) (1988).

Dufour, D. and Torre, A. (1985), 'Filières et structures polaires', in ADEFI (1985).

Duijn, J. J. van (1983), *The Long Wave in Economic Life*, Allen & Unwin, London.

Duke, J. and Brand, H. (1981), 'Cyclical behaviour of productivity in the machine tool industry', *Monthly Labor Review*.

ECE (1986), *Recent Trends in Flexible Manufacturing*, United Nations, New York.

Edgeworth, F. Y. (1913), 'Contributions to the theory of railway rates – IV', *The Economic Journal*.

Edquist, C. and Jacobsson, S. (1988), *Flexible Automation*, Blackwell, Oxford.

Edwards, B. K. and Starr, R. M. (1987), 'A note on indivisibility, specialization and economies of scale', *American Economic Review*.

Egidi, M. (1986), 'The generation and diffusion of new routines', in Arcangeli et al. (eds.) (1991).

(1989), 'L'impresa come organizzazione e la funzione di produzione: un binomio impossibile', in Zamagni (ed.) (1989).

Elster, J. (1983), *Explaining Technical Change. A Case study in Philosophy of Science*, Cambridge University Press, Cambridge.

Ergas, H. et al. (1988), *Firm-environment Interaction in a Changing Productive System*, F. Angeli, Milan.

Esposito, E. (1990), 'La misura del cambiamento tecnologico: un indicatore composito', *L'Industria*.

Faber, M. (ed.) (1986), *Studies in Austrian Capital Theory, Investment and Time*, Springer-Verlag, Berlin.

Faber, M. and Proops, J. L. R. (1990), *Evolution, Time, Production and the Environment*, Springer-Verlag, Berlin.

Fenneteau, H. (1985), 'La Structuration d'une filière et l'organisation des relations entre les firmes – le cas des industries liées à l'automobile', in ADEFI 1985.

Florence, P. S. (1953), *The Logic of British and American Industry*, Routledge & Kagan, London.

Francis, A. and Grootings, P. (eds.) (1989), *New Technologies and Work*, Routledge, London.

Frank, C. R. Jr (1969), *Production Theory and Indivisible Commodities*, Princeton University Press, Princeton.

Freeman, C. (1974), *The Economics of Industrial Innovation*, Pinter, London, 2nd edn 1982.

(1987), 'Information technology and change in techno-economic paradigm', in Freeman and Soete (eds.) (1987).

Freeman, C. and Soete, L. (1985), *Information Technology and Employment*, mimeo, SPRU, University of Sussex, Brighton.

Freeman, C. and Soete, L. (eds.) (1987), *Technological Change and Full Employment*, Blackwell, Oxford.

Frisch, R. A. K. (1962), *Theory of Production*, D. Reidel, Dordrecht, Holland 1965, translated from the Norwegian by R. I. Christophersen, *Innledning til Produksjonsteorien*, 1962.

Fuà, G. and Zacchia, C. (eds.) (1983), *Industrializzazione senza fratture*, Il Mulino, Bologna.

Gaibisso, A. M., Gros-Pietro, G. M., Leone, G., Rolfo, S. and Trentin, I. (1987), 'Gli FMS nel mondo alla fine del 1986', *Bollettino CERIS*.

Georgescu-Roegen, N. (1952), 'A diagrammatric analysis of complementarity', *Southern Economic Journal*.

(1964), 'Measure, quality and optimum scale', in C. R. Rao (ed.), *Essays in Econometrics and Planning*, Pergamon Press, Oxford, repr. in Georgescu-Roegen 1976.

(1965), 'Process in farming versus process in manufacturing: a problem of balanced development', in U. Papi and C. Nunn (eds.), *Economic Problems in Agriculture in Industrial societies*, Macmillan, 1969, London, repr. in Georgescu-Roegen 1976.

(1966), *Analytical Economics*, Harvard University Press, Cambridge, Mass.

(1967), 'Chamberlin's new economics and the unit of production', in R. E. Kuenne (ed.), *Monopolistic Competition Theory. Essays in Honor of E. H. Chamberlin*, J. Wiley & Sons, New York.

(1969), 'The economics of production', R. T. Ely Lecture, *American Economic Review*, 1970, repr. in Georgescu-Roegen 1976.

(1971), *The Entropy Law and the Economic Process*, Harvard University Press, Cambridge, Mass., 4th edn 1981.

(1976), *Energy and Economic Myths*, Pergamon Press, New York.

(1979), 'Energy analysis and economic valuation', *The Southern Economic Journal*, Italian translation of a longer version by P. L. Cecioni in Georgescu-Roegen N., *Energia e miti economici*, Boringhieri, Turin 1982.

(1986), 'Man and production', in M. Baranzini and R. Scazzieri (eds.), *Foundations of Economics*, Blackwell, Oxford.

Gershuny, J. (1983), *Social Innovation and the Division of Labour*, Oxford University Press, Oxford.

Giannini, C. (1981), 'Una nota sul cambiamento tecnologico nei sitemi input–output', *Il Giornale degli Economisti, Annali di Economia*.

Gold, B. (1981), 'Changing perspective on size, scale, and returns: An interpretive survey', *Journal of Economic Literature*.

Goldberg, V. P. (1985), 'Production functions, transaction costs and the new institutionalism', in G. R. Feiwel (ed.), *Issues in Contemporary Microeconomics and Welfare*, Macmillan, London.

Goodman, E., Bamford, J. and Saynor, P. (eds.) (1989), *Small Firms and Industrial Districts in Italy*, Routledge, London.

Grant, R. M. (1988), 'Diversification and firm performance in a changing economic environment', in Ergas et al., 1988.

Griliches, Z., Pakes, A. and Hall, B. H. (1987), 'The value of patents as indicators of inventive activity', in Dasgupta and Stoneman (eds.) 1987.

Grossman, S. J. and Hart, O. D. (1986), 'The costs and benefits of ownership: a theory of vertical and lateral integration', *Journal of Political Economy*.

Hagedoorn, J. (1989), *The Dynamic Analysis of Innovation and Diffusion: A Study in Process Control*, Pinter, London.

Hahn, F. H. (1973), *On the Notion of Equilibrium in Economics*, Cambridge University Press, Cambridge, repr. in Hahn 1984.

(1978), 'Review of *Evolution, Welfare and Time in Economics: Essays in Honor of Nicholas Georgescu-Roegen*, eds. A. M. Tang, F. M. Westfield and J. S. Worley, Lexington, Cambridge, Mass., 1976', *Journal of Economic Literature*.

(1981), 'General equilibrium theory', in D. Bell and I. Kristol (eds.), *The Crisis in Economic Theory*, Basic Books, New York, repr. in Hahn 1984.

(1982), 'The neo-Ricardians', *Cambridge Journal of Economics*, repr. in Hahn 1984.

(1984), *Equilibrium and Macroeconomics*, Blackwell, Oxford.

(1986), 'On Marx and Keynes and many things', *Oxford Economic Papers*.

Hahn, F. H. and McLeod, A. N. (1949), 'Proportionality, divisibility, and economies of scale: two comments', *Quarterly Journal of Economics*.

Hahn, F. H. and Matthews, R. C. O. (1964), 'The theory of economic growth: a survey', *The Economic Journal*.

Hahn, F. H. and Solow, R. M. (1985), 'Is wage flexibility a good thing?, *mimeo*, Sienna.

Håkansson, H. (1989), *Corporate Technological Behaviour. Co-operation and Networks*, Routledge, London.

Haldi, J. and Whitcomb, D. (1967), 'Economies of scale in industrial plants', *Journal of Political Economy*.

Haltmaier, J. (1984), 'Measuring technical change', *The Economic Journal*.

Harcourt, G. C. (1962), 'Review of W. E. G. Salter, productivity and technical change', in Harcourt (1982), repr. from *Economic Record*, n. 83.

(1966), 'Biases in empirical estimates of the elasticities of substitution of C.E.S. production functions', in Harcourt (1982), repr. from *Review of Economic Studies*, no. 95.

(1972), *Some Cambridge Controversies in the Theory of Capital*, Cambridge University Press, Cambridge.

(1976), 'Pricing and the investment decision', in Harcourt 1982, repr. from *Kyklos*, vol. 29.

(1977), *Microeconomic foundations of macroeconomics*, Macmillan, London.

(1979a), 'Conclusion: the social science imperialists', in Harcourt 1982, repr. from *Politics*, no. 2.

(1979b), 'Non-neoclassical capital theory', in Harcourt 1982, repr. from *World Development*, no. 10.

(1982), *The Social Science Imperialists*, Routledge & Kegan, London, ed. P. Kerr.

(1983), 'On Piero Sraffa's contribution to economics', in Harcourt, 1986b, Wheatsheaf, Brighton, repr. from P. D. Groenewegen and J. Halevi (eds.), *Altro Polo: Italian Economics Past and Present*, University of Sydney, Sydney 1983.

(1986a), 'On the contributions of Joan Robinson and Piero Sraffa to economic theory', in Harcourt 1986b, this essay is a longer version of an article entitled 'On the Influence of...', *The Economic Journal*, Supplement.

(1986b), *Controversies in Political Economy*, Wheatsheaf, Brighton, edited by O. F. Hamouda.

Harcourt, G. C. and Laing, N. F. (eds.) (1971), *Capital and Growth*, Penguin, Harmondsworth.

Hay, E. J. (1988), *The Just in Time*, J. Wiley & Sons, New York.

Hayami, Y. and Ruttan, V. (1971), *Agricultural Development: An International Perspective*, Johns Hopkins Press, Baltimore.

Hayek, F. A. von (1941), *Pure Theory of Capital*, Macmillan, London.
(1945), 'The use of knowledge in society', *American Economic Review*.
Heathfield, D. F. and Wibe, S. (1987), *An Introduction to Cost and Production Functions*, Macmillan, London.
Heertje, A. (1973), *Economies and Technical Change*, Weidenfeld and Nicolson, London.
Hellriegel, D. and Slocum, J. W. Jr (1974), *Management: a Contingency Approaches*, Addison-Wesley, Reading, Mass., 2nd edn 1978.
Hicks, J. R. (1932), *The Theory of Wages*, Macmillan, London, 2nd edn 1963.
(1965), *Capital and Growth*, Clarendon, Oxford.
(1973a), 'The Austrian theory of capital and its rebirth in modern economics', in J. R. Hicks and W. Weber (eds.), *Carl Menger and the Austrian School of Economics*, Clarendon Press, Oxford, repr. in J. R. Hicks, *Classics and Moderns, Collected Papers*, vol. 3, Blackwell, Oxford 1983.
(1973b), *Capital and Time. A Neo-Austrian Theory*, Clarendon Press, Oxford.
(1976), 'Some questions of time in economics', in A. M. Tang, F. M. Westfield and J. S. Worley (eds.), *Evolution, Welfare and Time in Economics: Essays in Honor of Nicholas Georgescu-Roegen*, Lexington, Cambridge, Mass.
Hippel, E. von (1988), *The Sources of Innovation*, Oxford University Press, Oxford.
Hirsch, W. Z. (1952), 'Manufacturing process functions', *Review of Economics and Statistics*.
Hirschman, A. O. (1958), *The Strategy of Economic Development*, Yale University Press, New Haven, repr. W. W. Norton & Company, New York, 1978.
Hirshleifer, J. and Riley, J. G. (1979), 'The analytics of uncertainty and information – an expository survey', *Journal of Economic Literature*.
Hodgson, G. M. (1988), *Economics and Institutions*, Polity Press, Oxford.
Holmstrom, B. R. and Tirole, J. (1989), 'The theory of the firm', in R. Schmalensee and R. Willig (eds.), *Handbook of Industrial Organization*, vol. 1, North-Holland, Amsterdam, 2 vols.
Hutchins, D. (1988), *Just in Time*, Gower, Aldershot.
Hyman, R. (1988), 'Flexible specialization: miracle or myth?' in Hyman, R. and Streeck, W. (eds.), *New Technology and Industrial Relations*, Blackwell, Oxford.
Jacquemin, A. and Rainelli, M. (1984), 'Filières de la nation et filières de l'entreprise', *Revue Economique*.
Jensen, M. C. and Meckling, W. H. (1979), 'Rights and production function', *Journal of Business*.
Johnston, J. (1958), 'Statistical cost functions: a reappraisal', *Review of Economics and Statistics*.
(1960), *Statistical Cost Analysis*, McGraw-Hill, New York.
Jones, B. (1988), 'Work and flexible automation in Britain: a review of developments and possibilities', *Work, Employment and Society*.
Jones, R. A. and Ostroy, J. M. (1984), 'Flexibility and uncertainty', *Review of Economic Studies*.
Kaldor, N. (1934), 'The equilibrium of the firm', *The Economic Journal*.
(1957), 'A model of economic growth', *The Economic Journal*, repr. in N. Kaldor, *Essays on Economic Stability and Growth*, Duckworth, London 1960, 2nd edn 1980.

(1972), 'The irrelevance of equilibrium economics', *The Economic Journal*.

Kalecki, M. (1971), *Selected Essays on the Dynamics of the Capitalist Economy 1933–1970*, Cambridge University Press, Cambridge.

Kamien, M. I. and Schwartz, N. L. (1982), *Market Structure and Innovation*, Cambridge University Press, Cambridge.

Kay, N. M. (1979), *The Innovating Firm*, Macmillan, London.

Kay, N. M., Robe, J. F. and Zagnoli, P. (1987), *An Approach to the Analysis of Joint Ventures*, EUI Working Paper no. 87/313, European University Institute, Florence.

Keeble, D. (1988), 'High-technology industry and local environments in the United Kingdom', in Aydolt P. and Keeble D. (eds.), *High Technology Industry and Innovative Environments: The European Experience*, Routledge, London.

Keynes, J. M. (1921), *The Treatise on Probability*, Macmillan, London, repr. in *The Collected Writings*, edited by D. Moggridge, Macmillan, London 1971–, vol. VIII.

(1936), *The General Theory of Employment, Interest and Money*, Macmillan, London, repr. in *The Collected Writings*, edited by D. Moggridge, Macmillan, London, 1971–, vol. VII.

(1937), 'The general theory of employment', *Quarterly Journal of Economics*, repr. in *The Collected Writings*, edited by D. Moggridge, 1971–, vol. XIV.

Kim, S. (1989), 'Labor specialization and the extent of the market', *Journal of Political Economy*.

Kline, S. J. and Rosenberg, N. (1986), 'An overview of innovation', in Landau, R. and Rosenberg, N. (eds.), *The Positive Sum Strategy*, National Academy Press, Washington.

Knight, F. H. (1921), *Risk, Uncertainty and Profit*, Houghton, Boston.

Knight, K. E. (1985), 'A functional and structural measurement of technology', *Technological Forecasting and Social Change*.

Koopmans, T. C. (ed.) (1951), *Activity Analysis of Production and Allocation*, J. Wiley & Sons, New York, 5th edn 1964.

(1957), *Three Essays on the State of Economic Science*, McGraw-Hill, New York.

(1964), 'On flexibility of future preference', in Shelley, M. W. and Bryan, G. L. (eds.), *Human Judgements and Optimality*, Wiley, New York.

Landau, R. and Rosenberg, N. (eds.) (1986), *The Positive Sum Strategy. Harnessing Technology for Economic Growth*, National Academy Press, Washington.

Landes, D. S. (1987), 'Small is beautiful. Small is beautiful?' in *Piccola e grande impresa: un problema storico*, F. Angeli, Milan.

Landesmann, M. A. (1986), 'Conceptions of technology and the production process', in M. Baranzini and R. Scazzieri (eds.), *Foundations of Economics*, Blackwell, Oxford.

Langlois, R. N. (1986), 'The new institutional economics: an introductory essay', in R. N. Langlois (ed.), *Economics as a Process*, Cambridge University Press, Cambridge.

Lanzara, R. (1988), *Le strategie di flessibilità produttiva*, Giappichelli, Turin.

Lawson, T. (1987), 'The relative/absolute nature of knowledge and economic analysis', *The Economic Journal*.

Leach, D. and Wagstaff, H. (1986), *Future Employment and Technical Change*, Kogan Page, London, with the collaboration of A.-M. Bostyn, C. Pritchard, D. Wight.

Leibenstein, H. (1982), 'The Prisoner's Dilemma in the invisible hand: an analysis of intrafirm productivity', *American Economic Review, Papers and Proceedings*, repr. in Putterman (ed.) (1986).

Leijonhufvud, A. (1986), 'Capitalism and the factory system', in Langlois (1986).

Leoni, R. (1989), 'Sulla definizione di industrie high-tech tramite indicatori di input', *L'Industria*.

Leontief, W. (1966), *Input Output Economics*, Oxford University Press, Oxford, second edition 1986.

Leontief, W. et al. (1953), *Studies in the Structure of the American Economy*, International Arts and Science Press, New York.

Leontief, W. and Duchin, F. (1986), *The Future Impact of Automation on Workers*, Oxford University Press, New York.

Loasby, B. J. (1983), 'Review of *An Evolutionary Theory of Economic Change*, by R. R. Nelson and S. G. Winter', *The Economic Journal*.

(1988), *Knowledge and Organisation. Marshall Theory of Economic Progress*, Marshallian Studies, no. 3, Department of Economics, University of Florence.

Lorenzoni, G. (1983), 'La costellazione di imprese. Una base di indagine sui processi di sviluppo', *Economia e Politica Industriale*.

Lorenzoni, G. and Ornati, O. A. (1988), 'Constellations of firms and new ventures', *Journal of Business Venturing*.

Lowe, A. (1955), 'Structural analysis of real capital formation', in National Bureau of Economic Research, *Capital Formation and Economic Growth*, Princeton University Press, Princeton.

(1965), *On Economic Knowledge*, Harper & Row, New York.

(1976), *The Path of Growth*, assisted by S. Pulrang, with an appendix by E. J. Nell, Cambridge University Press, Cambridge.

Luben, R. (1988), *Just-in-time Manufacturing*, McGraw-Hill, New York.

Lunghini, G. (1975), 'Teoria economica ed economia politica: note su Sraffa', in G. Lunghini (ed.) (1975), *Produzione, capitale e distribuzione*, ISEDI, Milan.

(1984), 'Dall'ordine naturale al caso: il denaro e le macchine', in G. Lunghini et al., *La scienza impropria*, Metamorfosi n. 8, F. Angeli, Milan, 1984.

MacDonald, S., Lamberton, D. McL. and Mandeville, T. (eds.), (1983), *The Trouble with Technology*, Pinter, London.

McGee, J. S. (1975), 'Efficiency and economies of size', in H. Goldschmid, H. M. Mann and J. F. Weston (eds.), *Industrial Concentration: The New Learning*, Little, Brown, Boston.

Manne, A. S. (1961), *Economic Analysis for Business Decisions*, McGraw-Hill, London.

Manne, A. S. and Markowitz, H. M. (1963), 'Introduction', in A. S. Manne and H. M. Markowitz (eds.), *Studies in Process Analysis*, J. Wiley & Sons, New York, proceedings of a Conference sponsored by the Cowles Foundation for Research in Economics at Yale University, 24–26 April, 1961.

Mariti, P. (1980), *Sui rapporti tra imprese in un'economia industriale moderna*, F. Angeli, Milan.

(1989), 'Constructive co-operation between smaller firms for efficiency, quality and product changes', Università degli Studi di Pisa, ed. Il Borghetto, forthcoming in O'Doherty, D. (ed.), *The Cooperation Phenomenon between Smaller Firms*, Kluwer Ac. Publishers, Lancaster, 1991.

Mariti, P. and Smiley, R. (1983), 'Cooperative agreements and the organization of industry', *Journal of Industrial Economics*.

Markowitz, H. M. and Rowe, A. J. (1963), 'A machine tool substitution analysis', in A. S. Manne and H. M. Markowitz (eds.), 1963.

Marris, R. (1964), *The Economic Theory of Managerial Capitalism*, Free Press, New York.

Marschak, T. and Nelson, R. R. (1962), 'Flexibility, uncertainty and economic theory', *Metroeconomica*.

Marshall, A. (1890), *Principles of Economics*, Macmillan, London, 8th edn 1920, reprinted 1982.

Marshall, A. and Paley Marshall, M. (1879), *Economics of Industry*, Macmillan, London.

Marx, K. (1864–94), *Capital. A Critique of Political Economy*, translated from German by B. Fowkes (vol. 1) and D. Fernbach (vols. 2–3), introduced by E. Mandel, Penguin Books in association with *New Left Review*, 3 vols., London, 1976, 1978, 1981.

Marzi, G. and Varri, P. (1977), *Variazioni di produttività nell'economia italiana: 1959–1967*, Il Mulino, Bologna.

Menger, C. (1871), *Principles of Economics*, New York University Press, New York, translated from German by J. Dingwall and B. F. Hoselitz, 1950, 2nd edition with an introduction by F. A. Hayek, 1981.

Menger, K. (1979), *Selected Papers in Logic and Foundations, Didactics, Economics*, Reidel, Dordrecht.

Merkhofer, M. W. (1975), *Flexibility and Decision Analysis*, Ph.D. dissertation, Department of Engineering – Economic Systems, Stanford University.

Metcalfe, J. S. (1981), 'Impulse and diffusion in the study of technical change', *Futures*.

(1988), 'The diffusion of innovations: an interpretative survey', in Dosi et al. (eds.) (1988).

(1989), 'Evolution and economic change', in A. Silberston (ed.), *Technology and Economic Progress*, Macmillan, London.

Metcalfe, J. S. and Gibbons, M. (1986), 'Technological variety and the process of competition', *Economie Appliqué*.

Mill, J. S. (1844), *Principles of Political Economy*, Longmans Green, London (1909).

Mills, D. E. (1986), 'Flexibility and firm diversity with demand fluctuations', *International Journal of Industrial Organization*.

Minsky, H. P. (1982), *Can " It " Happen Again?: Essays on Instability and Finance*, M. E. Sharpe, Inc., New York.

(1985), 'Review of "The Second Industrial Divide"', *Challenge*.

Momigliano, F. and Siniscalco, D. (1982), 'The growth of service employment: a reappraisal', *Banca Nazionale del Lavoro, Quarterly Review*.

Monden, Y. (1983), *Toyota Production System*, Institute of Industrial Engineering, Atlanta.

Monfort, J. (1985), 'L'Analyse des filières de production: objectifs, methodes et resultats', in ADEFI (1985).

Morroni, M. (1985), 'Costo', in G. Lunghini (ed.), *Dizionario di Economia Politica*, vol. X, Boringhieri, Turin, 16 vols.

Morvan, Y. (1985), *L'Analyse de filière*, in ADEFI (1985).

Moss, S. (1981), *An Economic Theory of Business Strategy*, Blackwell, Oxford.

(1984), 'The history of the theory of the firm from Marshall to Robinson and Chamberlin: the source of positivism in economics', *Economica*.

Mulligan, J. G. (1986), 'Technical change and scale economies given stochastic demand and production', *International Journal of Industrial Organization*.

Murray, F. (1987), 'Flexible specialisation in the "Third Italy"', *Capital and Class*.

Nabseth, L. and Ray, G. F. (eds.) (1974), *The Diffusion of New Industrial Processes*, Cambridge University Press, Cambridge.

Nelson, R. R. and Winter, S. G. (1977), 'In search of useful theory of innovation', *Research Policy*.

(1982), *An Evolutionary Theory of Economic Change*, Harvard University Press, Cambridge Mass.

Northcott, J. and Walling, A. (1988), *The Impact of Microelectronic. Diffusion, Benefits and Problems in British Industry*, Policy Studies Institute, London.

Oakey, R. (1984), *High Technology Small Firms. Regional Development in Britain and the United States*, Pinter, London.

Oakey, R., Rothwell, R. and Cooper, S. (1988), *The Management of Innovation in High-Technology Small Firm*, Pinter, London.

Oda, S. H. (1990), 'The application of Pasinetti's vertical hyper-integration to time-saving technical progress and the input-output table', *Cambridge Journal of Economics*.

OECD (1986), *Flexibility in the Labour Market. The Current Debate*, Paris.

(1988), *Employment Outlook*, chapter 6, Paris.

Pagano, U. (1985), *Work and Welfare in Economic Theory*, Blackwell, Oxford.

(1988), *Property Rights, Asset Specificity and the Division of Labour under Alternative Capitalist Relations*, paper presented at the Workshop on Economics and Institutions of the International School of Economic Research held at the Certosa di Pontigliano, 10–20 July 1988, Sienna, Discussion Papers of the Department of Political Economy, Sienna 1989.

Panzar, J. C. and Willig, R. D. (1977), 'Economies of scale in multi-output production', *Quarterly Journal of Economics*.

(1981), 'Economies of scope', *American Economic Review*.

Pasinetti, L. L. (1959), 'On concepts and measures of changes in productivity', *The Review of Economic and Statistics*, with a comment by R. M. Solow, and a reply by the author.

(1981), *Structural Change and Economic Growth*, Cambridge University Press, Cambridge.

Patinkin, D. (1965), *Money, Interest, and Capital*, Harper & Row, New York.

Pavitt, K. (1984), 'Sectoral patterns of technical change: towards a taxonomy and a theory', *Research Policy*.

Penrose, E. (1959), *The Theory of Growth of the Firm*, Blackwell, Oxford.

Perez, C. (1985), 'Microelectronics, long waves and world structural change: new perspectives of developing countries', *World Development*.

Phillimore, A. J. (1989), 'Flexible specialisation, work organisation and skill:

208   References

approaching the "second industrial divide"', *New Technology, Work and Employment*.
Piacentini, P. (1987), 'Costi ed efficienza in un modello di produzione a flusso lineare', *Economia Politica*.
— (1989), 'Coordinazione temporale ed efficienza produttiva', in Zamagni (ed.) (1989).
Piatier, A. (1984), *Barriers to Innovation*, Pinter, for the Commission of the European Communities, London.
Pigou, A. C. (1920), *The Economics of Welfare*, Macmillan, London.
Piore, M. J. (1980a), 'The technological foundations of dualism and discontinuity', in S. Berger and M. J. Piore (eds.) (1980).
— (1980b), 'Dualism as a response to flux and uncertainty', in S. Berger and M. J. Piore (eds.) (1980).
Piore, M. J. and Sabel, C. F. (1984), *The Second Industrial Divide: Possibilities for Prosperity*, Basic Books, New York.
Polidori, R. and Romagnoli, A. (1987), 'Tecniche e processo produttivo: analisi a "fondi e flussi" della produzione nel settore agricolo', *Rivista di Economia Agraria*.
Porter, M. E. (1985), *Competitive Advantage*, The Free Press, New York.
Pratten, C. F. (1971), *Economies of Scale in Manufacturing Industry*, Cambridge University Press, Cambridge.
— (1980), 'The manufacture of pins', *Journal of Economic Literature*.
— (1988), *A Survey of the Economies of Scale*, Economic Papers, Commission of the European Communities, Brussels.
Putterman, L. (ed.) (1986), *The Economic Nature of the Firm*, Cambridge University Press, Cambridge.
Rae, J. (1834), *Statement of some New Principles on the Subject of Political Economy, Exposing the Fallacies of the System of Free Trade, and some other Doctrines Maintained in the 'Wealth of Nations'*, Boston, republished in the care of C. W. Mixter with the title *The Sociological Theory of Capital*, 1905.
Rees, R. D. (1973), 'Optimum plant size in United Kingdom industries: some survivor estimates', *Economica*.
Reichlin, L. (1986), 'Un approccio istituzionale alla determinazione del salario: il caso italiano', *Politica Economica*.
Reid, G. C., Jacobsen, L. R. Jr (1988), *The Small Entrepreneurial Firm*, Aberdeen University Press, Aberdeen.
Rey, G. M. (1989), 'Small firms: a profile of their evolution', in Goodman, E. et al. (eds.) (1989).
Richardson, G. B. (1972), 'The organization of industry', *The Economic Journal*.
Robertson, D. H. (1930), 'Wage-Grumbles', in D. H. Robertson, *Economic Fragments*, P. S. King & Son, London, 1931.
Robinson, E. A. G. (1931), *The Structure of Competitive Industry*, Cambridge University Press, Cambridge, revised and reset edition 1958.
Robinson, J. (1937–8), 'The classification of innovation', *Review of Economic Studies*.
— (1953–4), 'The production function and the theory of capital', *Review of Economic Studies*, partly repr. in J. Robinson, *Collected Economic Papers*, MIT Press, vol. II, Cambridge, Mass. 1980.
— (1971), *Economic Heresies*, Basic Books, New York.

(1980a), 'Time in Economic Theory', in J. Robinson, *Further Contributions to Modern Economics*, Blackwell, Oxford, repr. from *Kyklos*, 1980.

(1980b), *Spring Cleaning*, mimeo, Cambridge.

Romagnoli, A. (1989), 'Teoria del processo produttivo: il caso dell'azienda agricola', in Zamagni (ed.) (1989).

Rose, H. et al. (1986), 'Opening the black box: the relation between technology and work', *New Technology, Work and Employment*.

Rosegger, G. (1980), *The Economics of Production and Innovation*, Pergamon, Oxford, 2nd edn 1986.

Rosenberg, N. (1969), 'The direction of technological change: inducement mechanisms and focusing devices, *Economic Development and Cultural Change*, repr. in Rosenberg (1976b).

(1975), 'Problems in the economist's conceptualisation of technological innovation', in N. De Marchi (ed.), *History of Political Economy*, repr. in Rosenberg 1976.

(1976a), 'Marx as a student of technology', in Rosenberg 1982, repr. from *Monthly Review*, 1976.

(1976b), *Perspectives on Technology*, Cambridge University Press, Cambridge.

(1976c), 'On technological expectations', *The Economic Journal*, repr. in Rosenberg 1982.

(1978), 'The historiography of technical progress', in Rosenberg, 1982, the English version of 'Progresso tecnico: l'analisi storica', in M. Carmignani and A. Vercelli (eds.), *Il mondo contemporaneo*, vol. VIII–, La Nuova Italia, Florence, 1978.

(1981), 'How exogenous is science?' in Rosenberg 1982, paper presented at a conference held at Harvard University in April 1981.

(1982), *Inside the Black Box. Technology and Economics*, Cambridge University Press, Cambridge.

(1990), 'Why do firms do basic research (with their own money)?' *Research Policy*.

Rosenberg, N. and Birdzell, L. E. (1986), *How the West Grew Rich. The Economic Transformation of the Industrial World*, I. B. Tauris & Co, London.

Rothwell, R. and Bessant, J. R. (eds.), (1987), *Innovation: Adaptation and Growth*, Elsevier, Amsterdam.

Rothwell, R. and Zegveld, W. (1979), *Technical Change and Employment*, St Martin's Press, New York.

(1982), *Innovation and Small and Medium Sized Firms*, Pinter, London.

Rowthorn, B. (1974), 'Neo-classicism, neo-Ricardianism and Marxism', *New Left Review*.

Rubery, J., Tarling, R. and Wilkinson, F. (1987), 'Flexibility, marketing and the organisation of production', *Labour and Society*.

Rullani, E. (1987), 'L'impresa come sistema artificiale: linguaggi e apprendimento nell'approccio evolutivo alla complessità', *Economia e Politica Industriale*.

(1988), 'Flessibilità del lavoro e flessibilità di impresa: le nuove regole dello sviluppo industriale', in M. Regini (ed.), *La sfida della flessibilità*, F. Angeli, Milan.

Rullani, E. and Zanfei, A. (1988a), 'Area networks: telematic connection in a traditional textile district', in Antonelli (ed.) (1988a).

(1988b), 'Networks between manufacturing and demand: cases from textile and clothing industries', in Antonelli (ed.) (1988a).

Russo, M. (1985), 'Technical change and the industrial district: the role of inter-firm relations in the growth and transformation of ceramic tile production in Italy', *Research Policy*, repr. in Goodman et al. (eds.) (1989).

Sabel, C. F. (1982), *Work and Politics. The Division of Labour in Industry*, Cambridge University Press, Cambridge.

Sabel, C. and Zeitlin, J. (1982), 'Historical alternatives to mass production', *Past and Present*, English translation of 'Alternative storiche alla produzione di massa', *Stato e Mercato*, 1982.

Sahal, D. (1981), *Patterns of Technological Innovation*, Addison-Wesley, London.
(1984), 'The innovation dynamics and technology cycles in the computer industry', *Omega*.

Salomon, G. L. (1985), 'Accounting rates of return', *American Economic Review*.

Salter, W. E. G. (1960), *Productivity and Technical Change*, Cambridge University Press, second edition 1966, Cambridge, with an 'Addendum' by W. R. Reddaway.

Salvadori, N. (1986), 'Il capitale fisso come "specie" del "genere" produzione congiunta', *Economia Politica*.
(1988), 'Fixed capital within the Sraffa framework', *Journal of Economics*.

Salvati, M. (1988), 'Flessibilità e occupazione. Quanto possono ragionevolmente dire gli economisti', in M. Regini (ed.), *La sfida della flessibilità*, F. Angeli, Milan.

Samuelson, P. A. (1948), *Economics*, McGraw-Hill, New York, 12th edition with the collaboration of W. D. Nordhaus, 1985.

Santarelli, E. (1987), 'Generation and diffusion of new technologies', *Rivista Internazionale di Scienze Economiche e Commerciali*.

Sato, R. and Suzawa, G. S. (1983), *Research and Productivity*, Aburn House Publishing Company, Boston, Mass.

Saving, T. R. (1962), 'Estimation of the optimum size of plant by the survivor technique', *Quarterly Journal of Economics*.

Saviotti, P. P. and Metcalfe, J. S. (1984), 'A theoretical approach to construction of technological output indicators', *Research Policy*.

Sbriglia, P. (1988), 'Recent developments in the theory of innovation and technical change', *Studi Economici*.

Scazzieri, R. (1981), *Efficienza produttiva e livelli di attività*, Il Mulino, Bologna.
(1982), 'Scale and efficiency in models of production', in M. Baranzini (ed.), *Advances in Economic Theory*, Blackwell, Oxford.
(1983), 'The production process: general characteristics and taxonomy', *Rivista Internazionale di Scienze Economiche e Commerciali*.

Scherer, F. M. (1980), *Industrial Market Structure and Economic Performance*, Rand McNally, Chicago.
(1984), *Innovation and Growth*, The MIT Press, Cambridge, Mass.

Schneider, E. (1934), *Theorie der Produktion*, Verlag von Julius Springer, Vienna, Italian translation from a revised and enlarged version by F. Di Fenizio, *Teoria della produzione*, Casa Editrice Ambrosiana, Milan 1942.

Schumpeter, J. A. (1911), *The Theory of Economic Development*, Harvard University Press, Cambridge, Mass., 1934, 8th edn 1968, translated by Redvers Opie, *Theorie der wirtschaftlichen Entwicklung*.

(1935), 'The analysis of economic change', in R. V. Clemence (ed.), *Essays of Schumpeter*, Addison-Wesley Press, Cambridge, Mass., 1951, repr. from *Review of Economic Statistics*.

(1939), *Business Cycles*, McGraw-Hill, New York.

Semlinger, K. (1990), 'New developments in subcontracting-mixing markets and hierarchy', *mimeo*, paper presented at the EAEPE 1990 Conference, Florence, 15–17 November.

Sforzi, F. (1989), 'The geography of industrial districts in Italy', in E. Goodman et al. (eds.) (1989).

Sharp, C. (1981), *The Economics of Time*, M. Robertson, Oxford.

Shepherd, W. G. (1967), 'What does the survivor technique show about the economies of scale', *Southern Economic Journal*.

Signorini, L. F. (1988), 'Innovation in Tuscan firms', Paper presented to the Regional Science Association's European Summer Institute, Arco, 17–23 July, Trent.

Silberston, A. (1972), 'Economies of scale in the theory and practice', *The Economic Journal*, Supplement.

Silverberg, G. (1988), 'Modelling economic dynamics and technical change: mathematical approaches to self-organisation and evolution', in Dosi et al. (eds.) (1988).

Singh, A. and Whittington, G. (1968), *Growth, Profitability and Valuation*, Cambridge University Press, Cambridge.

Smith, A. (1776), *An Inquiry into the Nature and Causes of the Wealth of Nations*, Clarendon Press, 2 vols., Oxford, 1976.

Smith, C. A. (1955), 'Survey of empirical evidence on the economies of scale', in G. J. Stigler et al., *Business Concentration and Price Policy*, Princeton University Press, Princeton.

Soete, L. (1987), 'Employment, unemployment and technical change: a review of the economic debate', in Freeman and Soete (eds.) (1987).

Soete, L. and Turner, R. (1984), 'Technology diffusion and the rate of technological change', *The Economic Journal*.

Solow, R. M. (1957), 'Technical change and the aggregate production function', *Review of Economics and Statistics*.

Sorge, A., Hartmann, G., Warner, M. and Nicholas, I. (1983), *Microelectronics and Manpower in Manufacturing*, Gower, Aldershot.

Sraffa, P. (1925), 'Sulle relazioni tra costo e quantità prodotta', *Annali di Economia*, repr. in P. Sraffa, *Saggi*, Il Mulino, Bologna, 1986.

(1926), 'The laws of returns under competitive conditions', *The Economic Journal*.

(1930), 'A criticism – increasing returns and the representative firm: a symposium', *The Economic Journal*.

(1960), *Production of Commodities by Means of Commodities*, Cambridge University Press, Cambridge.

Staehle, H. (1942), 'The measurement of statistical cost functions: an appraisal of some recent contributions', *American Economic Review*.

Stevens, B. (1988), 'From stability to flexibility in corporate manpower utilization', in Ergas et al. (1988).

Stigler, G. J. (1939), 'Production and distribution in the short run', *The Journal of Political Economy*.

(1951), 'The division of labour is limited by the extent of the market', *Journal of Political Economy*.

(1958), 'The economies of scale', *Journal of Law and Economics*.

Stoneman, P. (1981), 'L'Impact d'une nouvelle technologie sur l'emploi', *Revue d'Economie Industrielle*.

(1983), *The Economic Analysis of Technological Change*, Oxford University Press, Oxford.

(1986), 'Technological diffusion: the viewpoint of economic theory', in Arcangeli et al. (eds.) 1990.

(1987a), *The Economic Analysis of Technology Policy*, Clarendon Press, Oxford.

(1987b), 'Some analytical observations on diffusion policies', in Dasgupta and Stoneman (eds.) 1987.

Stoneman, P. and Ireland, N. (1983), 'The role of supply factors in the diffusion of new process technology'. *The Economic Journal*, Supplement.

Storey, D. J. (1982), *Entrepreneurship and the New Firm*, Croom Helm, London.

(ed.) (1983), *The Small Firm: An International Survey*, Croom Helm, London.

Storper, M. (1989), 'The transition to flexible specialisation in US film industry: external economies, the division of labour, and the crossing of industrial divides', *Cambridge Journal of Economics*.

Summers, L. H. and Wadhwani, S. B. (1987), *Some International Evidence on Labour Cost Flexibility and Output Variability*, Discussion Paper n. 292, Centre for Labour Economics, London School of Economics, London.

Swann, G. M. P. (1986), *Quality Innovation*, Quorum Books, New York.

Sylos Labini, P. (1956), *Oligopoly and Technical Progress*, Harvard University Press, Cambridge, Mass., 1962, revised edn 1969, translated by E. Henderson, *Oligopolio e progresso tecnico*, Einaudi, Turin 1964, third edition.

Tani, P. (1976), 'La decomponibilità del processo produttivo', in G. Becattini (ed.), *Mercato e forze locali: il distretto industriale*, Il Mulino, Bologna, 1987, revised version of 'La rappresentazione analitica del processo di produzione: alcune premesse teoriche al problema del decentramento', *Note Economiche*, 1976.

(1979), *Alcune questioni di teoria della produzione*, Faculty of Economics and Commerce, University of Florence.

(1986), *Analisi microeconomica della produzione*, La Nuova Italia Scientifica, Rome.

(1988), 'Flows, funds, and sectorial interdependence in the theory of production', *Political Economy*.

(1989), 'La rappresentazione della tecnologia produttiva nell'analisi microeconomica: problemi e recenti tendenze', in Zamagni (ed.) 1989.

Teece, D. J. (1980), 'Economies of scope and the scope of the enterprise', *Journal of Economic Behavior and Organization*.

(1988), 'Technological change and the nature of the firm', in Dosi et al. (eds.) 1988.

Termini, V. (1984), 'Sequenze e tempo nel ragionamento economico', in G. Lunghini et al., *La scienza impropria*, Metamorfosi no. 8, F. Angeli, Milan, 1984.

Tinacci Mossello, M. (1989), *Innovative capacities of industrial districts. Hypothesis and verification; the case-study of Prato in Tuscany*, Department of Economics, University of Florence.

Torriero, A. L. (1989), 'Factorizations of M-matrices in input-output analysis', *Optimization*.

Ure, A. (1835), *Philosophy of Manufactures*, Bohn, London, 3rd edn (1861).

Vercelli, A. (1986), 'Uncertainty, technological flexibility and long term fluctuations', in M. Di Matteo, R. M. Goodwin and A. Vercelli (eds.), *Technological and Social Factors in Long Term Fluctuations*, Springer-Verlag, Berlin, 1989, Proceedings of an International Workshop Held in Siena, 16–18 December, 1986.

— (1988), 'Technological flexibility, financial fragility and recent revival of Schumpeterian entrepreneurship', *Recherches Economique de Louvain*.

Vickery, G. and Campbell, D. (1989), 'Advanced manufacturing technology and the organisation of work', *STI Review*, no. 6, OECD, Paris.

Viner, J. (1931), 'Cost curves and supply curves', *Zeitschrift für National-oekonomie*.

— (1961), *The Intellectual History of Laissez Faire*, The University of Chicago Law School, Chicago.

Walras, L. (1874), *Elements of Pure Economics. Or the Theory of Social Wealth*, G. Allen and Unwin 1954, 2nd edn (1965), London, translated by W. Jaffe, *Eléments d'économie politique pure*, 1926.

Walsh, V. (1990), 'Inter-firm technological alliances: A transient phenomenon or new structures in capitalist economies?' *mimeo*, paper presented at the EAEPE 1990 Conference, Florence, 15–17 November.

Walters, A. A. (1963), 'Production and cost functions: an econometric survey', *Econometrica*.

Warnecke, H. J. and Steinhilper, R. (eds.) (1985), *Flexible Manufacturing Systems*, IFS & Springer-Verlag, Kempston, Bedford.

Weiss, L. W. (1964), 'The survival technique and the extent of suboptimal capacity', *Journal of Political Economy*.

— (1976), 'Optimal plant size and the extent of suboptimal capacity', in R. T. Masson and P. D. Qualls (eds.), *Essays on Industrial Organization in Honor of J. S. Bain*, Blaainger Publishers, Cambridge, Mass.

Wibe, S. (1980), 'Engineering production functions and technical progress', in Puu, T. and Wibe, S. (eds.), *The Economics of Technical Progress*, Macmillan, London.

Wiles, P. J. D. (1956), *Price, Cost and Output*, Blackwell, Oxford.

Williams, K., Cutler, T., Williams, J. and Haslam, C. (1987), 'The end of mass production? Review article of M. Piore and C. Sabel, *The Second Industrial Divide: Possibilities for Prosperity*', *Economy and Society*.

Williamson, O. E. (1985), *The Economic Institutions of Capitalism*, Free Press, New York.

Winston, G. C. (1974), 'The theory of capital utilization and idleness', *Journal of Economic Literature*.

— (1982), *The Timing of Economic Activities*, Cambridge University Press, Cambridge.

Wodopia, F. J. (1986), 'Time and production: period versus continuous analysis', in Faber, M. (ed.) (1986).

Zagnoli, P. (1988), *Inter-Firm High Technology Agreements: A Transaction Cost Explanation*, Centre for Research in Management, Berkeley, Cal.

Zamagni, S. (1982), 'Introduzione', in N. Georgescu-Roegen, *Energia e miti*

214   References

economici, Boringhieri, Turin, partial Italian translation by P. L. Cecioni of Georgescu-Roegen, 1976.

(1984a), *Microeconomic Theory. An Introduction*, Blackwell, Oxford 1987, translated by A. Fletcher, *Economia politica. Teorie dei prezzi, dei mercati e della distribuzione*, La Nuova Italia Scientifica, Rome, 1984.

(1984b), 'Ricardo and Hayek effects in a fixwage model of traverse', *Oxford Economic Papers*, November, Supplement.

(ed.) (1989), *Le teorie economiche della produzione*, Il Mulino, Bologna.

Zenezini, M. (1989), 'Wage and unemployment in Italy, a long-term perspective', *Labour*.

Author index

Subject index

activities analysis, 92–3, 102, 150
adaptability, 28, 98, 105, 112, 123, 148, 171–3, 178
administrative activities, *see* service processes
aircraft industry, 20, 81
alterability, 171
applied analysis, 4, 81, 85–6, 99–102, 137–8, 190
based on interviews, 100, 104–5,
appropriability of technology, 20, 22
artisan production, *see* production
automation, 103, 181, 185–6, 190, 194–5
flexible, 95, 174, 185–6
rigid, 174–6, 178, 185
automobile industry, 70, 81, 183

Babbage's factory principle, 63–4
batches (lots, runs), 1, 27, 74, 95, 106, 110, 140, 174, 180, 183–4, 191
bounded rationality, 165
business unit, *see* production unit

capital
depreciation of machines and premises, 82–3, 90–1, 105–8, 114, 126, 150, 172
locked-up, 82–3, 91, 105–6
of different vintages, 33, 87–8, 90–1, 107, 151
working capital, 181
see also degree of use of funds and technical change, capital-embodied
classic economists, 5, 14
clock industry, 183–4
coefficients of production, 13, 28–30, 88, 92
complementarity of goods and processes, 28–31, 93
and fixed coefficients, 28–30
and productive capacity, 30
and returns or economies of scale, 137, 142–4, 146–7, 151, 156

and team production, 29
and technical change, 30–1, 137–9, 143
computer-based technology, 4–5, 42, 98, 102–3, 113, 121, 123, 127, 130, 138–40, 154–5, 166, 171, 176f., 192ff.
CAD (computer-aided design), 75, 187
CAM (computer-aided manufacturing), 75, 185, 187, 194
CIM (computer-integrated manufacturing), 185–6, 193
FMS (flexible manufacturing system), 194
contingency theory, 43
convertibility, 171
costs of production, 4–5, 13, 27, 31–2, 39, 70, 72, 79, 81–3, 90–2, 98, 105–15 and *passim*, 123, 126, 141ff., 158ff., 170ff. *passim*
methods of collecting data on, 139, 150–2
see also economies of scale, returns to scale, sunk costs, transaction costs

decomposability of an elementary process, 68–72, 75–80, 85–9, 91–3, 104, 109, 139, 152, 154
defective products, 93–4, 98, 109
degree (intensity) of use of funds or microeconomic units, 13, 55–64 and *passim*, 82, 88–91, 112, 141, 147, 156
demand
for labour, *see* employment.
of inputs and/or outputs, 15, 21–2, 27, 90, 93–6, 98, 101–2, 123, 144, 172, 174, 179, 180, 187, 193
development path of a production unit, 31, 34–6, 143, 146, 149, 181, 186
see also learning processes, practical knowledge, specificity
differentiation of product, 101, 106–7, 143, 170, 172, 176–7, 182
diffusion of new techniques, 9

219